THE VIKINGS

by Robert Nicholson and Claire Watts

Editorial Consultant: Gareth Binns, Education Officer,
York Archaeological Trust & Council for
British Archaeology

TWO-CAN

First published in Great Britain in 1991 by
Two-Can Publishing Ltd
27 Cowper Street
London EC2A 4AP

Copyright © Two-Can Publishing Ltd, 1991
Text copyright © Robert Nicholson, 1991
Design by Millions Design

Printed in Italy by Amadeus - Rome

The JUMP! logo and the word JUMP! are registered trade marks.

British Library Cataloguing in Publication Data

Nicholson, Robert
    Vikings
    1. Vikings
    I. Title II. Watts, Claire III. Series
    948.022

    ISBN: 1-85434-024-7

Photographic credits:
Werner Forman: p. 3, p. 6, p. 7, p. 8, p. 9, p. 10, p. 11, p. 12, p. 13, p. 16, p. 17, p. 20 (top)
p. 21, p. 23, p. 30 (top), p. 32 (bottom); Toby Maudsley: p. 20 (craft) p. 22; Ronald Sheridan:
p. 30 (middle); York Archaeological Trust: p. 19, p. 24

Illustration credits:
Kevin Maddison: p. 9, p. 11, pp. 12-13, p. 14, p. 17, pp. 18-19, pp. 22-23, p. 24
Maxine Hamil cover: pp. 25-29

Contents

All words marked in **bold** can be found in the glossary.

▼ Eric the Red founded a settlement in Greenland.

▲ The Vikings were the first Europeans to reach America.

Lindisfarne was an island whose wealthy, unprotected monastery was an easy target for the Vikings.

"on 8 june the ravages of heathen men miserably destroyed god's church on lindisfarne with plunder and slaughter ..."

(ANGLO-SAXON CHRONICLE, 793)

The Viking World

The first glimpse many European people had of the Vikings was when the fierce dragon-heads of the Viking longships appeared off their coasts. No-one was prepared for the invading warriors and few countries could resist the Vikings. From the first attacks in 793, Viking raids were a frequent occurrence all over north-western Europe for the next 200 years.

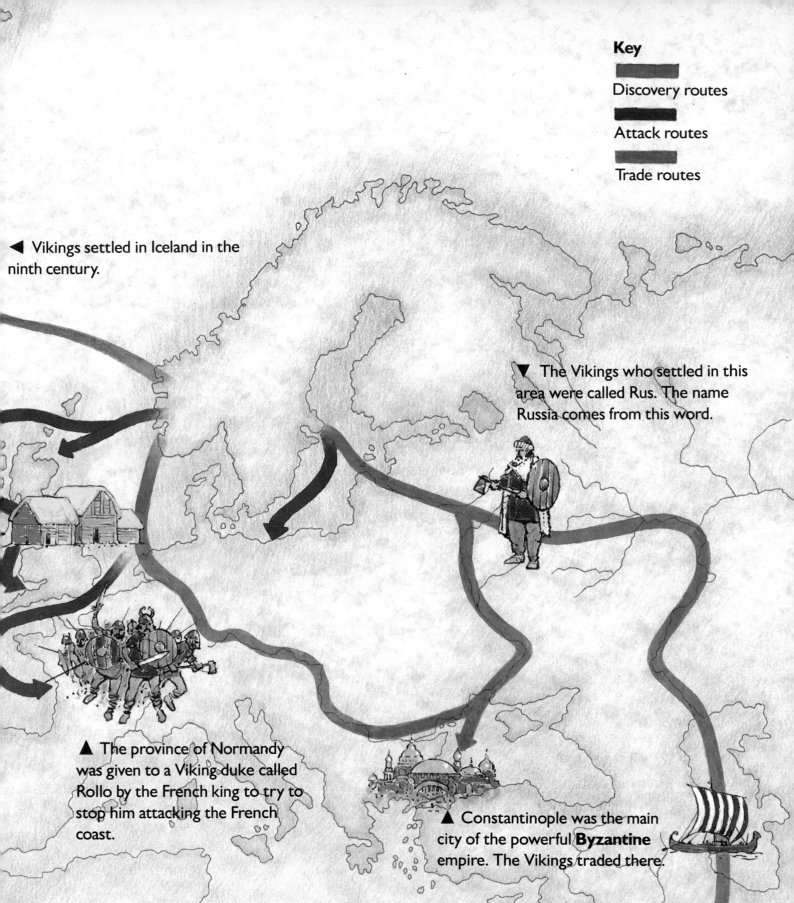

Key

Discovery routes

Attack routes

Trade routes

◄ Vikings settled in Iceland in the ninth century.

▼ The Vikings who settled in this area were called Rus. The name Russia comes from this word.

▲ The province of Normandy was given to a Viking duke called Rollo by the French king to try to stop him attacking the French coast.

▲ Constantinople was the main city of the powerful **Byzantine** empire. The Vikings traded there.

Viking Lands

The Vikings came from the countries which are now called Sweden, Norway and Denmark. These lands are cold and bleak, with deep rivers, rocky coasts and mountains. There was not enough good farm land to produce sufficient food for all the Vikings, even though they also fished and hunted wild animals.

Many Vikings chose to leave their homes rather than try to farm the meagre land. They set out to seek riches using their skills as seamen and warriors.

Viking lands were divided into several different kingdoms. The richest and most powerful men became leaders and were called kings and dukes. These leaders would sometimes call all the **free men** to a meeting known as the **Allthing** where they would discuss plans about expeditions to other countries or make decisions about local problems. There were often wars between the different kingdoms, particularly over pieces of good land.

▼ Men gathering for the Allthing.

▼ The narrow, deep-watered fjords of **Scandinavia** form perfect natural harbours.

Pirates or Traders?

Pirates

The Vikings attacked lands around them, particularly Britain and France, stealing food and treasures and carrying people off to become slaves. People who lived in isolated areas on the coast or on islands were terrified of the Vikings' attacks. They were mostly farmers, and were not used to defending themselves and their families. They added to their daily prayers the words "God deliver us from the fury of the **Northmen.**"

▲ Viking helmets like this one have been found at a number of gravesites in Europe. Soldiers were often buried with all their weapons because the Vikings believed they would need them on the way to heaven.

▼ Rope was wrapped around the hilt of Viking swords to protect the warrior's hand.

Traders

In certain places the Vikings got food and goods by trading rather than by attacking and stealing property. They usually chose to trade rather than attack when the inhabitants were stronger or more organised and could defend themselves better. Viking traders travelled as far south as the Black Sea trading their furs, jewellery and slaves for spices and wine.

▶ Goods were sold by weight of gold or silver rather than for a number of coins. Merchants used tiny portable scales to weigh the gold or silver. If they needed to give change they would break up the coins.

Longships

The Vikings were superb seamen and used ships for travelling on the lakes, seas and fjords of Scandinavia as well as further afield. The ships were measured by the number of oars they had, the smallest, a **faering**, with 4 and the largest, a **longship**, with about 32. A big longship might be nearly 30 m long and would travel at up to 32 km per hour under full sail. Ships were so important to the Vikings that their language contained dozens of ways of saying "ship".

The Vikings managed to navigate without any of the modern equipment that is used today. They found their way by watching the stars and Sun as well as familiar landmarks like islands and mountains. They also looked out for birds which are found in different places at different times of year, like puffins and fulmars.

▲ Viking ships were among the first to have a **keel** which helped them to cut through the water very fast and made them stable even in rough weather.

▲ Oars were used if the sail was not up, when there was no wind or on inland waters. Each rower sat on a box which held his belongings and a waterproof reindeer-skin sleeping bag.

▶ The gaps between the oak planks of the ship were made waterproof by filling them with sheep's wool dipped in tar.

◀ The ship used one huge square sail. In bad weather this was lowered over the ship and then fastened down like a tent to protect the men inside. The sail was made of thick, coarse material.

◀ The **prow** of a Viking ship was elaborately carved, usually with the head of a dragon or another animal. The ships had names which reflected the shape of their prows, like "Long Serpent", "Snake of the Sea", and "Horse of the Home of Ice".

Heroes

The Vikings admired bold and fearless men and their heroes were all soldiers, sailors or explorers. The deeds of heroes were told again and again until they became more like myths than real historical fact.

Leif Ericson

Eric the Red's son Leif, who was known as "Lucky", arrived in northern America 500 years before Columbus reached the continent. He landed to the south of Newfoundland in a place which he called Markland. He travelled on south to a place called Vinland, which may have been south of modern New York. The Vikings left America after about two years when they were attacked by Indians.

King Cnut

In 1016 England had suffered 200 years of Viking raids, which had made the country very weak. When King Cnut of Denmark attacked England, the English king had just died and so Cnut took over. The English accepted him because he was a wise ruler and brought peace.

Harald Haardraade

As the fame of the Vikings spread throughout Europe, many kings paid Vikings to work in their armies. The Byzantine Emperor had an elite fighting force of Vikings called the **Varangarian Guard.** Harald Haardraade, or Hard-nose, was a famous member of the Guard, who later became king of Norway. He was the last Viking to land with an army in England.

Sagas and Runes

Viking children did not go to school to learn. Lessons came in the form of long stories, or **sagas**, which told the adventures of the gods or of great Viking heroes. These stories were important ways of teaching history, geography and navigation. Children would also learn whilst helping their parents around the house and farm.

Storytellers travelled around reciting sagas at feasts and festivals. They were especially sought after on dark, cold winter nights, when everyone sat inside around the fire.

▲ Some buildings were decorated with pictures from famous sagas. The wood carving above shows Sigurd the Dragon-Slayer attacking a dragon.

▲ This stone carving shows one of the tales of Odin. You can see Odin in the centre at the top, handing a sword to an old man.

The Futhark

The Viking alphabet, the **Futhark**, was quite different from ours. The letters, or **runes**, are made up mostly of straight lines. This is because they were usually carved into wood or stone and it is easier to carve straight lines than curves.

► These are all the runes of the Futhark. Underneath you can see how all the letters were pronounced. Try writing your name in runes – it's like a secret code!

a b c d e f g h

ij k l m n o p q

r s t uvw x y z

The Viking Gods

The Vikings believed that there were lots of different gods who lived in a place called **Asgard.** Each one was responsible for a different thing, like war, travel or the home. In stories the gods were not perfect. They had very human qualities, and also human weaknesses like jealousy and greed.

If a Viking died fighting it was believed that he went to a hall in Asgard called **Vallhalla,** where everybody fought all day and feasted all night.

Some Important Gods

Thor

Freyja

Odin

THOR, the god of thunder, was the most popular god. He was short-tempered and a little stupid, but very good-hearted. He had the qualities that the Vikings thought most important: strength and determination.

ODIN or Woden was the god of war, who rode an eight-legged horse. He often doubted himself and spent too long trying to decide whether to do things or not.

FREY made sure that the sun shone, rain fell and the crops grew. He owned a magic boat which could carry all the gods at once, but folded up in his pocket when not needed.

FREYJA was Frey's sister. She was the goddess of love and war. She could turn herself into a bird by putting on a magic falcon-skin.

LOKI was half god, half fire-spirit. He caused the other gods a lot of trouble.

▲ When Viking warriors died their bodies were often placed in longships, which were buried or set alight and pushed out to sea.

▶ Towards the end of the Viking age the Vikings began to convert to Christianity. This is a mould made in the tenth century for making Christian crosses, but it could also be used for making copies of **Mjollnir**, Thor's hammer.

At Home

The Vikings were not only skilled soldiers, seamen and traders. Most Vikings were farmers and lived with their families, growing and making all the things they needed for their daily lives. Children helped their parents as soon as they were able to. Even very small children had their own jobs around the farm, like feeding the animals or gathering firewood.

Viking women worked on the farm and wove material for clothes and blankets on small looms. When their husbands were away fighting, they took care of the whole farm.

Viking houses were made of timber planks and woven branches, with turf or thatched roofs. Stone was used in places where there was no wood, like Shetland and Iceland. Inside, the houses were not divided into rooms. Areas were separated off by stretching cloth or skins between the pillars which supported the roof.

A typical farm would contain the family house, or more than one house if the family were large. There were also sheds for the animals, a workshop with a furnace for making metal tools, and small huts for slaves.

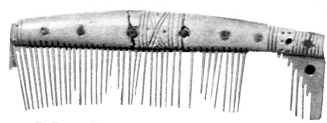

Rubbish!

● Viking homes were not as clean as our houses are. Meat bones and vegetable peelings might be left on the floor all winter and only cleared out in the spring.

● Rubbish was buried outside.

● All the Vikings had combs because they had lice in their hair.

Games

Viking children did not spend all their time helping their parents. They had some time to themselves for playing games and carving wooden toys. Girls and boys went skating in winter, using skates made of carved bone. These were strapped to the children's shoes with strips of leather.

When it was too dark and cold to go outside, Viking children may have played a game called **hnefatal**. This was a board game rather like chess but with simple pieces, like draughts.

Crafts

Vikings were very skilled craftsmen, making marvellous objects from stone, wood and metal. Many of the most beautiful objects were not made by specialist artists, but by ordinary people. A farmer might make a brooch using the same furnace he used to make his plough.

As there were no banks, people wore their wealth in the form of jewellery. This was the best way to keep it safe.

Smiths were very highly respected and often became very wealthy. Thor, one of the most important Viking gods, used a smith's hammer as his main weapon.

▲ Some jewellery was made specially for burial with a dead person. This arm-ring was found at a burial site.

Make Some Viking Jewellery

Look at the decoration on the Viking objects in this book. Can you see how all the figures are woven around one another? The Vikings loved to use complicated patterns for decoration.

Try making a bracelet or brooch using Viking designs. Modelling clay that you can bake hard in the oven is good for making jewellery.

◀ Use four balls of clay to make the heads.

▼ Roll out three long strands and plait them together.

▼ This is a mould which was used to make part of a helmet. Once the mould was made, many helmets could be made with this pattern.

▶ This gold pendant was worn around the neck as a magical amulet. Look at the elaborate patterns that cover it.

▶ The symbol of Thor's hammer was used in much Viking jewellery. This hammer head is made in silver but many were much simpler than this.

Food

Finding food was a very important part of a Viking's life. Little of the land was fertile and the winters were very long and harsh, so as well as growing and raising food on their farms, the Vikings hunted and fished for food. They ate rich stews of beef or mutton from their farms, or fish and whale meat. They grew vegetables like cabbage, peas and beans and also ate wild leeks and garlic.

Trestle tables would be set up in the middle of the room for meals, and members of the family would sit on the same wooden benches that they slept on at night. They ate off rectangular wooden platters or from soapstone bowls, using spoons and the knives that were carried on their belts at all times.

The Vikings used drinking horns as well as cups. Because the horns did not have flat bottoms, they had to be passed on around the table until they were empty. A man who could drain a drinking horn at one go was very highly thought of! The usual drink was mead, a sweet beer made from honey.

Food Facts

● When the Vikings had no other grain they would use peas to make bread.
● Salt was made by boiling sea-water.
● The Vikings ate two meals a day: the **day meal** after the early farmwork and the **night meal** at the end of the day.

Cooking was done over an open hearth fire. Meat was roasted on huge spits, and stews were made in big iron cauldrons. Sometimes a **gridiron** made of coiled iron was used. Does it remind you of part of a modern cooker? Bread was baked in stone ovens or in the ashes of the fire.

▼ Bowls were made from pottery or soapstone.

Clothes

Most Viking clothes were made from coarse woollen cloth, although some rich people wore imported silk or linen. In winter people wore furs to keep warm.

Men wore an undershirt and breeches, covered by long woollen trousers and a tunic which reached to the knees. All this was held up with a leather belt. A purse and knife were carried on the belt.

Women wore long wool or linen dresses with a woollen tunic rather like an apron attached with brooches. Hanging from their belts they carried a knife and keys.

▲ Shoes were made from leather or goatskin, laced up with strips of leather.

Thor Visits the Land of the Giants

This story is part of a Viking saga. It is about Thor, the god of thunder, and the journey he set out on to prove his strength. The journey and the trials of strength would have been very familiar to the Vikings.

One summer day, Thor, Loki and their two servants set off to visit Utgard, the land of the giants. After a long journey, they arrived at the gates of Utgard to find them locked. Thor thumped and hammered on the gates, calling out for someone to come and and let them in, but Loki grinned and slipped through the bars, dragging the others after him. They walked into the great hall of Utgard. In the middle of the hall was a long table around which hundreds of giants were seated on benches, eating and drinking and making the most enormous noise. The giants all began to laugh

as Thor marched up to the Giant King who was seated on a chair at the far end of the hall.

"Greetings, Giant King," said Thor, politely.

The Giant King sat chewing bones and did not even look at Thor. From time to time he tossed a bone over his shoulder and picked up a new one.

Thor spoke again, a little louder: "Greetings, Gi . . ."

The Giant King interrupted: "So you're the great thunder god Thor, are you? Well, you look like a scrawny little piece of work to me. I suppose you've come to test your strength?"

Thor was furious at the Giant King's rudeness, but it did not seem a very good idea to lose his temper when he was surrounded by giants.

"What skill would you like to challenge us with?" continued the Giant King.

Thor looked around him at the giants.

"I doubt if anyone here can drink as much as I can," Thor replied.

The Giant King signalled to a servant, who brought forward a huge drinking horn.

"This is the horn used by all my followers," he said. "A good drinker can finish it in one draught, and all here can down it in two at the most. Let us see what the great Thor can do!"

Thor took the horn. It was certainly not the largest he had ever drunk from. He raised it to his mouth and began to swallow. He felt sure he could drink it all, but he ran out of breath before the horn was empty. He looked into the horn and found that it was no less full than before. He drank a second time, and again had to stop for breath. This time the horn was no longer brimming full. He took a third draught, gulping down the liquid until he was sure he must empty the horn, but although the level was lower than before, the horn was by no means empty.

"You don't seem to be much of a drinker," said the Giant King. "Why not try your strength? Some of the younger giants like to test themselves by lifting my cat. We don't think this much of a feat, but perhaps you'd like to try?"

Standing beside the Giant King's chair was the most enormous cat Thor had ever seen. He braced himself and then put both arms under the cat and heaved. The cat simply arched its back. Thor heaved again and managed to make the cat lift one paw off the ground before he had to admit defeat.

"As I thought," said the Giant King scornfully. "You may be strong in Asgard and in the realms of men, but your strength is nothing here."

At this Thor grew angry. "I can match any of your men in a fight. Just let anyone here wrestle with me."

There was a roar of laughter from all the giants in the hall.

"Everyone here feels that wrestling with you would be too easy," said the Giant King. "Perhaps you could fight Elli, my foster mother."

A wrinkled old woman hobbled forward leaning on a stick. Thor thought that the Giant King was making fun of him until Elli threw down her stick and took hold of him. He knew at once that his strength would be sorely tested. They struggled and fought, but eventually Elli threw Thor off balance so that he landed on one knee.

"Enough, enough!" shouted the Giant King. "You have shown us that you have no strength as a wrestler either. As you pose no threat to us, you may eat with us and spend the night here in Utgard."

Thor and his companions were very hungry and tired after their long journey. When they had eaten, the tables were pushed back, and they spread their bedding in a space on the floor among the giants.

Thor awoke early, before any of the giants, and roused his companions.

"Come, let's go before the giants wake up," he whispered.

They tiptoed over the sleeping giants and out of the gates of Utgard. To their surprise, they found the Giant King already outside waiting for them. He walked with them across the plain for a while.

At last he stopped: "This is where I must leave you. Thor, do not feel too badly about your failures last night."

Thor was puzzled. "But I have never before been so soundly beaten," he said.

The Giant King replied: "You were not competing in a fair fight. I feared your strength, so I used magic to deceive you. The other end of the horn that you drank from was in the sea. When you reach the shore you will see just how much you have lowered its level. The cat you lifted was really the giant serpent whose body is wrapped around the world. You managed to lift it until its back touched the sky. And as for Elli, it was a wonder you withstood her for so long. You see, Elli is Old Age, which defeats all men in time."

Thor was furious that he had been tricked. He seized his hammer Mjollnir and swung it around his head, but the Giant King and Utgard had vanished, as if they had never been.

29

How We Know

Have you ever wondered how, although the Vikings lived over 1000 years ago, we know so much about their daily lives?

Evidence from the Ground

Certain objects have been found preserved in wet earth or water. Often these are very ordinary objects which were thrown away by the Vikings because they were broken or not needed. Archaeologists piece them together and work out how the Vikings used them.

Some important Vikings were buried in ships full of their possessions. When these ships are discovered, archaeologists can gain a lot of information about the Vikings.

Evidence from Books

Many of the stories told by the Vikings were written down, and so it is quite easy to find out who the important gods were and what various historical figures did. We even know that when Eric the Red discovered Greenland, he gave it that name in spite of its cold iciness because "many would want to go there if it had so promising a name".

Evidence around us

Many place names in Europe were originally Viking names, and so we can tell where the Vikings settled.

The whole of Normandy in France was taken over by the Vikings, and the name means land of the Northmen.

In Britain many place names have the Viking endings "-thorpe" and "-by", like Scunthorpe and Grimsby. Can you find any others on a map?

And what about our days of the week? Did you know that Wednesday was originally Woden's day, and Thursday Thor's day?

Glossary

Allthing
a council of free men which met when problems arose. This was the only form of government the Vikings had.

Asgard
the place where the Vikings believed that their gods lived, and where they would go when they died.

Byzantine
the strongest world power at the time of the Vikings was the Byzantine empire in the east which lasted from the 6th to the 15th century.

day meal
the first meal of the day, eaten after the early farmwork had been done.

free men
all the men who were not slaves. Slaves were usually people who had been captured on raids.

faering
the smallest type of Viking ship, with four oars.

Futhark
the runic alphabet used by the Vikings. The word is taken from the sound of the first six letters.

gridiron
a coiled metal strip which was placed in the fire to heat pots on.

hnefatal
a board game played by the Vikings.

keel
the long timber which forms the lowest part of a ship and helps it to balance.

longship
the long, low ships used by Vikings.

Mjollnir
Thor's hammer. He carried it with him at all times.

night meal
the meal eaten after all the work was done, when it began to grow dark.

Northmen
most of the people the Vikings attacked or traded with knew them as "Northmen". "Viking" was a term they used to describe themselves.

prow
the front end of a ship.

rune
a letter of the Viking alphabet. Runes are made up of straight lines because they were intended to be carved on wood or stone.

saga
storytelling adventure of gods or heroes. Although sagas were usually passed on by word of mouth, some were written down.

Scandinavia
The group of countries which include Denmark, Norway, Sweden and Iceland.

Vallhalla
the hall in Asgard where warriors hoped to go when they died. Here they could fight all day and feast all night.

Varangarian Guard
a section of the Byzantine army made up of Vikings. The Varangarian Guard were the Emperor's bodyguard.

Index

The Making of the

English
Patient

The Making of the
English
Patient

A Guide to Sources for the
Social History of Medicine

JOAN LANE

SUTTON PUBLISHING

First published in 2000 by
Sutton Publishing Limited · Phoenix Mill
Thrupp · Stroud · Gloucestershire · GL5 2BU

British Library Cataloguing in Publication Data
A catalogue record for this book is available from the British Library

ISBN 0 7509 2145 5 (hardback)
ISBN 0 7509 2146 3 (paperback)

Typeset in 10/11pt Baskerville MT.
Typesetting and origination by
Sutton Publishing Limited.
Printed and bound in England by
J.H. Haynes Co. Ltd, Sparkford.

For M.R.L.

CONTENTS

LIST OF ILLUSTRATIONS

ACKNOWLEDGEMENTS

Those of us who use English local record offices often become indebted to the archivists who work there, frequently for drawing our attention to a newly acquired research source, and this has been my experience during the last twenty years when I have been collecting many of the manuscript extracts that make up this selection. Material is included from the following record offices, and I am grateful to all – to some more than to others – for their services and permission to include material they hold: Bath, Birmingham, Coventry, Derbyshire, Essex, Gloucestershire, Herefordshire, Lichfield, Northamptonshire, Somerset, Staffordshire, the Shakespeare Birthplace Trust, Warwickshire and Worcestershire. I should also like to thank the Bodleian Library, the Library of the Royal College of Surgeons of England and the Wellcome Library for allowing me to use their records. Owners of portraits have been extremely generous in permitting photographs to be included, as have the county record societies for copyright permissions. At a personal level, I should like to thank Ann Bennett for her photographic skills and patience over the years. My students at Warwick will, I hope, be pleased to see in print many of the sources about which I have enthused to them and understand why sources for medical history matter.

Joan Lane,
Leamington Spa, November 2000

INTRODUCTION

The history of medicine has, in the last twenty years, aroused considerable interest in both specialist and amateur researchers. This is largely because it has shifted its emphasis from the traditional approach – the study of great scientific discoveries and figures, often researched by medical practitioners – to the broader one of the social history of medicine. This newer emphasis is essentially patient-orientated and far wider in scope. Just as we are all patients at various times in our lives, so a vast array of English history archives can be approached as having a medical content and interest, albeit unexpected and not regarded essentially as such. Some of these sources are clearly identifiable as medical history, for example, hospital records and practitioners' case notes, but information is also contained in a huge variety of other sources, such as personal papers, poor law and friendly society material, even works of art and religious monuments. These diverse sources, however, require more detective work by the researcher and the purpose of this collection is to indicate representative material that can be used. Most of the papers are accessible in English record offices, but some material is still held in private hands, especially letters, diaries and portraits. There is also a substantial amount of information on health and medical services in parish registers, parliamentary publications, trade directories and local newspapers, often not indexed, all again requiring painstaking detective work by the researcher.

The emphasis of this collection is the patient, what medical treatment was available, how it was viewed by the sufferer and how patients experienced their illness, a common topic in contemporary correspondence and diaries. In addition, how practitioners became qualified, how prosperous they might be and how a profession was created are also of considerable interest in the present century. Records, though, that are strictly medical (hospital admission registers, patient case notes and the like) are closed to public access for a hundred years, because of personal confidentiality, a limit also inevitably affecting this collection. Many local historians and especially those tracing their family roots will need to use medical history sources in their search, seeking ancestors as either practitioners or patients; records such as the Warwick workhouse listing, Birmingham Hospital admissions or the Stratford-upon-Avon smallpox survey are important and usually overlooked material about our forebears.

A problem of medical history sources, however, remains the erratic level of their survival and undeniably many have been destroyed, as, for instance, the papers belonging to Dr William Johnston (p. 17) and mentioned in his probate inventory, which were presumably his letters, case notes and prescriptions. Sometimes, papers are divided between different repositories, so that some of Richard Wilkes's journals and case notes are in the Lichfield Record Office (pp. 101–3) while others are in the

Wellcome Library in London. Deliberate destruction of such manuscripts by later generations seems to have been commonplace, yet some family papers still contain a medical ancestor's student lecture notes and letters, as, for example, those of Henry Ward (pp. 7–8). In other instances patient records have survived undisturbed and ignored in a very long-established practice, as the obstetric notes of Thomas Jones illustrate (pp. 106–10). The most difficult sources, yet the most interesting, especially in personal terms, are the accounts of illness, professional advice and treatment written by the patients themselves. Diaries and journals almost always note when the writer is unwell, the medical attention available and the outcome. Some also record illness beyond their own families, especially a local epidemic. Often it is clear that, like Samuel Pepys, diarists record their sufferings and later refer back to the account if they experience similar symptoms again; a journal is, naturally, generally intended to be read only by the writer. Letters, on the other hand, clearly contain a patient's description of suffering to a friend or relative, invariably including the medical opinion and often the fees charged. The advice is sometimes quoted verbatim, so that one eighteenth-century gentleman was told by his physician that 'Dr Horse is the best medicine' while another complained that 'The Doctor scolds me and brings me more of his vile nostrums', obviously patients unwilling to change their lifestyles on medical advice.

There are also certain categories of official sources for medical history that are national and wide ranging, for example, the great Apprenticeship Registers at the Public Record Office, listing the details of boys indentured to surgeons and apothecaries in the first half of the eighteenth century. Parish registers of baptism, marriage and burial are, of course, a well-known and essential source for tracing changing patterns of population and outbreaks of disease, even if the causes of death are usually unspecified. Regional sources include bishops' licences to practise medicine held in diocesan record offices, usually dating from before 1700, and the records of apprentices in the major trading companies and cities, some of whom were practitioners' sons. Although printed material, large numbers of parliamentary papers also contain medical information, especially those reporting on the poor law, specific trades and sanitary conditions in the nineteenth century. Most include evidence from practitioners and other commentators, often surprisingly detailed. Individual reformers also described the health of the poor, for example Sir F.M. Eden and the Revd David Davies, while the local press was always eager to print items of medical interest, including pieces on longevity, infanticide, infirmary news and advertisements for medical services, both qualified and quack.

A largely unexplored source for medical history are the many hundreds of portraits and memorials to practitioners in all parts of the country. Clearly the grandest physicians and surgeons sat to the best, most fashionable artists, but many practitioners of the middling sort also had their portraits painted, often by artists now unfortunately anonymous. A practitioner's standing in his own community is often illustrated by a memorial erected after his death, from the sumptuous Victorian creation to the simple plaque of stone or brass commemorating the 'peritissumus medicus' (most skilful physician) interred. For instance, one in Ripon Cathedral dated 1914 carried the inscription 'Honour a physician with the honour due to him'. Cartoons, of course, projected the unflattering view of practitioners, certainly from the age of Hogarth onwards, suggesting that they were not always universally admired and respected by their contemporaries. Sometimes a medical innovation, such as inoculation or vaccination, would be caricatured, while government inaction on a particular health problem would also be depicted as, for example, *Punch*'s drawing of personified diseases emerging from the River Thames in 1853 to threaten London. The nineteenth century saw the creation of a number of sentimental poverty-genre paintings, especially by such artists as Sir Luke Fildes, and many of these comprised a bedside scene showing a compassionate medical practitioner, the patient and grieving relatives. They are an interesting example of the doctor-as-saviour perception of practice, whereas in earlier paintings practitioners were usually not included.

Sources for the history of medicine are among the most diverse of all archives found in all English record offices, even if they are not catalogued as such. They can by careful and persistent detective work be made to yield an enormous amount of new information both about the practitioners themselves and their patients, even of the humbler sort, to give us a clearer picture of sickness and health in society during the centuries before the welfare state.

Pre-decimal currency
1*s* (shilling) = 5p, 1*d* (penny) = twelfth part of a shilling. A guinea (£1 1*s*) = £1.05p.

I
MEDICAL APPRENTICESHIP AND TRAINING

❖ ❖ ❖

A s in all skilled occupations, traditional apprenticeship was the means of training to be a surgeon or apothecary until the later nineteenth century, while physicians were always university-educated men. Apprenticeship involved the choice of a life-style as well as a career, with an accepted place in society and a lifelong commitment to that occupation. Medical apprenticeships were usually for seven years, although in the early nineteenth century apothecaries reduced the term by two years, and fourteen was usually the youngest age at which a child might be indentured. A boy's parents chose a surgeon-apothecary as a master; he agreed to bind the youth as his apprentice, taking a substantial sum of money, the premium, to cover the cost of tuition, board and lodging for the whole period, the term. The youth received no wages and had only limited free time; he lived as part of his master's family, often far from his own home. The indenture was a legal requirement of an apprenticeship, stating the master's and the apprentice's responsibilities. The master was *in loco parentis* to the child and could administer corporal punishment. If the training were not completed, the boy could be transferred to another master, with an appropriate financial adjustment. Medical apprentices, among the highest status trainees, were generally well treated in their masters' households, did not abscond and invariably completed their terms to set up in practice on their own account eventually. Many new young practitioners in advertising their

An apprenticeship indenture, 1676.

professional services stressed the name of the master with whom they had trained.

After the 1709 Stamp Act (8 Anne, *c.* 9), which fixed a tax scale (6*d* on every £1 of premiums less than £50, 1*s* on larger sums, plus 6*d* stamp duty), medical apprentices can be traced in the great apprenticeship registers in the Public Record Office, although these are less satisfactory after 1760. Individual indentures, however, survive in family and personal papers for a much longer period. The premium varied greatly (between £20 and £100 in London in 1747, for example), depending on what the parents could afford, but a famous medical practitioner could always attract large sums; thus Caesar Hawkins took £200 in 1736 and William Cheselden received £150, £250 and £310 in the years 1712–30. Men apprenticing their own sons did not pay premiums. Larger premiums were paid in cities, especially to a master with a hospital appointment. The few medical apprentices whose diaries have survived were mostly dissatisfied with their lives, either at the menial tasks they had to perform or their food and general living conditions. Most men were in single-handed practice, although family partnerships were beginning to develop by the mid-eighteenth century.

AN APPRENTICESHIP INDENTURE TO A SURGEON, 1705

[modernised spelling]
This Indenture witnesseth that John Beale of Woolscot in the county of Warwick puts himself apprentice to William Edwards[1] surgeon of Kenilworth to learn his art and with him after the manner of an apprentice to serve for four years from this date. During the term the apprentice shall faithfully serve his master, his secrets keep, his lawful commands gladly obey; the apprentice neither to do damage to his master nor see it done; the apprentice not to waste his master's goods nor lend them unlawfully. The apprentice not to commit fornication nor contract matrimony during the term; the apprentice not to play at cards or dice or any unlawful game that may cause his master loss. The apprentice not to haunt taverns nor ale-houses nor be absent unlawfully day or night from his master's service but in all things behave as a good and faithful apprentice towards his master.

William Edwards, in consideration of the sum of £53 16*s*, shall teach the apprentice all the art he uses by the best means he can. William Edwards shall find the apprentice in meat, drink, washing and lodging during the term.

1 May 1705. Signatures of William Edwards, John Beale and two witnesses.

Warwickshire County Record Office, CR 556/364.

APPRENTICESHIP EXPERIENCES

Joseph Hodgson in Birmingham, c. 1805

I was an apprentice of Mr Freer's,[2] who then lived in New St., and Mr Blount[3] lived in Temple Row. . . . I used to pass Mr Blount's house every day on my way to the hospital; [James Russell][4] stopped me one day as I was passing to the Hospital; he was not in attendance there but had a great longing to go; he asked me if I was going to the hospital, I told him I was & asked him to go with me. After that we became intimate, I asked him to call on me & then he used to come frequently. I seldom went to him as Mr Blount's rooms were not so convenient as ours, but he often used to come to me.

I used to dissect a great deal, and inject: & [Russell] was very fond of coming to help me: Mr Blount was very kind in letting him come to me, but Mr Freer did not much like my going out. [Russell] used to bring pieces to dissect, from the Workhouse, to which Mr Blount was surgeon.

At last we were constantly together; I used to call for him when I went to carry out medicines, for at that time we pupils used to take out the medicines . . . we had a little society which used to meet in our room at Mr Freers; . . . we used to lecture, & I have by me now the lectures on anatomy which I wrote.

R.E. Franklin, 'Medical Education and the rise of the General Practitioner, 1760–1860', unpublished PhD thesis, University of Birmingham, 1950, pp. 67–8.

John Taylor in Bolton, Lancashire, c. 1825

I studied hard; learned the Linnean names and doses of drugs; attended seven surgical operations; worked from nine to nine daily, Sundays included; made mercury ointment in the old style by turning a pestle in a mortar for three days in succession, to amalgamate the quicksilver with the pig's grease; made up what the doctor called his 'Cathartic acid bitter mixture', as a sort of fill-up for every purgative bottle, and almost every disease that 'flesh is heir to'; made up boluses of a teaspoonful of preserve with half-a-grain of opium, as a sedative; drew a tooth for 6d; and took 4d if the sufferer had no more; and did many things during that six months which gave me a distaste for the practice of medicine, and made me desirous of another employment.

John Taylor (b. 1811) left medicine to enter the law; he became a coroner in Bolton, Lancashire and kept a legal diary from 1844.

Autobiography of a Lancashire Lawyer, ed. J. Clegg (Bolton, 1883), p. 16.

THE DUTIES OF A HOUSE-PUPIL AT THE MIDDLESEX HOSPITAL, 1761

He must not absent himself from the business of the Hospital at the same time as the apothecary. He must supervise the work of the apprentices and pupils in the surgery; he must report any incident of swearing or other misbehaviour to the first surgeon who next comes to the Hospital; in default of which the whole blame shall be at his door and leave him open to be censured or even expelled as the Board shall think proper. He must attend constantly at the dressing of the patients and carry pen, ink and paper to minute down all messages to the physicians or instructions relating to the patients.

H. Campbell Thomson, The Story of the Middlesex Hospital School (1935), p. 12.

SIR ASTLEY COOPER'S EVIDENCE TO THE SELECT COMMITTEE ON MEDICAL EDUCATION, 1834

Astley Cooper (1768–1841) was the fourth son of a cleric. He served as anatomy lecturer at St Thomas's Hospital and as consultant to Guy's Hospital. He was created a baronet in 1821 and published extensively. Cooper was one of the sixteen distinguished medical witnesses to appear before the Select Committee. He had himself been apprenticed in 1784 to a London surgeon for seven years for the extremely high premium of £535.

Question. What is the present expense of hospital attendance in London?
Astley Cooper. There are three classes. The first is the apprentice, who usually pays about £500 or £600 to be boarded and lodged in the house of the surgeon to whom he is attached.
Q. Do you mean of the hospital surgeon?
A.C. Yes. The second is the dresser, who pays £500 for the advantage of dressing for 12 months. The third is the pupil, who pays £26 5s. to be considered as a perpetual pupil, but in reality to enter only for 12 months; because it was thought right to hold over him, if he did not conduct himself properly, the power of disposing of him at the end of the year.
Q. Will the lectures which an apprenticed pupil is required to attend, be the lectures given in the hospital to which the master-surgeon is attached; or is the apprentice generally allowed to select, at his own discretion, the lecturers whose courses he will attend?
A.C. He enters, when he first embarks in the profession, at the lectures delivered at the hospital; but if he chooses afterwards to attend any particular lectures, he is at liberty to do so. For example, I myself, whilst I lived with Mr Cline,[5] attended Mr Hunter's[6] lectures.
Q. What is the minimum expense incurred by a surgical student, studying in London?
A.C. As an apprentice, it would cost him £2,000 for the six or seven years of education, before he could embark in practice. That is the sum which a man ought to calculate that his son would spend, under such circumstances.
Q. How many months need he actually study in London?
A.C. About 15 months.
Q. What items of expense would the education in London involve?
A.C. If he be an apprenticed pupil, he pays £600 as an apprentice fee. Then he has to enter the anatomical lectures, which would be £21; the lectures on surgery about £5 5s.; the lectures on physic about £8 8s.; the lectures on chemistry about £8 8s., midwifery about £10, if he were a perpetual pupil to them.
Q. What is the expense for dissection?
A.C. The expense of anatomy is quite uncertain. It depends upon the price of subjects, whether you give £14 or three guineas. I hold that every man should dissect two bodies, at least, if not three. You may put that at nine guineas. Then materia medica would be about four guineas. Physiology is a separate course at our hospital. Two courses of physiology would be three guineas. Twelve months of surgical practice, in a recognized hospital in London, is, as I have stated, £26 5s. as a pupil.

Report from the Select Committee on the Education and Practice of the Medical Profession in the United Kingdom (1834), pp. 96–7.

A MEDICAL STUDENT IN EIGHTEENTH-CENTURY LONDON

John Coakley Lettsom (1744–1815), a Quaker, was born in the West Indies, a planter's son, and was sent to England in 1750 to be educated at Penketh, Lancashire before being indentured, aged sixteen, to a surgeon-apothecary, Abraham Sutcliff, at Settle, Yorkshire, the third of seven apprentices, for five years with a premium of £60. He went to London in 1766 with an introduction to John Fothergill MD (1712–80), then at the height of his reputation, whose brother was Lettsom's guardian. Lettsom was entered as a surgeon-dresser under Benjamin Cowell (1716–83) at St Thomas's Hospital, where Mark Akenside MD (1721–70) was one of three consultants. Lettsom very much wanted to study under Akenside, a noted poet as well as a physician, but seems to have been quickly disillusioned at Akenside's manner towards patients, of which he wrote an account in his diary.

Lettsom returned briefly to the West Indies to practise, then studied at Edinburgh and Leiden before settling in London, where he founded the Aldersgate Dispensary and the London Medical Society. He was influential in the Royal Humane Society and in establishing the Sea-Bathing Infirmary. He lived in a villa, Grove Hill, at Camberwell and was an extremely popular and successful practitioner. A philanthropist and scholar, he died a very wealthy man.

Lettsom's account of Dr Mark Akenside at St Thomas's Hospital

> Great was my disappointment in finding Akenside, the most supercilious and unfeeling physician that I had then, or have since known. If the poor affrighted patients did not return a direct answer to his queries, he would often instantly discharge them from the hospital. He evinced a particular disgust to females, & generally treated them with harshness. I was informed that this moroseness was occasioned by disappointment in love; but hapless must have been that female that should have been placed under his tyranny. I was inexpressibly shocked at an instance of his inhumanity exercised towards a patient of Abraham's ward, to whom I had ordered bark boluses; who, in consequence of not being able to swallow them, so irritated Akenside, as to order the sister of the ward to discharge him from the hospital, adding "he shall not die under my care". As the sister was removing him in obedience to the doctor, the patient expired.

> James Johnston Abraham, *Lettsom, his Life, Times, Friends and Descendants* (1933), p. 40.

BEGINNING A MEDICAL CAREER IN THE NINETEENTH CENTURY

The future career of a young man in medicine could follow different paths in the nineteenth century, but with few variations. If he or his parents could afford it after apprenticeship, a training period at a hospital was followed by an infirmary post before setting up in practice. General practice itself comprised several sources of income – private patients, poor law work, new and traditional institutional appointments (to a dispensary, hospital, friendly society, asylum or prison), as well as an increasing number of bureaucratic tasks (inspecting apprentices and militia men or attending inquests). Junior hospital posts, however, were considered a good early step in a young man's career, providing a guaranteed salary, training under local consultants and a chance to become known to potential private patients before setting up in practice. Such posts were usually advertised in local newspapers, which had a far wider readership than in the immediate area.

Henry Ward was one such young man. He was baptised at Castle Bromwich in 1786, a gentleman's son, and indentured to a Birmingham surgeon-apothecary and man-midwife, John Taylor, in 1804 with a premium of £100 for four years. Ward may have been bound to an earlier master but he seems to have been the last of Taylor's five apprentices. In 1809–10 Henry Ward trained at the Westminster Hospital, London, where he was taught surgery by William Lynn and Anthony Carlisle. He was also a house-pupil for nearly two years to Charles Bell at the Middlesex Hospital, while from John Abernethy he learned surgery, with anatomy, dissection and midwifery taught by James Roberton. His teachers' references praised his 'greatest diligence' and the 'general propriety of his conduct' making him 'fitted for the Place of House Surgeon at any Hospital'. He had certificates of attendance from all his London courses. He became a Member of the Royal College of Surgeons in 1809.

Ward's period of training coincided with the opening of a new county infirmary at Derby and in March 1810 the governors decided to advertise the post in the press, including the Hull and Manchester newspapers, as well as in existing hospitals and in the London anatomy lectures. The applicants' letters were to be answered, testimonials requested and an appointment made on 5 April; the infirmary would open on 4 June 1810. There were eight candidates, including Henry Ward, who began canvassing support in Derby. After failing to secure the hospital appointment, Ward became a surgeon-apothecary at Atherstone, north Warwickshire in 1811 as the partner of an established practitioner, Benjamin Hector. However, their partnership was dissolved three years later. From Atherstone Ward treated poor law patients in four nearby parishes for many years.

Letters of application for a hospital post, 1810

Ladies and Gentlemen,
The Situation of House Surgeon and Apothecary being vacant {I take the liberty} I now take the earliest opportunity of offering myself as a candidate for the situation, and do most earnestly and respectfully solicit your support.
        I have the Honour to be
                Your Obedient Servant, Henry Ward.
I beg Leave to solicit the favour of your Votes and interest at the ensuing election of House Surgeon and Apothecary to the General Hospital.
Should I succeed in the object of my Wishes, it shall be my constant endeavour to promote the welfare of that /excellent/ Institution. I have the Honour to be Ladies and Gentlemen your humble servant. . . .

Henry Ward also felt the need to promote himself in Derby and wrote of his efforts to a Mr Wheelwright:

I have now just arrived at Derby and I found my first place was to call upon Mr Simpson Clarke to the Governors,[7] and he informed me that there was several candidates;[8] and one or two of them now in Derby, acanvassing, I feel myself much obliged to you for the Letter you wrote for me. Mr Barr did not know any body in Derby, or else he would have given a letter, but Mr Burton [?] gave me a letter to Mr Webster[9] at the Kings Arms Hotel in Derby, and the aforesaid Mr Webster promises me all as interest and behave very kind to me inform what Gentlemen to go to. As I think there will be a good deal of opposition, I will thank you to send that satificate of Roberton down to Hodge Hill being I shall leave Derby on Friday and so return again next week.

Derbyshire Record Office, D 1190 and Warwickshire County Record Office, CR 1020/106/1–40.

RESURRECTIONISTS AND MEDICAL TRAINING

The criminal activities of Burke and Hare in providing corpses for dissection at the Edinburgh medical school are widely known. However, the growth in the number of medical students and schools by the later eighteenth century meant that there was a widespread demand for bodies for anatomical demonstrations, while numbers legally available were controlled. The Barber Surgeons' Company under an Act of 1530 (22 Henry VIII, c. 12) were allowed the corpses of four malefactors, taken from the gallows, for post-mortem examination every year and these dissections were publicly advertised and widely attended. Hogarth's engraving, *The Reward of Cruelty* (1751), illustrates a public dissection at Surgeons' Hall. Dissection was always regarded as a further punishment imposed in addition to the death penalty. The surgeons were inevitably involved in criminal activities to secure bodies. They would pay quite substantial sums to the resurrectionists and pass these charges on to their students, even forming themselves into an Anatomical Club to regulate prices. Not all bodies were exhumed, however, but stolen or obtained by false pretences before burial. The resurrection-men regularly bribed the custodians of burial grounds and some grave-diggers colluded with them; several bodies could thus be removed from a single graveyard in one night, in spite of the 'patrols'. A deceased's relatives could hire grave-watchers to protect the burial at night until the decomposed body was unsuitable for dissection or a large iron cage, a mortsafe, could be erected over the burial plot. An iron coffin was a further precaution. A unique archive source, a London resurrectionist's working diary, has survived from the early nineteenth century; the original is now in the Library of the Royal College of Surgeons of England. It records that an adult corpse cost surgeons at least £4 4s and bodies were graded as large, small and 'foetus'. During the period from 28 November 1811 to 5 December 1812 receipts in this diary came to £1394 8s. There are no entries during May, June and July, when warmer weather meant that dissection was not taught and when summer nights were long and light. Anatomy schools' sessions ran from October to May and corpses were sent to some of the most famous medical names in London, often to order, and also to Edinburgh on several occasions.

The Reward of Cruelty from William Hogarth's *The Four Stages of Cruelty*, 1751.

The diarist was Joseph Naples, born at Deptford in 1774 and serving as a sailor by 1797. He then became a grave-digger at the Spa Fields burial ground. He continued as a resurrectionist until the passing of the Anatomy Act in 1831, when he worked as a servant in the dissecting room of St Thomas's Hospital. The gang of eight was led by Benjamin Crouch, a carpenter's son, who was employed at Guy's Hospital.

W. Austin, 'The Anatomist overtaken by the Watch . . . carryng off Miss W . . . [ts] in a Hamper'.
The anatomist has dropped a paper, 'Hunter's Lectures'.

Joseph Naples's diary, November–December 1811

Thursday 28th November At night went out and got 3, Jack & me Hospital Crib,[10] Benj[n], Dan[l] & Bill to Harpers,[11] Jack & me 1 big Gates,[12] sold 1 Taunton[13] D[o] St Thomas's.

Friday 29th November At night went out and got 3, Jack Ben & me got 2, Bethnall Green, Bill & Dan[l] 1 Bartholo[w] Crib opened;[14] whole at Barth[w].

Saturday 30th At night went and got 3 Bunhill Row, sold to Mr Cline,[15] St Thomas's Hospital.

Sunday 1st December We all look[d] out, at Home all night.

Monday 2nd December Met at St Thomas's, Got paid for the 3 adults & settled with Mordecai[16] and made Him up £2 5s. 6d. and Receipt of all demands. At Home all night.

Tuesday 3rd December Went to look out and brought the Shovils from Barthol[w]. Met early in the evening at Mr Vickers[17] did not go out that night. Butler and me came home intoxsicated.

Wednesday 4th December At night went out and got 10, whole [all the gang] went to Green[18] and got 4, Black Crib 1, Bunner fields[19] 5.

Thursday 5th December The whole at home all night.

Friday 6th December Removed 1 from Barthol. to Carpue.[20] At night went out and got 8, Dan[l] at home all night. 6 Back St Lukes & 2 Big Gates: went 5 Barthol. 1 Frampton,[21] 3 St Thomas's, 3 Wilson.[22]

Saturday 7th December At night went out & got 3 at Bunhill Row. 1 St Thomas's, 2 Brookes.[23]

Sunday 8th December At home all night.

Monday 9th December At night went out and got 4 at Bethnall Green.

Tuesday 10th December intoxsicated all day: at night went out & got 5 Bunhill Row. Jack all most buried.

Wednesday 11th December Tom & Bill and me removed 5 from St Barthol[w], 2 Wilson, 2 Brookes, 1 Bell;[24] in the evening got 1 Harp[er]s, went to St Thomas, at home all night.

Thursday 12th December I went up to Brookes and Wilson, afterwards me Bill and Daniel went to Bethnall Green, got 2; Jack, Ben went got 2 large & 1 small back St Luke's,[25] came home, afterwards met again & went to Bunhill row got 6, 1 of them with [her throat cut] named Mary Rolph, aged 46, Died 5th Dec. 1811.

Friday 13th December At Home all day & night.

Saturday 14th December Went to Bartholomew took[d] two Brookes: Pack[d] 4 and sent them to Edinborough, came Home to Ben[n], settled £14 6s. 2d. each man, came home, got up at 2 me Jack & Bill went to Bunhill Row and got 3. Ben & Daniel staid at home.

Sunday 15 December At home all day Got up at 3 a.m. The whole party went to Harp[er]s, got 3, Went to St Thomas's.

Monday 16th December At home all day & night Ill.

Tuesday 17th December At home all day & do. night.

Wednesday 18th December At home all day & do night.

Thursday 19th December Went to Bartholomew, At home all night.

Friday 20th December Went to St Thomas's, came home and went to the play, came home: at 3 A.M. got up and went to the Hospital Crib got 5 large.

Saturday 21st December Went to St Thomas's sent 1 to Mr Taunton, 2 to Edinburgh, St Thomas's took 6 of the above this week, came home and stopt home all night.

Sunday 22nd December Went and look'd out, at 4 o'clock, got up, party went to Harp[er]s got 3 large and 2 small, the whole went to Barth[m].

Monday 23rd December Went for orders to Wilson and Brookes, Met Bill, Brought one to Capue, Sent him back to bring 2 from Bartol[w] 1 for Brookes, 1 for Bell, Ben[n] and Jack got 5 small at Harpers.

Tuesday 24th December At twelve at midnight a party went to Wygate got 3 small, came back and got 2 large at Newington, Came home then settled at Ben[n], Each man's share £8 16s. 8d., at home all night.

Wednesday, 25th December At home all day and night.

Thursday 26th December At home all day and night.

Friday 27th December Went to look out, Came home met Ben and Dan[l] at 5 o'clock, went to Harp[er]s, got 1 large and took it to Jack's house, Jack, Bill and Tom not with us, Geting drunk.

Saturday 28th December At 4 o'clock in the morning got up, with the whole party to Guy's and St Thomas's Crib, got 6 took them to St Thomas's Came home and met at Thomas's again, pack[d] up 3 for Edinbro, took one over to Guys.

Sunday 29th December At home all day and night.

Monday 30th December Butler and Dan[l] took 1 large to Framton, large small to Hornig.[26]

Tuesday 31st December Met at the Harty Choak,[27] had dispute about the horse.

January 1812

Wednesday 1st January Got up at 3 in the morning, the whole party went to Guys and St Thomas', got three adults, 1 from Guys and 2 from St Thomas', took them to St Thomas', came home and met again, took one of the above to Guys, settled for the Horse £24. At home all night.

Thursday 2nd January Went down to St Thomas's, got paid £7 17 6 for one adult open D° not. Came home, met by agreement at St Thomas's, did not go out, Bill not there. Came home again, at home all night.

Friday 3rd January Went to St Thomas's, took the Foetus to the London, Rec^d 10s. 6d. Came back to St Thomas's Rec^d £4 4s 0d, Went home, Met by agreement, Went to the Green got 5, Jack, Benⁿ and me; Danl and Bill at home, took the above 5 to Barthol^w at home all night.

Saturday 4th January Met at Bartholo^w, they took 4 of the above, 1 sent to Edinburgh, I went to Brookes, Carpue and Wilson for orders, Came back, at home all night.

Sunday 5th January At home all day. Met at 5, whole went to Newin[gton] got 3. Jack and me took them to Wilson, Came home, met at 12, got 5 & 2 small at Harp[er]s, afterwards went to the Big Gates, got 3 adults, left Danl at home, took the whole to Bartho^m.

Monday 6th January Went to Barth^w., took 1 to the London, Jack & Tom 1 to Harnige, D° 1 to St Thomas's. Came home, in all night.

Tuesday, 7th January At home all day, Tom removed 1 from the borough to Bartholom^w fetched £2 from there, took 2 to Mr Wilson, D° to Brookes.

Wednesday 8th January At 2 am got up, the Party went to Harp[er]s, got 4 adults and 1 small, took 4 to St Thomas's, came home and went to Mr Wilson & Brookes, Danl got paid £8 8s 0d from Mr Wilson I recd. 9 9 0 from Mr Brookes, Came over to the borough, sold small for £1 10 0, Recd £4 4 0 for adult, At home all night.

Thursday 9th January Went down to St Thomas's, got paid £8 8 0, 2 adults: at home all night.

Friday 10th January Met at St Thomas's, settled each man's share £12 12 0, 3 things on hand.

Saturday 11th January At 4 am got up & went to the Hospital Crib, got 2 adults, met at Barthol^w, packed up 2 for the Country, sold 1 at St Thomas's: at home all night.

Sunday 12th January At home all day, at 11 pm met & the whole went to Wygate, got 2 adults & 2 small, afterwards went to the Green, got 2 large & 1 small, Took them to Barthol^w.

Monday 13th January Took 2 of the above to Mr Brookes & 1 large & 1 small to Mr Bell, Foetus to Mr Carpue, small to Mr Framton, Large small to Mr Cline. Met at 5, the party went to Newington, 2 adults. Took them to St Thomas's.

Tuesday 14th January At 1 am got up, Benⁿ, Bill & me went to St Lukes, 2 adults; Jack, Danl Big Gates, 1 large & 1 small, took them to Bartholo^w. Came home & went to St Thomas's, afterwards went to the other end of the town for orders. At home all night.

Wednesday 15th January Went to St Thomas's, Came back, pack'd up 2 large & 1 small for Edinburgh. At home all night.

Thursday 16th January The party met at the Hartichoak. Settled the above, Each man's share £8 4s. 7d. At home all night.

Friday 17th January Went & look out: came home met at 11, party except Danl. Went to the Hospital Crib, & got 4, was stopt by the patrols, Butler, Horse & Cart were taken.

Saturday 18th January Went to the White horse, Butler bailed: at home all night.

Sunday 19th January Went & look'd out, at home all night, Could not get the horse out of the Stable.

Monday 20th January At home all day & night, Butler & Jack got drunk.

Tuesday 21st January Look'd out, Jack & Butler drunk as before, hindred us of going out. At Home.

Wednesday 22nd January At 4 o'clock in the morning got up, Bill & me went to the Hospital Crib and 1 for Mr Cooper's[28] Lectures, had a dispute with the party, at home all night. Ben got drunk.

Thursday 23rd January Met at 10 at night, went to Wygate, got 4 large and 1 small, went to the Green got 3 large. Dan[l] not with us.

Friday 24th January Met at 11 at night. Met the patrols. Got one Hospital Crib and 6 at Bermondsey, took them to Barthol[w], sent 3 to the Country.

Saturday 25th January Met at Bartholomew. Took 1 to Mr Carpue; St Barthol[w] took 2; at home all night.

Sunday 26th January Went to Big Gates to Look out, came home, at home all night.

Monday 27th January At 2 o'clock in the morning, got up, met the party except Dan[l]. Went to the Big gates, got 4 Took them to Barthol[w]. Afterwards met, took 1 to Mr Cline, 2 to Mr Wilson, came home. Tom & Bill got drunk, did not go out.

Tuesday 28th January Went to Barthol[w], could not sell, came back to the Borough & came home, at home all night.

Wednesday 29th January Went to Bartho[w], brought remaining 2 to St Thomas's, at home all night.

Thursday 30th January Went to St Thomas's, at home all night.

Friday 31st January Went to look out, at night went out, got 2 Guys & Thomas's, same night 3 Harp[er]s 2 small: same night the Cart broke down, took 2 to Guys.

James Bailey Blake, *The Diary of a Resurrectionist, 1811–1812* (1896), pp. 139–51.

PRESS REPORTS OF BODY-SNATCHING

Many aspects of the crime of body-snatching were widely reported in the eighteenth- and nineteenth-century press, often as merely a scandalous and horrific news item, but also as a warning to would-be resurrectionists and to the medical practitioners who were their clients. By 1753 a Bill had reached parliament making it a felony, with a death sentence, to steal corpses from consecrated ground. However, the trade continued until the passing of the Anatomy Act in 1831, enabling corpses to be legally dissected in medical schools.

London. We hear that in searching the Lodgings of a Woman who was taken up with the Head and Arm of a Man in a Sack, a Child's Hand and other Parts were found; and that it is since discovered that the Head and Arm were part of a Corpse taken out of a Burying Ground belonging to St. George's Hospital.

Aris's Gazette, 13 May 1754.

On Tuesday the 23 of December last, Mr. S., professor of anatomy, Great Queen-street, employed a man to procure him a dead body, that he might demonstrate the muscels the day following to his young pupils, amounting to upwards of seventy. The man according to agreement brought the body in a sack the same evening to his dissecting room, but shocking to relate, on examining the body, he found it to be his own sister, that was buried at Kensington on the 14th, the sight of which threw Mr. S. into strong convulsions, and he now lies dangerously ill.

Bristol Journal, 10 January 1784.

Yesterday a man was whipt through High-street, in the Borough, for stealing dead bodies out of the Church-yard of St. George's in the East.

Whitehall Evening Post, 20–22 January 1784.

The curiosity of the public was yesterday much excited by the exposal of the heads of two lascars at Stepney. It seems that two of those personages, vulgarly called resurrection men, were detected by the watchman with them in a sack and (soon after they were stopped) found means to make their escape. It is presumed, that as the bodies were not taken with them, they were stolen merely with a view to the profits arising from the sale of their beautiful long black hair, which is particularly valuable.

Gazeteer and New Daily Advertiser, 21 June 1784.

Some bodies having been stolen from the church-yard of a remote parish in Northumberland, the owner of the estate, to prevent such depradation in the future, has directed the graves to be made rather shorter than the coffin, and to be excavated at the bottom, so as to admit the head under the solid ground. It is then impossible to raise it by the feet and the ground must be cut away above the head – a work of more time than could always be commanded by the operation. In addition, a mixture of percussion powder and gunpowder, placed on a wire in the inside of the coffin, to explode on its being opened, has been resorted to. This will retain its explosive power for a month, in which time the corpse will be generally unfit for dissection.

The Carlisle Journal, quoted in *The Times,* 17 February 1824.

RECOMMENDATIONS TO PRACTISE MEDICINE

We the Minister Church Wardens and other Inhabitants of the Parish of Road whose Names are hereunto Subscribed Do Certifye that William Gawen hath performed many Extraordinary Cures in the Art of Surgery and hath Practised the Same for many Years past, with good Success: and We do recommend him as a proper Person to be Licensed for that Practice Witness our hands this 11th day of May 1742.
James Churchward Minister
William Crabbe & Thomas Barnes Churchwardens
James Gerish   William Stevens junr   James Barnes   Thos Gerrish

Somerset Record Office, D/D/Rn.

To The Worshipful Richard Smalbroke Doctor of Laws, Chancellor of the Diocese of Litchfield and Coventry.

We whose names are Subscribed do hereby Certify that Mr Richard Wicksteed of Whitchurch in the County of Salop and Diocese of Litchfield and Coventry hath practised as An Apothecary for the Space of thirty years at Least, with Skill and Judgment, and we do recommend him as A proper person to obtain a License to practise Physick given under our hands this sixteenth day of October in the year of our Lord 1749.
Peter Colthurst   John Whitfield

Lichfield Record Office, B/A/11/5.

MEDICAL PARTNERSHIP AGREEMENT, 1777

Single-handed practice was by far the commonest way of making a medical living until well into the nineteenth century. However, family practices, really medical dynasties, certainly existed and in 1777 George Weale, surgeon-apothecary of Warwick, took his son, Edward, into partnership with a formal written agreement. George Weale served as poor law surgeon to four parishes and also attended prisoners at the county gaol. He was master to three apprentices. George Weale died in March 1797. Edward Weale, his son, was also a parish surgeon. Their separate professional spheres were clearly set out in the partnership deed – George Weale was to retain his gaol appointment, worth £20 a year, and Edward Weale was to keep his own midwifery fees.

Clauses in a partnership agreement between George Weale and Edward Weale, May 1777

1. The partnership is to last for seven years from 16 April last.
2. Edward Weale to pay his father for half the drugs in the shop and surgery.
3. Edward Weale to pay £60 to enter the partnership.
4. Future drugs etc. to be bought jointly.
5. Work to be done only on behalf of the partnership.
6. George Weale to retain his personal appointment as county gaol surgeon and keep the fees from the appointment.
7. Edward Weale to practise midwifery and keep the fees.
8. Neither to pay for drugs used in the above [6 and 7] or in treating their own families.
9. Accounts to be kept relating to drugs, visits and attendances. Profits and debts to be shared equally.
10. Each partner to provide and keep one horse at his own expense.
11. A servant to be paid jointly by the partners to look after the horses, attend the shop and other necessary tasks.
12. Edward Weale to pay George Weale £3 a year as half the rent of the shop and surgery and for the use of drawers, counters, shelves, mortars, stills, stillhorse, instruments and articles.
13. If either partner should die, his share is to belong to his executors.

Warwickshire County Record Office, CR1596/Box 90.

PRACTITIONERS' PROBATE INVENTORIES

Inventories were made at death to value the deceased's goods and chattels; the document was proved and retained by the diocesan authorities. Land was not included in the deceased person's assets, but the value of personal possessions, livestock, tools, household goods and cash was noted and listed by two or three local inhabitants. Inventories, in conjunction with wills, indicate a person's prosperity. The document is usually arranged as if going round the house room by room, providing valuable information about changing domestic fashions and individual occupations. Although wills never ceased to be made, inventories become rare after the later eighteenth century. Inventories are usually found in diocesan record offices.

The inventory of John Parker, apothecary of Lichfield, 1711

John Parker had acquired a bishop's licence to practise medicine in February 1685 and he died a comparatively wealthy man. His apothecary supplies were very valuable indeed at £70. He owned silver plate and pictures and his house had five bedrooms. At his death he was owed for his services a total of £10, part of which was noted as 'desperate', or unlikely to be recovered.

An Inventory of the Goods and Chattells of Mr John Parker late of the City of Lichfield Apothecary deceased valued and apprized this 19th Day of May 1711 by Wm Berwick and Xtopher Barker as followeth (viz.)
Impris In the Shop and Wairhouse Drugs, Plaisters, Oyntments, Oyles, Speritts, Syrups, conserves, simple-water, Gally potts, Glasses, Morters, pestells, Scales and Weights, Counters, Boxes and all other Utensills belonging to his trade valued at £70

In the Parlour
  Chairs, Pictures, fire shovell, and tongs and other goods there vallued at   £4 0 0
In the Kitchen Brass, Pewter, fire irons Dresser, Bookes and all other Goods there £3
In the Scullery Some od things there valued at   5 0
In the Pantry and Buttery Ticknall Wair and other goods at   8 0
In the Cellars Barrells and bottles and other od things there at   £1 0 0
In the best Chamber or Chamber over the Parlour
  One Bed with all the furniture therto belonging Caine Chairs,
  a Chest of Drawers one table, one picture, one Chimney peice,
  Grate Window Curtains and Glass   £5 0 0
In the Chamber over the Shop One Bed and furniture 6 cane Chairs at   £3 0 0
In the Chamber over the passage One Couch one Chest one trunk
  Boxes pictures and other od things   £2 0 0
In the Chamber over the Pantry One Bed and furniture looking
  glass table Chairs and other od things   £1 0 0
In the Chamber over the Kitchen Two Beds and furniture one
  Chest of Drawers two Chests Books table Glass Chairs and
  other furniture at   £3 0 0
In the Garretts One Garner, gally potts, Glasses, Boxes
  and other Lumber at   £1 0 0
In a little Room by the Garrett One old Bed and furniture vallued at   10 0

	£	s	d
Linnen of all sorts vallued at	£6	0	0
Plate of all sorts at	£4	0	0
Wearing Apparell and Money in his pockett	£10	0	0
Book Debts hopeful and desperate	£10	0	0
In the Brewhouse Two furnaces one Still one Linebeck, tubs,			
Dresser, Grate fireshovel and other Lumber at	£3	10	0
In the Stable Hay and Straw at		10	0
In the Yard Lumber and some wooden Waire at		5	0
	£128	8	0

Lichfield Record Office, B/C/5/1711/32.

William Johnston MD of Warwick

William Johnston (1643–1725) gained an MD at both Angers in 1673 and at Cambridge in 1682, three years later becoming a Fellow of the Royal College of Physicians. He was the most senior practitioner in Warwick and the only physician in the town. He was obviously a wealthy man, owning portraits, silver and land. Although his patients' records have not survived, it is clear that he attended the local aristocracy after his arrival in Warwick in 1675. His large new house, built in 1692–3, and its contents are described in detail when his widow, Ann, died in 1733 and an inventory was made by a local surveyor, James Fish. As well as the usual domestic areas and servants' quarters, there were eight bedrooms and five living rooms, including William Johnston's study, where intriguingly Fish noted 'The Doctor's Bookes' were worth £12. The house was later the home of the poet, Walter Savage Landor.

Extracts from Ann Johnston's inventory

The Parlour	£	s	d
One Black Card Table		2	0
One corner Table		6	0
One Great Looking Glass	1	16	0
Six Glass schonces		10	6
One clock and clock case	5	0	0
One broken weather Glass		4	6
The Fire Grate with Brass Faces		10	0
The Fender, Fire shovel and Tonges		2	0
Two hand Fire skreens			6
Eight Kain chaires		12	0
The chimney Peece Picture	1	1	0
The Drs and Mrs Johnstons			
Pictures	2	2	0
Miss Heyingtons Picture	1	1	0
Sir John Bowyers and two			
other Pictures		8	0
Eight yellow silk cushions		8	0
Two yellow silk window seats		2	0
Window shutters and Iron barrs	—	—	

The Kitchen Chamber	£	s	d
One bedstead, curtains lined and			
Counterpaine	2	0	0
Featherbed, bolster, pillows	4	7	6
Two Blankets		7	6
Easie chaire and cushion		10	6
Three Old Kaine chairs		6	0
Four Green cushions		5	0
One square Table and Drawer		2	0
One Scrutone under the clock		16	0
The Eight Day clock	7	0	0
One Great Skrewtone wallnut	2	0	0
Tapestry Hangings	2	0	0
Grate, Fender, fireshovel and			
Tonges and Poker		11	6
One Paire of Bellows		1	6
One Close stoole and Pewter Pan		2	6
The Chimney Peece Picture		8	0

Medical equipment sold in 1733

	s	d
Mr Hall's[29] man Lancet case and sissors etc.	2	0
Mr Chernock 1 marble mortar & glass pestle	3	0
ye silver syringe	13	0
Chirurgeon's case of Instruments	12	6
tweeser case	1	0

Warwickshire County Record Office, WA6/113–154,
the property of Warwick District Council.

The inventory of the shop of William Freeman of Wellesbourne, 1785

William Freeman was a surgeon-apothecary at Wellesbourne, Warwickshire, born in about 1755, whose inventory was made on 3 February 1785. Apart from the usual household goods, the contents of the shop and his books were listed and separately valued at £31 18s 2d by John Freer, the Birmingham surgeon. There was also an eight-page list of 'drugs, chymicals etc.' and some thirty bills for medical treatment. He did occasional poor law work. Freeman had had two apprentices bound to him, in 1775 and 1781, and was among the subscribers to John Jordan's poem, *Welcome Hills*, in 1777.

Shop

12 Large Glass Jarrs & Stopper, Flint Glass
26 Smaller Do Do Do
1 Large Do Do
24 Jarrs Tin Tops
88 Small Bottles
62 Smaller Do
26 Large Mouth^d Do
86 Glass Bottles Diff^t Sizes
46 Earthen & Stone Pots
6 Stone Jarrs
26 Galley Pots
Marble Pestle & Mortar
A Stone Mortar
5 Pewter Measures 4 Tin Funils
6 Brass Weights 1 Iron Do 2 Lead Do
4 Beams & Scales
Pr Money Scales
5 Salve Knives Iron Ladle & Large Slate
Marble Slab 2 Tools to Spread Plasters
Small Box w^t Instruments
2 Powdering Sceives
Small Pr Steps 4 Small Boxes & Tub
Counter 8 Nests of Drawers Glass Case

Part of Counter 25 Shelves 2 Viol Racks & Scale
Do & Shew Board at the Door
2 Vols of Town & Country
2 Vols Beauties of Spectators & Tatlers
1 Do Lind on Hot Climates
2 Vols Practice on Physick
1 Vol. Freemans Letters
9 Physical Books
11 Pamphlets

Warwickshire County Record Office, CR 1596/Box 92.

PRACTITIONERS IN LIVERPOOL IN 1773

At least a century before Samuel Foart Simmons published his *Medical Registers*, practitioners had been listed in commercial directories compiled for the largest English towns and cities. However, practitioners were not normally separated from the general listing although, as in Sketchley's *Directory* for Birmingham (1767), physicians were included in the first section, 'Some of the Professors of the Polite Arts, &c', which also gave the names of musicians and drawing masters. Apothecaries and surgeons (twenty in all) were placed between anvil makers and attorneys in the town's trades. Liverpool's directories, beginning in 1766, are some of the earliest in the country, presumably because of its status as a port and trading centre. The Gore family were responsible for a range of these, John Gore for the years 1766–1803 and Johnson Gore from 1805 to 1855. The 1773 directory was the fourth they published.

Physicians, Surgeons, Dentists, Apothecaries and Druggists

Alanson, Edward, surgeon, Cable Street
Antrobus, Thomas, surgeon, Chapel Street
Bostock, John, physician, Paradise Street
Bromley, Stephen, surgeon, Love Lane
Cahoun, Walter, surgeon and apothecary, Castle Street
Cheshyre, Mary, druggist, Dale Street
Day, William, surgeon, Custom House Lane
Despleit, Bernard, French Doctor, Strant Street
Dobson, Matthew, physician, Harrington Street
Gerrard, Richard, surgeon and apothecary, Church Street
Girod Abraham, surgeon, Dale Street
Gleave, Wright, surgeon, Dale Street
Goldie, Joseph, surgeon, King Street
Green, Walter, physician, Union Street
Hemingway, Jane, druggist, Redcross Street
Hesketh, Birch, operator for the teeth, Cook Street
Holt, Ralph, surgeon and apothecary, Redcross Street
Houlston, Thomas, apothecary and bookseller, High Street
Kenion, John, physician, Drury Lane
King, James, surgeon, Lord Street
Leigh, James, apothecary, Prieston's Row
Lowdnes, John, druggist, Prieston's Row
Lyon, John, surgeon, College Lane
Park, Henry, surgeon, Paradise Street
Pickering, William, surgeon, James's Street
Pinder and Renwick, druggists, North Side Old Dock
Renwick, Michael, surgeon, King Street
Richmond, Henry, physician, St Paul's Square
Richmond, Thomas, apothecary, Derby Square
Robinson, Thomas, physician, Chapel Street
Shertcliffe, John, surgeon and apothecary, Edmund Street

Slater, John, druggist, East Side Dry Dock
Stephenson, James, druggist, Pool Lane
Timons, Miles, surgeon and operator for the ears, Dale Street
Turner, Matthew, surgeon, John Street
Wetwood, William, surgeon, Paradise Street
Worthington, James, surgeon, Temple Lane
Wright, Henry, druggist, Castle Street
Wright, Phillip, druggist, High Street

G.T. Shaw and I. Shaw (eds), *Liverpool's fourth directory* (Liverpool, 1931), pp. 88–9.

PHYSICIANS IN WESTMINSTER IN 1774

Electoral registers did not exist before 1832 and poll books varied from one area to another. In Westminster, residents were listed by parish and addresses given, as well as occupations or status. The Westminster 1774 poll book lists over 7,000 voters, living in 7 parishes. Of these, 30 were physicians and a further 46 were surgeons. St James's parish, where most physicians lived, included such famous practitioners as Addington, Fordyce, William Hunter and Manningham.

page			
85	Anthony Addington	Dr	Clifford St
72	George Baker	Dr	Jermyn St
122	Robert Bromfield	ph	Gerrard St
56	John Burows	ph	Haymarket
67	George Caverhill	ph	Nohill St
56	Thomas Denman	ph	Queen St, Golden Square
150	John Elliot	MD	Cecil St
102	James Ford	Dr	Albemarle St
82	William Fordyce	Dr	Warwick St, Golden Square
22	Anthony Geisler	ph	Tufton Street
81	William Heberden	Dr	Pall Mall
132	Bryan Higgins	MD	Greek St
52	Richard Huck	MD	Spring Gardens
60	William Hunter	ph	Windmill St
106	Robert James	Dr	Bruton St
5	Richard Jeff	Dr	Great George St
124	Alexander Kennedy	ph	Nassau St
110	Robert Knox	Dr	George St
143	Thomas Lawrence	MD	Essex St
92	Daniel P. Layard	MD	Lower Brook St
68	Thomas Manningham	ph	Jermyn St
58	Donald Munroe	ph	Jermyn St
63	John Lewis Pettit	ph	Great Marlborough St
122	William Philips	Dr	Richmond Buildings
53	William Rowley	Dr	Castle St

37	Patrick Russell	MD	Buckingham St, York Building
35	John Scott	MD	Salisbury St
131	James Smith	MD	Newport St
82	Noah Thomas	Dr	Old Burlington St
55	Richard Warren	MD	Sackville St

Note: Dr = Doctor in physic; ph = physician

THE MEDICAL REGISTER FOR THE YEAR 1783

In 1779 Samuel Foart Simmons, a London physician, published the first edition of his *Medical Register*, which was so successful that two further editions were produced in 1780 and 1783. It was the first listing of members of a profession, although earlier trade directories, such as Sketchley's for Birmingham, Walsall and Wolverhampton in 1767, included various practitioners of medicine, both fringe and qualified. Simmons's list, on the other hand, excluded the unqualified (bonesetters, female midwives and the like) and emphasised the academic qualifications of those named. By the third edition, the *Register* included lists of staff at London and provincial hospitals, those serving overseas, as well as officers of the medical societies and members of the three main professional bodies, the physicians, surgeons and apothecaries. The main section of the *Register*, however, consisted of the names of practitioners in London and the provinces, on a county basis, for England, Wales, Scotland and Ireland. A name index was also added and an appendix of recent deaths.

Simmons's standard style for a county entry was, as for Cheshire reproduced below, a brief account of a county's hospital and any other institutions, followed by the names of those practising in the different communities, often with their qualifications and publications, occasionally with a note that a practitioner had recently moved to the area. He clearly relied heavily on his medical network for information and for updating earlier editions. Occasionally, in the 1779 edition, Simmons was obliged to add a testy footnote that information had not been provided for a particular area, but all the counties seem to have cooperated by 1783.

The 1783 *Register* provides a wonderful picture of late eighteenth-century medical services and personnel in Britain. It illustrates the scarcity of physicians and their concentration in county towns and cathedral cities, as well as the rarity of professional partnerships, although Cheshire was above average in this respect. Presumably intended primarily for practitioners, who might wish to refer a patient, the *Register* also sold to the lay public, and copies have been found in gentlemen's libraries. The modern type of medical register, where inclusion meant recognised professional qualifications, did not appear until 1858 and thus Simmons's work, some seventy-five years earlier, is all the more remarkable.

Cheshire

Chester A General Infirmary* was instituted here in 1755. It is a handsome building, in an airy situation, and contains seventy beds. It is attended, gratis, by

Derbyshire and
Devonshire entries in
Samuel Foart Simmons's
*The Medical Register for the
Year 1783.*

DERBYSHIRE.

Alfreton. SURGEONS and APOTHECARIES. Mr. Nathaniel Spencer.

Ashbourne. Messrs. Robert Dickfey and G. Jones; Messrs. Richard and §Samuel Riddledden.

Ashford. PHYSICIAN. William Bullock*, M.D. (Leyden 1765).

Ashover. SURGEON and APOTHECARY. Mr. Thomas Radford.

Bakewell. PHYSICIAN. Joseph Denman, M.D. SURGEONS and APOTHECARIES. Mr. Edward Buxton, Mr. Mellard. Mr. Beech.

Belsover; Mr. Buxton.

Buxton.

Chesterfield. PHYSICIAN. Richard Milles, M.D. (Edinburgh). SURGEONS and APOTHECARIES. Mr. Thomas Skiner, Mr. John Elam, Mr. Samuel Holland.

Chapel in le Frith. Mr. John Bennet, Mr. Edward Bennet, Mr. John Green.

Derby †. PHYSICIANS. Erasmus Darwin, M.D. (Cambridge 1759) F.R.S. removed hither from Litchfield. John Berridge, M.B. (Oxford). John Hollis Pigot, M.B. (Cambridge 1779) removed hither from Mansfield. SURGEONS and APOTHECARIES. Messrs. John Meynell and R. Wright, Mr. Richard Wright, Mr. Francis Brookfield, Mr. F. Meynell, Mr. Edward Ley, Mr. Richard Cook, Mr. Harrison, Mr. Fox, Mr. Moredbye.

Duffield. Mr. R. Beaumont.

Melbourne. Mr. Charles Watkins.

Repton. Mr. Charles Davenport.

Ripley. Mr. Richard Heigh.

Tifshudt. Mr. Anthony Goodwin, Mr. Thomas Southern,

Winkfworth. Mr. William Frogat, Mr. Peach.

* Dr. Bullock attends at Buxton during the Bathing Season.
† Dr. Butter, late of this town, is removed to London.

DEVON.

DEVONSHIRE.

Exeter. The EXETER and DEVON HOSPITAL contains one hundred and sixty beds. It was opened for the reception of patients in the year 1743, and is attended, gratis, by four † Physicians and four Surgeons. The Apothecary, Mr. Arthur White, resides in the house.

PHYSICIANS. Thomas Glafs, M.D. (Leyden 1731) Fellow of the Royal Medical Society at Paris, and formerly Physician to the Hospital. *Thomas Okes, M.D. (Cambridge 1769). *Bartholomew Parr, M.D. (Edin. 1773). *Thomas Ruffon, M.D. (Edin. 1765).

SURGEONS. Mr. George Abraham Gibbs, late Surgeon to the Hospital, (retired from practice). *Mr. Samuel Lutcombe, *Mr. Barthol. Parr, *Mr. John Patch, Mr. Robert Patch. Mr. Pippin, Mr. John Symons. § Mr. Nicholas Arthur.

APOTHECARIES. Messrs. John Codrington and Philip Drake, Mr. Peter Cornifh, Mr. James Green, Mr. Edward Holwell, Mr. Richard Liccrofi, Mr. Matthew Lufcombe, Messrs. William Lufcombe, and Robert Roe, Mr. William Pitfield, Mr. Richard Radford, Messrs. Edward Walker and ____ Gater, Mr. Benjamin Walker, Mr. Tucker.

Ashburton. SURGEONS and APOTHECARIES. Mr. Tripe, Mr. Jervis, Mr. Moggridge. Messrs. Bragg and Son, Mr. Robert Gammet, Mr. William Robbins.

Axminster. Mr. John Pike, Mr. William Wren.

Appledore.

Barnstaple ‡. PHYSICIANS. George Corryne, M.D. Jafper Porter, M.D. (Edin. 1769). SURGEONS and APOTHECARIES. Mr. Edward Hourdle, Messrs. James and §Thomas Hiern, Mr. H. Gardener Tippetts, Mr. John Bellew, Mr. John Glewat, §Mr. John Hafwell, Mr. Philip Scott, §Mr. John Exeter.

† Four is the stated number, according to the Rules of the Hospital; but at present there are only three, Dr. Harvey, one of the Physicians, having lately retired from practice, and quitted Exeter.
‡ Dr. Hardy, late of this town, is removed to Northampton.

Bampton.

the three Physicians at Chester and by three Surgeons. The Apothecary, Mr. Peter Wilkinson, resides in the house.

Physicians	Dr. Denton.
	John Haygarth, M.B.(Cambridge) F.R.S.
	William Currie, M.D. (Edin. 1770).
Surgeons	Mr. Ogden, +Mr. Johnson, +Mr. Daniel Orred,
	+Mr. Morral, Mr. Freeman
Surgeons	Messrs Crew and Harrison, Messrs Brodhurst and
and Apothecaries	Williamson, Messrs Johnson and Owen, Mr. Sambach,
	Mr. Tomlinson, Mr. Green.
Altrincham	Mr. Charles Poole.
Congleton	Messrs John Barret and Joseph Clubbe, Mr. John Eaton,
	sen, Mr. John Eaton, jun, Mr. William Reade,
	Mr. Samuel Troutbeck.
Frodsham	Mr. Jackson, Mr. Nooly.
Knutsford	Messrs Billingham and Cowley, Mr. Daniel Howard,
	Mr. Peter Penny, Mr. James Coppock.
Macclesfield	Physician Dr. Norton.
	Surgeons and Apothecaries Mr. Samuel Stone,
	Mr. Coxton, Mr. Halley, Mr. James Walthall.
Malpas	Mr. Rowe, Mr. Skerratt.
Middlewich	Mr. Becket, Mr. Greaves, Mr. Henderson.
Nantwich	Physician Dr Gorst.
	Surgeons and Apothecaries Messrs Edward and John
	Wickstead, Mr. Wrench, Mr. Edwards, Mr. Priest.
Neston	Mr. Wolstonholme.
Northwich	Mr. Thoms Filkin, Mr. William Thursby.
Sambach	Mr. Millington.
Stockport	Mr. Briscall, Mr. Thompson, Mr. John Hewitt,
	Mr. Young.
Tarpaly	Mr. Gregory.
Upton	Mr. Houghton.
Wilmslow	Mr Grey.

* A Society has been established at Chester for promoting Inoculation, and preventing the fatality of the Small-pox. The Inspector of the Society is authorized to give a reward to the person who first informs him that a fresh family is infected.
+ Surgeons to the Infirmary.

THE PROVINCIAL MEDICAL DIRECTORY, 1848

The demand for a reliable and modern list of medical practitioners was considerable even before the 1858 Act of Parliament that made it compulsory for qualified men to be listed. *The Provincial Medical Directory* was set out in two sections. The first part was a geographical listing, arranged by towns within a county, and with each practitioner's name given under the town. In this list, the degree of MD was noted, but no other qualifications. The majority of men were in single-handed practice, with only two partnerships given in the Wiltshire list, for example, although several places, such as Swindon, clearly had a medical dynasty. The second section was an alphabetical list of practitioners, with their qualifications and dates when these were obtained, their address in a particular town and when an institutional post was held, for example, as Medical Officer to a Poor Law Union. Older practitioners were noted as 'in practice before 1815' to justify their inclusion.

Wiltshire

Amesbury G.B. Batho; C. Pyle
Aylesbury G. Pickess
Bedwin (Great) J. Liddersdale
Bishopstone — Clifton
Box C.C. Langworthy; W.W. Monckton
Bradford A. Adye; J. Baines; N.J. Highmore
Calne J.F. Chittenden; R. Greenup;
    H. King; T.H. King; G. Page;
    J. Pownall
Chilmark — Richardson
Chippenham C. Bailey; C. Bayliffe;
    W. Colbourne; F. Spencer; G.S. Stiles
Christian Malford C.F. Edwards
Clifton-on-Terne W.G. Tiley
Codford (St Peter) I. Flower
Collingbourne S. Lawes
Corsham G.W. Dyke MD; W. Kemm;
    A. Little; T. Washbourne
Cricklade C. Brooks; E. Parker
    T. Taylor; W. Wells
Devizes T.B. Anstie; W.G. Everett MD;
    R. Montgomery; W.R. Seagram MD;
    C. Trinder; G. Waylen; W. Waylen
Donhead L.A. Lawence; L.A.L. Rowberry
Downton R.H. Hooper
Elston E.W. Turner
Fennings J.C. Spicer
Forant G. Wylde
Grinstead (West) T.M. Wilmot
Heytesbury W.G. Davis; W.C. Swayne
Highworth C. Smith
Hullavington — Wright
Lacock J.C.S. Jennings
Laverstock W. Finch MD; J.D. Hewson
Malmesbury A.F.W. Jeston; E.O. Lyne
Market Lavington C. Hitchcock,

(Hitchcock & Ives); J. Heriott;
    J. Ives (Hitchcock & Ives)
Marlborough C.P. Fitzgerald; J. Gardner;
    D.P. Maurice; H.W. Somerset
Melksham G.C. Kendrick; T.R. King;
    G. Plimmer
Mere M. Newman; C. Rumsey;
Milford M. Fowler MD
Nether Avon J. Hornbrook
Pewsey — Barrett; C.H. Carter
Purton H. Dixon; W. Finch MD;
    — Washbourn
Rowley Regis D. Timmins
Rushall J. Bartlett
Salisbury J. Andrews; W. Andrews; T.G. Blake;
    H. Coates; W.M. Coates; H. Finch;
    — Hole; J.A. Lush; J. Miles; T. Moore MD;
    G. Tatum; J. Toone; J. Winzar
Shrewton J. Nicholls; — Turner
Steeple Langford D.E. Hamilton
Sutton Benger E. Butler
Swindon A. Davis; J. Gay; J. Gay jun; I. Gay;
    W. Gay
Tisbury T. Jukes
Tisbury (East) C. Barrett
Trowbridge J. Carey; J.W. Carey;
    J.W. Stapleton; G. Sylvester;
    G.M. Sylvester; C. Taylor
Warminster C. Bleeck; P. Grubb;
    J. Lampard; F.F. Seagram;
    C. Vicary; G. Vicary; G.T. Vicary
Westbury J.H. Gibbs; G. Shorland
Weston J.F. Martin
Wilton W.J. French (French & Son);
    G. Langstaff
Wootton Bassett G. D. Hooper; R. Hooper

MEDICAL ADVERTISING

Both qualified and quack regularly advertised their services and products to the general public, especially by means of the rapidly growing number of provincial newspapers of the eighteenth century catering for an increasingly literate population. As well as some extravagant claims of success, the advertisements often included recommendations from satisfied former patients and lists of symptoms, and the shops where the preparations could be bought, frequently from the newspaper office. If the advertiser were offering a service, such as inoculation, ophthalmic or midwifery attention, further details would be given. Sometimes the qualified practitioner mentioned the surgeon-apothecary to whom he had formerly been apprenticed, presumably as a recommendation in the locality, and a willingness to treat the poor free might be stated.

Medical practitioners' advertisements

John LARDNER, Surgeon, Apothecary and Manmidwife of Alcester, will deliver any poor Woman, in Town, or any Part of the County, (for Half-a Guinea) with GOD'S Permission. N.B. He has already deliver'd several, in the most difficult Cases, with great Success.

Worcester Journal, 8 November 1750.

JOHN BLICKE, Surgeon and Apothecary, at Stourbridge, in Worcestershire, Hereby gives Notice, That he shall now begin to Inoculate the SMALL POX for the current Season, and hopes for the Continuance of the Favours of his Friends in all Parts as they may depend upon the most just and honourable Treatment. He has been so happily successful in this Branch, that he never lost a Patient; and, from the peculiar Care, &c. with which he shall continue to treat that Distemper, he flatters himself he shall meet with the like Success in his future Practice.

He likewise begs Leave to inform the PUBLIC, that he performs all Operations that are requisite in curing Diseases of the EYES, EARS and TEETH, having perfectly cured many, who, for several Years, had been absolutely deaf, and deemed incurable.

N.B. He undertakes none but those that are curable, and gives his Advice gratis.

Aris's Gazette, 25 November 1754.

Coleshill – Mrs Watkins, widow of the late surgeon, man midwife and apothecary,[30] hereby acquaints her Friends in general That she is determined to carry on, with the Assistance of a Person unquestionably qualified for the Undertaking, the Business of her late Husband in all its Branches; and humbly hopes that the Debt of Gratitude already subsisting for their past Favours to the Deceased, may remain upon her, by a Continuation of those Favours to A. Watkins.

Coventry Mercury, 15, 22 and 29 September 1760.

Mr STAPLES, Surgeon, who has removed to Mr Keene's late House out of Bishopgate, Coventry TAKES this public Method to acquaint those who are afflicted with any of the several Species of Consumptions or Dropsies, that he has a more Efficacious Method in treating of, and curing those Chronical Diseases, different from the Common Mode of Practice. Head achs, tho' ever so inveterate, (which often terminates in Vertigo, Epilepsy, Apoplexy, Palsy &c) instantaneously relieved, and cured in a few Days.

Coventry Mercury, 29 September 1760.

Atherstone, 4 November Dr Seager[31] takes this Method to inform his friends and the public, notwithstanding he has had the honour of the Degree of Doctor of Physic conferred upon him, he intends to practice the art of surgery, midwifery, and pharmacy on the usual terms.

Coventry Mercury, 11 November 1771.

Mr MILBOURN[32] Finding that his Absence from Coventry the last Winter, in Consequence of his Attendance upon the Hospitals in London, has given Rise to a Report that he means to decline the Practice of Inoculation, begs Leave to acquaint his Friends and the Public, That he continues the Practice of Inoculation as usual, together with Surgery and Pharmacy in all their different Branches.

Coventry Mercury, 22 June, 6, 13 and 20 July 1772.

1 March 1773 Mr Wilmer,[33] Surgeon, is removed from High Street, to his House in Midsford Street, late in the occupation of Mr Turton, where he hopes to receive the Continuance of the Encouragement he hath hitherto experienced from his Friends, and which upon every Occasion he will make his particular study to deserve.

Coventry Mercury, 27 February 1773.

Garner PICKERING,[34] Surgeon, Apothecary and Man Midwife Takes this Method to inform his Friends That he has taken the House on S. Johns Bridge, late the Navigation Office, where he intends practicing all the Branches of his Profession. Those who chuse to employ him may depend on the utmost Diligence and Attention, and their Favours will be gratefully acknowledged by Garner Pickering. N.B. Innoculation performed with greatest Care and Safety.

Coventry Mercury, 27 December 1773 and 3 January 1774.

Mr Gibbs'[35] Practice in Surgery, Midwifery and Pharmacy, being too Extensive to Admit of his paying a proper Attention to the Retail Business; takes the Liberty of informing the Public he has declined it, and is removed to a large and more convenient House, opposite the Bulls Head in Bishops Street, where he hopes for a continuance of the Favours of his Friends, who, in Cases requiring his Assistance, may depend on being treated with Diligence, Attention and Humanity.

Coventry Mercury, 30 September 1776.

William Bouchier Lennard,[36] Surgeon and Man-Midwife, after an extensive Practice in his Majesty's Service by Sea and Land . . . has open'd a Shop four Doors below the New-Kings-Arms, in Briggate, Leeds . . . Inoculation according to the Suttonian Method – He will bleed and dress the Poor gratis every Sunday Morning, from Seven o'clock till Half past Eight – and at all times give them his Advice.

The Leeds Mercury, 24 July 1781.

Quack advertisements

FRANCES DEANE, Oculist of New Street, by Fleet-Street, London, gives this Notice
THAT She is to be advis'd with in all Cases relating to Eyes on Mondays, Wednesdays and Fridays, at any Time of the Day, from Nine in the Morning till Six at Night, which Days have been set apart for those Purposes for upwards of one hundred Years past, without any Intermission, by the same Family, she being the only Survivor, and brought up in the useful Art by the well known Mrs. Jones, and having practised with great Success herself for upwards of twenty Years past, and in the same House.
   N.B. Those Persons that live out of Town, whose Cases require Couching, such, till cured, will find Accommodation at her House, or any other Case that wants her close Application, she having a large, airy House, and good apartments.

Aris's Gazette, 11 July 1743.

We hear from Oldswinford that Mr Tristram, who formerly advertised himself for Curing Stammering, Squinting, Hollow Roofs, and has had great Success in causing the Deaf and Dumb both to understand and be understood, and has given Directions to several young Gentlemen and Ladies to prevent Squinting, and but few (being left to their own Liberty) have followed his Advice, therefore he will undertake no more without having them under his own immediate Care. Any Gentleman or Lady that has Occasion to make use of him in either respect, may direct to him at the Post Office in Stourbridge, where he will (the first Opportunity) receive and answer all Letters being post paid.

Aris's Gazette, 22 August 1743.

This is to inform the Publick THAT William Pool, Professor of Physick, Surgery and Botany, hath cured, and doth continue curing, the following Disorders, if not so long neglected as to render them incurable, as Coughs, Wheezes, Hoarseness, Shortness of Breath, Asthmas, and Consumptions in their Kinds, Ulcers in the Lungs, &c., internal and external, even in the Legs, where Humours are most subject to fall, by Preparations from our own native Plants, &c. by which more effectual Cures were performed when they were more used in the Shops, than ever were done in many Cases since they have been rejected; and he intends, during this Summer, to be at the Angel at Kidderminster every Thursday, and at the Bush in the Corn-Market in Stourbridge every Friday, if God permit. He also calculates Nativities.

Coventry Mercury, 19 March 1753.

We hear from Farnborough, near Banbury, that Mr Freekland of that Place, who was blind several Years, was brought to Sight by Mr Grant,[37] in one Minute. The Reputation this Gentleman has acquired by his Integrity as well as Skill in his Profession, has encouraged Numbers to apply to him, after being tampered with by others, without effect, many of whom he has relieved, and some effectually cured, after the heavy Calamity, of many Years Blindness. Mr Grant will be at the Three Swans Inn, in Walsall, on Tuesday the 30th Instant, at the Swan in Wolverhampton, May the 1st; at the Hen and Chickens in Birmingham, on Thursday the 2nd; at the Crown in Stourbridge, on Friday the 3rd; and at the New Bush in Dudley, on Saturday the 4th.

Coventry Mercury, 29 April 1754.

DOCTOR NASH[38] At the Golden Urn, in High-Street, Bromsgrove, gives his advice any hour on Tuesdays and Sundays, and between the hours of six and twelve any other day.

It is now more than ten years since the doctor first communicated to the world that he infallibly discovered diseases by inspecting the patients urine. His unbounded success has sufficiently evinced this assertion.

As the efficacy of medicines are rendered precarious by a number of superfluous ingredients, the Doctor (to avoid any perplexity, error, and connfusion) has reduced their luxuriance within the bounds of science, by pruning away the fruitless branches, and using only those parts which are profitable, he having by a series of experiments, investigated the real principles, constituence, and essential properties of the various minerals, animals, and vegetables, of every different nation and climate.

Date of the Year	Number of Patients cured
1761	820
1762	974
1763	1,440
1764	1,307
1765	1,270
1766	1,450
1767	1,540
1768	1,509
1769	1,700
1770	3,040
	15,150

Now residing under the Doctor's care 368.

Coventry Mercury, 11 November 1771.

With pleasure we inform the public, that Health and Strength are daily restored, and the following disorders effectually cured, at a trifling expence, without medicine, bathing, sweating, or journies to the Continent, viz. the gout, rheumatism, palsey, lameness, nervous complaints, debilitated constitutions; weak, wasted, and contracted limbs; corpulency, bad digestion, &c. The certainty of success is supported by a list, which is given gratis to ladies and gentlemen only, at Mr. BUZAGLO's,[39] opposite Somerset-house, Strand, of 159 surprising cures in similar cases, performed on many of the most distinguished personages; whose testimony will confirm that their cures were effected by muscular exercise only, after all physic and bathing had failed, and pronounced incurable by the most eminent of the Faculty. Mr. BUZAGLO at first sight tells every patient the benefit he has to expect; which generally surpasses his most sanguine expectations. One week's exercise in warm weather, is found preferable to six in winter. Patients in general should apply for relief in the intervals of the fits, whilst they have the use of their limbs; and not wait till they are laid up helpless.

Whitehall Evening Post, 5–7 August 1784.

NOTES

1. When William Edwards died childless in 1723, a wealthy man, he left money to found two charity schools and provide clothes for the poor in the area. The Kenilworth school is now a private residence. No further trace has been found of John Beale, whose home was in Grandborough, not far from Rugby.
2. Joseph Hodgson (1788–1869) was apprenticed in March 1805 to George Freer, a leading surgeon in Birmingham and at the town's general hospital, who belonged to a midland medical family. Freer had two other apprentices then nearing the end of their terms, and with these youths Freer had received £157 each, but Hodgson was bound for only four years with the very large premium of £200. Hodgson left Birmingham for London, became FRS and was the first provincial practitioner to be president of the Royal College of Surgeons.
3. John Blount, a surgeon-apothecary, was apprenticed in 1769 to a Leominster, Herefordshire surgeon and then practised in the county at Bromyard before moving to Birmingham. James Russell became one of his three apprentices there in August 1803 for seven years with a premium of £150. Blount had moved to Warwick by 1807 to set up a private madhouse and later established an asylum at Great Wigston, Leicestershire.
4. James Russell FRCS (1786–1851) became a senior surgeon in Birmingham.
5. Henry Cline (1750–1827), a surgeon, taught anatomy at St Thomas's Hospital.
6. John Hunter (1728–93), the most famous of all contemporary surgeons, was the brother of William, the physician.
7. Robert Simpson was a jewellery manufacturer and goldsmith in Derby.
8. The unsuccessful candidates included Henry Lilley Smith, later to found the Southam Self-Supporting Dispensary; John Hall was actually appointed.
9. John Webster was landlord of the King's Arms in Jury Street, Derby.
10. The burial ground at the hospital.
11. Harper seems to have been the name of the keeper of a graveyard.
12. Big Gates must have been the entrance to an unidentified burial ground.
13. John Taunton MRCS (1769–1821), the founder of the London Truss Society, a demonstrator at Guy's Hospital under Henry Cline and at this time the principal lecturer to the London Anatomical Society.
14. The burial ground at St Bartholomew's Hospital.
15. Henry Cline MRCS (1750–1827), anatomical lecturer at St Thomas's Hospital.
16. Michael Mordecai, a noted receiver of stolen goods, kept a shop in New Alley.
17. Presumably a publican.
18. Possibly the Green Churchyard of St Giles's, Cripplegate or at St Bartholomew the Great.
19. Bunhill Fields.
20. Joseph Constantine Carpue FRCS, FCP (1764–1846), founder of the Dean Street Anatomical School.
21. Algernon Frampton MD, FCP (1766–1842), physician at the London Hospital.

22. James Wilson MRCS (1765–1821), of Great Queen Street.
23. Joshua Brookes MRCS (1761–1833), the founder of the Blenheim Street Anatomical School.
24. Charles Bell FRSE, FRS, FRCSE (1774–1842), professor of surgery at Soho and Edinburgh, later knighted.
25. Either St Luke's church or St Luke's Hospital in Old Street.
26. Possibly Thomas Hornidge MRCS of Hatton Street.
27. The Artichoke public house.
28. Astley Cooper MRCS, FRS (1768–1841), anatomical lecturer at St Thomas's Hospital, formerly a pupil of Cline, created a baronet in 1821.
29. John Hall, surgeon-apothecary of Warwick, was licensed to practise by the Bishop of Worcester in 1730.
30. John Watkins had worked as poor law surgeon to nearby Shustoke parish and in 1756 had taken an apprentice, James Steel, for seven years with a premium of £50.
31. Edmund Seager gained an MD qualification at St Andrews. He took three apprentices and continued to practise at Atherstone, in north Warwickshire, including some poor law work.
32. In January 1771 Milbourn printed a denial in the press that a patient had died from inoculation, with 100 guineas offered to anyone who could prove the contrary. Later that year 'the eminent inoculator' married a young lady with a 'genteel fortune' and by 1774 was riding at Warwick Races. However, he was not listed as practising at Coventry in the 1779 *Medical Register*.
33. Bradford Wilmer (1747–1813) was one of Coventry's leading practitioners. He practised in a 15-mile radius of the city, including poor law work; he was a consultant for ophthalmic cases and an expert witness against John Hunter in the notorious Boughton poisoning trial of 1783. He was the author of two books on surgery and one on toxic plants. His first wife, Sarah (d. 1791), was Garner Pickering's sister. He indentured five apprentices with substantial premiums. Unusually for the period, he belonged to a four-man practice in Coventry. He married four times and died a comparatively wealthy man.
34. Garner Pickering (1730–74) came from a local medical family, with a city barber-surgeon among his ancestors in the 1670s. He was apprenticed in Coventry in 1745; after his death his apothecary's shop was advertised for sale.
35. Joseph Gibbs did occasional poor law work in the Coventry area and in 1791 took an apprentice for three years with the substantial premium of £105.
36. No evidence has been found in civilian, military or naval records of Lennard's existence as a qualified practitioner.
37. Roger Grant began life as a tinker and Anabaptist; he became Sworn-Oculist-in-Ordinary to Queen Anne. His extensive advertising included his own portrait.
38. A practitioner at Bromsgrove, Worcestershire, had long provided a uroscopy service to the area. Earlier in the century, this man was John Woodcock, a qualified surgeon-apothecary, who died in 1759. His widow, still living at the Old Shop, opposite the Market House in the High Street, advertised his services and medications, but the practice was taken over by Thomas Nash, claiming that he had Woodcock's original secrets. Nash was born at Droitwich and been apprenticed to the Birmingham surgeon, Henry Hollier, in 1740. Woodcock's son seems to have practised in Bromsgrove towards the end of the century. Nash later became a Freeman of Bromsgrove.
39. Buzaglo had become famous by inventing a heating apparatus and then successfully set up as a 'gout doctor'; he had inserted a similar advertisement a month earlier giving details of how an alderman was cured of gout.

II
NURSES AND MIDWIVES

❖ ❖ ❖

Professionally qualified nurses and midwives are relatively recent groups of medical attendants. Nursing the sick was seen as a family duty and only the wealthier paid for such assistance. Under the poor law provisions, nursing was invariably carried out by the poorest women in a parish, paid two or three shillings a week by the Overseers to attend a sick pauper. Nursing in workhouses was always severely criticised for its poor quality. Even in hospitals, nurses were modestly paid and of low status. However, Florence Nightingale published her *Notes on Nursing* in 1860 and nursing gradually developed recognised training programmes and professional status.

Midwives were always regarded as more skilled than nurses and able to command better fees for their services. But there was no formal midwifery qualification until the late nineteenth century and training was largely by experience. The emergence of the *accoucheur* in the eighteenth century considerably reduced the midwife's status and ladies would increasingly choose to be delivered by a male practitioner rather than by the local midwife. Midwives were also unfortunately seen as drunkards (Sairey Gamp a well-known example), while some were suspected of practising abortion, in the style of Defoe's Mother Midnight.

THE DIARY OF ISAAC ARCHER OF MILDENHALL, 1670–82

Isaac Archer was born in north Suffolk in 1641, educated at Cambridge University and became a cleric. In 1667 he married Anne Peachey (b. 1643), but eight of their nine children born in a thirteen-year period died in infancy; his son and heir, William, died at the age of three and Frances in 1679, when she was only five. Anne lost her sight in the late 1680s and Archer nursed her until her death in September 1698. Archer died two years later and was buried at Mildenhall. His diary began in 1665.

27 November 1670 My wife growing neerer her time was troubled with feares she should die; and I feared it too. She was much taken up, I saw, with such thoughts, and I was glad, because it was an occasion of seeking God, as I know she did. . . . This day she was ill, and her reckoning just out; I wish't it might not distract mee (being the Lord's day) and so she did not cry out till about 8 of clock at night; and at 11 was delivered of a girle, fatter, and stronger, otherwise very like my other. Her paines were sharpe, but short; and she bore them without sicknes (not so as before) and with great courage. It seems the child came with the face upwards, and did not cry till an hour, and more after 'twas borne.

Thus my heart was full of joy, thinking all over; and praysing God for his mercy: but about 1 of clock my wife began to faint, through an overflow of blood, and was without sensible pulse, or colour; we gave her over, and she took leave of mee (which much concerned mee); the women told mee she would loose all her blood etc. I sent to Isleham for blood stones (tying her fingers in the meane time, and burning feathers), but God was better than meanes, who stayed the flow, and she began to revive, and by degrees mended so as we had hopes of her.

6 October 1677 About 4 of the clock in the afternoon my wife was delivered, 2 months before her reckoning, and of a girle, which came wrong, and stuck so long with the head in the birth, that it was dead when fully borne, though alive in the time of travaile, and so next day 'twas buried in Frecknam chancell, on the north side of the little boy, under a stone. My wife was in danger of miscarrying often, and was not well, or as she used to be, severall times, especially a week before her delivery . . . perhaps I am not worthy of a son etc. . . . The losse is the lesse because 'twas a girle, though we could have wished the life of it.

14 July 1681 My wife was ill, we went to her father's house; on the 23 [July] I was just come home and word was brought that she was in danger of miscarrying, for she was quick; 'twas late, and Satterday night, so I went not, but was in great affliction, and prayed with many teares, in bitterness of spirit, that God would spare mother, and child etc. . . . I loved my wife most tenderly now in danger, and promised to be kinder then ever, and not so angry with her as had bin, and to govern myself better in my carriage etc.

9 August 1681 My wife was ill, and we thought she would have miscarried, but did not, only went on ill, and the child wasted, as we concluded. She went on in that case til the month came about, August 20, and next morning about 4 of clock was delivered of a girle; after 3 houres sharp paines, she came wrong, and was wasted; it lived halfe an houre, and died. I buried it at Frecknam by Isaac, in hopes of resurrection! I sce God is soveraigne. . . . My wife may be the better, the distemper she had (which she had 3 summers besides this) caused her coming 8 weeks before her reckoning. I begg of God health for her! Amen. I have too eagerly desired children. . . .

25 March 1682 My wife is quick, and I begged of God, after all the breaches made upon us, a child to live with mee!

3 September 1682 My wife, after ilnes at times 7 weeks together, was delivered of a lusty girle, fatter, and larger then any yet, for she had her [health] well, and a good stomach. She was in extremity from 1 to 4 in the morning, being the Lord's day, when, after great danger, God heard us, and she [was] delivered. I bless God that we have a living child. . . . And September 16 we had it baptized by the name of Frances in remembrance of that deare child, whom God took away so suddenly, and putt her to nurse.

10 December 1682 We were frighted betimes in the morning with the sad newes of my little girle's death. She was well the night before, and never sick in it's life, only came out with heat, and had a cough, which yet was gone, and thrived to admiration. She had a tender hearted nurse, but we feare 'twas overlaid, as many that saw it did positively say.

Matthew Storey (ed.), *Two East Anglian Diaries* (Suffolk Record Society, XXXVI, 1994), pp. 125–6, 155, 164, 165, 166.

JANE SHARP, *THE MIDWIVES BOOK*, 1671

As well as the practical skills required to provide medical treatment, as given in an apprenticeship, a crucial part of any professional medical training was the existence of textbooks to which the novice could refer and which encapsulated contemporary best practice. Until the eighteenth century, such manuals, including those on midwifery, were written in Latin, thus denied to virtually all female readers, and certainly those who might have to earn a living. However, in 1671 *The Midwives Book, Or the Whole ART of Midwifry Discovered*, written in English, was published. Its author, Mrs Jane Sharp of London, claimed to have been a midwife for over thirty years and the book was addressed to her 'Sisters, the Midwives of England'. She dedicated the work to Lady Eleanor Talbot. Although quite a lengthy text of 418 pages, it was small, only 93 mm by 142 mm and sold, bound, for 2s 6d; the fourth edition of 1725 was published after Jane Sharp's death. The book is divided into six sections, discussing conception, pain management, post-natal attention to the mother and advice on infant care. There is technical advice on dealing with malpresentations, on embryotomy and on treating venereal infections. Jane Sharp supported the humoral theory and cited the work of many authorities, especially Culpeper, usually anonymously. She included jokes and anecdotes, criticisms of male medical practitioners and widely held folk beliefs about pregnancy and parturition, such as an inexplicable taste for strange foods as a sign of pregnancy. Percival Willoughby had read her book and appears to have misunderstood her references to the use of instruments in delivery, but approved her treatment of convulsions. Virtually no details of her life are known.

Some perhaps may think that then it is not proper for women to be of this profession, because they cannot attain so rarely to the knowledge of things as men may, who are bred up in universities, schools of learning, or serve their apprenticeships for that end and purpose, where anatomy lectures being frequently read, the situation of the parts of both men and women, and other things of great consequence, are often made plain to them. But that objection is easily answered by the former example of the midwives among the Israelites; for though we women cannot deny that men in some things may come to a greater perfection of knowledge than women ordinarily can, by reason of the former helps that women want, yet the Holy Scriptures hath recorded midwives to the perpetual honour of the female sex. There being not so much as one word concerning *men-midwives* mentioned there that we can find, it being the natural propriety of women to be much-seeing in that art; and though nature be not alone sufficient to the perfection of it, yet farther knowledge may be gained by a long and diligent practice, and be communicated to others by our own sex. I cannot deny the honour due to able physicians and chyrurgions, when occasion is; yet we find even that amongst the Indians, and all barbarous people, where there is no men of learning, the women are sufficient to perform this duty; and even in our own nation, that we need go no further, the poor country people, where there are none but women to assist (unless it be those that are exceedingly poor, and in a starving condition, and then they have more need of meat than midwives), the women are fruitful, and as safe and well delivered, if not much more fruitful, and better commonly in childbed, than the greatest ladies of the land.

Elaine Hobby (ed.), The Midwives Book (1999), pp. 11–12.

AN ANONYMOUS LONDON MIDWIFE'S CASEBOOK

The name of the midwife who kept these case notes is unknown, although there are clues to the identity of her family in the notebook, which covers twenty-nine years from December 1694 until March 1723. During that time she recorded a total of 676 births, 433 of which were of women she had attended more than once. She noted eight sets of twins and four stillbirths. Her busiest years were from 1702 until 1711, and in 1703 she attended forty-two women. Her practice, based on the Old Bailey area, included some thirty London parishes; she recorded the addresses of most clients and occasionally their husbands' occupations. The patients' own status is indicated by the way she enters their names; for example, Madame Clarke of Chancery Lane (later Lady Clarke), Mrs Bowman of Canon Street or 'the woman in Tam Lane'. Her grandest and most regular clients were the Barnardiston family of Leytonstone, Essex. However, the most valuable and unusual part of this account book, arranged in two columns on seventy-three pages, are the fees that the midwife received. These seem to have been based entirely on patients' status and their ability to pay; 119 women were not charged, but fees ranged from 2s 6d to £8 10s, and although most were less than £2, the commonest sum for a delivery was 10s. Her largest annual income in the notebook was £50 2s 8d in 1704. It is not known if she were a widow or had a husband's earnings in addition. She noted occasional cash gifts from clients over the years. She must have been at least middle-aged, for she delivered her own daughters' babies as well as women whose mothers she had attended earlier. The account book is obviously written by the midwife herself, barely literate and often with phonetic spelling. The outer cover of the notebook is annotated that it was for Mr Thomas Barnardiston of Saffron Walden.

Case notes, 1703

patient	son/daughter	address	date	£	s	d
Mme Preston	daughter	–	5 Jan	2	10	0
Mrs Hall	son	Fox Court, Grusen Lane	? Jan	1	5	0
Mrs Hakins	son	Scoldin Alley, Poultry	13 Jan		5	0
Mrs French	son	Smithfield	19 Jan		5	0
Mrs Shephard	son	Minories	25 Jan		–	–
Mrs Tabron	daughter	–	7 Feb		7	6
Mrs Dupore	daughter	Blackfriars	15 Feb		5	0
Mme Winter	daughter	–	22 Feb	1	1	0
Mrs Jude	son	Butcher Hall Lane	1 Mar		15	0
Mme Sims	daughter	Sudrocke	4 Mar	1	12	3

Bodleian Library, Oxford, Rawlinson MS D 1141, f. 49.

THE BIRTHS OF CHILDREN TO EDMOND AND CHRISTIAN WILLIAMSON, 1709–20

The Williamsons lived at Husborne Crawley, Bedfordshire, and noted the details of the births of their children on two loose sheets of paper that appear to have been torn from a ledger or account-book. The entries were made by both husband and wife. Three of these children survived. Except between the first two births, when the interval was thirty months, there were less than two years between Christian Williamson's pregnancies, and only a year between two. Mrs Howe was the midwife at the first delivery in 1709, but Mrs Mann attended all the later births; no midwife was noted in 1720. Four different women were named as nurses and these were clearly dry-nurses. No mention of wet-nursing was made although Nurse Ward could have been Francis's wet-nurse when he was in Hampstead at his death in 1720 because his mother had died only two months before. The entries make it clear that, at this level of society, the status of the officiating cleric, the godparents, the gossips and even the place of baptism were of considerable importance, to judge from the regularity with which these details were noted.

E[dmond] W[illiamson] An account of the birth of my children by my second wife. 1709 March 29 My wife fell into labour and a little after 9 in the morning was delivered of a son. Present: aunt Taylor, cousin White, sister Smith, cousin Clarkson, widow Hern, Mrs. Howe, midwife, Mr[s] Wallis, nurse, Mrs. Holms, Eleanor Hobbs, servants.

April 4 He was baptised by Doctor Battle by the name of John. John, Duke of Newcastle, and Eveling, Marquis of Dorchester, and my mother Cromwell were gossips. My sister smith stood for Mrs. Cromwell.
[April] 16 The child died about 1 o'clock in the morning.

1711 Sept. 17 My said wife was delivered of a son just before 4 in the morning. Present: Mr. Thomas Molyneux's lady and maid, Mrs Mann, midwife, Margaret Williamson, nurse, Susan Nutall, servant.
Oct. 4. He was baptised by Mr. Trabeck by the name of Talbot after my grandmother's name.[1] Sir John Talbot and John Pulteney esquire were gossips, with my sister Smith godmother. Major William Bisset stood for Sir John Talbot. Present: my nieces Charlotte Lee and Rebecca Smith.

1713 June 9. About 8 at night my said wife began her labour.
June 10. Half an hour after 1 in the morning was brought to bed of a son. Present: Mrs. Molyneux, Mrs. Bisset, Mrs. Mann, midwife, Nurse Williamson, Susan Nuthall and Betty Ginger, servants.
June 30. Baptised by Mr. Mompesson of Mansfield by the name of Edmond. Sir Hardolf Wasteneys, St. Andrew Thornhaugh and Lady Howe, gossips. Note: Mrs. Bisset stood for Lady Howe. Present: Lady Mary Wortley, Lady Wasteneys, aunt Knight, cousin Margaret Cornwallis, Mrs. Molyneux, Major Bisset, Mr. Gilby of Lincoln, Mr. Mompesson's son.

1715 March 7. My said wife was brought to bed of a daughter 10 minutes before 6 in the morning. Present: Mrs. Molyneux, Mrs. Mann, midwife, Nurse Williamson, Mary Evans, Mary Cole and Mary Wheeler, servants.
March 29. Was baptised by Dr. Mandivel, Chancellor of Lincoln, by the name of Christian; Mrs. Dorothy White, Mrs. Ann Nanny and Colonel John Hopkey, gossips. Present: Mrs. Nanny the mother, Mrs. Westby, Mrs. White, Mrs. Hopkey, Mr. Westby, Mary Cole, servant.

1716 March 9. My wife was delivered of a daughter at 7 at night. Present: aunt Taylor, Mrs. Molyneux, Mrs. Oliver, Mrs. Man, midwife, Mary Smith, nurse, Jane Kensey and Mary Wheeler, servants.
March 31. Was baptised by Mr. Widmore, the Reader of St. Margaret's, by the name of Elizanna; Brigadier Robert Peyton, aunt Knight of Langold and Ann Knight, gossips. Registered in St. Margaret's, Westminster, as all the rest were.
April 27. Died, was buried in the new chapel yard in the Broadway.

C[hristian] W[illiamson]
1718 Jan. 21. I was brought to bed of a son about 2 in the morning. Mrs. Man, midwife, nurse Chatty, drying-nurse, present; Mrs. Taylor, Mrs. White and Mrs. Molyneux, Jane Beadle; servants: Mary Wells, Jane Griffith, Edmond Kinward. He was baptised by Mr. Widmore, Reader of St. Margaret's, Westminster, by the name of Francis. Sir Francis Molyneaux's eldest son and Mr. Francis Henry Lee, godfathers; my cousin Bridget Cornwallis, godmother. Mem.: Mr. Thomas Molyneaux stood for his nephew.

1719 Feb. 21 I was brought to bed of a son between 6 and 7 in the evening. Mrs. Man, midwife, nurse Chatty, dry-nurse; present: aunt Taylor, Mrs. Molyneux, and Jane Beadle; servants: Rebecca Shippy, Betty Hall and Mathew Dowcet.

March 7. He was baptised by Mr. Widmore, Reader of St. Margaret's, Westminster, by the name of William; General Seymour and Mr. Plumptre, godfathers; cousin Ann Cornwallis, godmother.
[no date] Died and buried at Hadley.

E[dmond] W[illiamson]
1720 June. My wife brought to bed of a daughter, but the child did not live a minute.
July 21. My wife died and was buried at Isleworth.
Sept. 9. [Francis] died of the smallpox at Nurse Ward's at Hampstead.

F.J. Manning (ed.), *Some Bedfordshire Diaries* (Bedfordshire Historical Record Society, XL, 1959), pp. 35–6.

LETTERS TO THE 3RD EARL OF CARDIGAN ABOUT HIS SONS, 1727

Daniel Eaton (1689–1742) was a tanner's son who became steward to the Brudenell family at Deene Park, Northamptonshire, writing regularly to George, 3rd Earl of Cardigan (1685–1732) about personal and estate affairs when his lordship was absent from home. Lord Cardigan had two daughters and four sons, 'Master James' (1725–1811) was the second and 'Master Robert' (1726–68) the third.

8 May 1727
My Lord,
Munday morning. Master James & Master Robert Brudenell are very well; but yesterday about 3 o'clock the poor nurse[2] fell down in the stone court, it being wet and slippery, and broke both the bones of her arm about 3 inches above her right hand. I sent immediately for Mr. Fryer,[3] who came and set it before eight. We do not suffer Master Robert to suck for these five or six days, for these things are always attended with a feaver. My mother and Mrs Bradshaw[4] will take care of the child, and the nurses sister is with her.

Tuesday, 11 May 1727
My Lord,
Master James & Master Robert are very well; and the nurse is intirely free from pain, and has not been at all feavourish as we could perceive, so that in a day or two the child may suck without any manner of danger. Her breasts have been very regularly drawn all this time, and Master Robert has born the loss of the pap with a great deal of patience.

Sunday, 14 May 1727
My Lord,
Mr. James and Mr. Robert are extreamly well, and the nurse continues free from pain and has not been at all feavourish, so that yesterday Mr. Robert began to suck again. I receiv'd the honour of your Lordship's of the 11th instant. We hope that Lady Frances[5] is better, because your Lordship says nothing of her.

The Letters of Daniel Eaton to the third Earl of Cardigan, 1725–1732, eds J. Wake and D. Champion Webster (Northamptonshire Record Society, XXIV, 1971), pp. 116–18.

EPISCOPAL LICENSING OF MIDWIVES

The moral character of a midwife and her Christian principles were considered as crucial as her professional skills and thus women who wished to practise with authority and status required a licence from the bishop of their diocese to do so. Several character sponsors were also essential. Such certificates are fairly uncommon survivals after the Commonwealth and certainly far rarer than surgeons'; for example, there were only 9 female midwives licensed by the Bishop of Worcester compared with 185 men practitioners in the years 1661–1712. In some dioceses women gained licences surprisingly late. The testimonial for Nancy Littlewood in 1787 was supported by her vicar and two churchwardens; the four women who signed were probably patients she had delivered. Frances Tutt's recommendation was signed by a local surgeon and five women she had presumably attended.

Chard Augt 19 1738
We whose names are hereunto subscrib[ed] having experienced the usefulness of Frances Tutt of this parish both in Surgery and Midwifery which she hath practiz'd with good success for several Years past and therefore recomend her as one well qualify'd for License.
Hen: Edwards, Vicar of Chard   John James   Hannah James   Betty Edwards
Henry Smith, surgeon   William James, Curchwardn   Henry Smith, Overseere
Jane Hippisley   Joan James   Ann Smith

Somerset Record Office, D/D/Rn.

To the Worshipful Richard Smallbroke Doctor of Laws Chancellor of the Diocese of Lichfield and Coventry his Surrogate.
We whose names are under written do hereby Certify that Nancy Littlewood wife of Jeremiah Littlewood of the parish of Womborne in the County of Stafford and Diocese of Lichfield and Coventry is a person of sober life and Conversation and well known to us and that she is well skilled in the practise of midwifry and a person fit to be admitted and Licensed to practise that Art Witness our hands this Eighteenth day of June in the year of our Lord 1787.
J. Honeyborne Vicr of Womborne   Ann Tongue
Thos Parker ⎱ Church   Mary York
John Rogers ⎰ Wardens   Mary Cartwright
Waltr Stubbs   Pru Hill

Lichfield Record Office, B/A/11/5.

MIDWIVES' OBITUARY NOTICES

Salisbury, June 1 On Sunday, the 24th. of May, died Mrs. Mary Hopkins, of Wilton, in this County, widow; a person well practised in the art of midwifry, and who, during the space of forty-five years last past, delivered upwards of 10,000 women, with the greatest success, and is therefore greatly lamented by all who knew her.

Adams Weekly Courant, 9 June 1767.

A midwife's certificate to practise, 1715, diocese of Worcester.

Died a few days ago at Horseley, in Derbyshire, a woman named Francis Barton, at the astonishing age of 107. She followed midwifery upwards of 80 years. It is said she remembered the Revolution in 1688, and that she danced at a merry-making on that glorious occasion.

The Newcastle Chronicle, 23 January 1790.

MARGARET STEPHEN, *THE DOMESTIC MIDWIFE,* 1795

Margaret Stephen was a highly experienced midwife practising in London from her home at Ely Place, Holborn; herself the mother of nine children, she attended Queen Charlotte in some of her many confinements. She believed midwifery to be work for women, that pregnancy was not an illness as such, and deplored the increasing influence of male practitioners in the field. She was not, however, as vitriolic about *accoucheurs* as the earlier midwifery author, Elizabeth Nihill, had been in 1760. Margaret Stephen claimed to be a 'teacher of midwifery to females', having been in practice for over thirty years and having been taught by a former male pupil of William Smellie. She used models in her physiology and anatomy teaching and also demonstrated how instruments should be employed; she considered that forceps could save lives if correctly used. She wanted to see midwives properly trained and examined, with more respectable, educated women joining the profession. Their literacy was presumed. She disapproved of giving 'cordials' (alcohol) to patients and refuted the charge that midwives drank excessively. She explained how she taught pupil midwives and also had decided views on remuneration for midwifery.

I teach my own pupils the anatomy of the pelvis &c., and of the fœtal skull, on preparations which I keep by me, with everything else relative to practice in nature at labours; also turning, and the use of the forceps and other obstetric instruments, on a machine which I believe few teachers can equal, together with the cases and proper seasons which justify such expedients; and I make them write whatever of my lectures may prove most useful to them in their future practice, for which they are as well qualified as men. I intend to continue my lectures as usual to women entering upon the practice of midwifery, until the men who teach that profession render them unnecessary, by giving their female pupils as extensive instructions as they give the males.

Be always ready to the calls of distress, and do not stand out because you do not know how you are to be paid. Never distress the distressed, nor turn your back upon a patient because she is become poor, and raise not your demands because you are come into great practice. If circumstances admit, people will be ready to put a proper value upon your time; and when you think they do not, you should be delicate in telling them of it, for some may think they have given you as much as you should expect, though you are of a very different opinion. Avarice is a very bad qualification, or rather a bad vice, in those who have the health and life of their fellow creatures under their care.

Margaret Stephen, *The Domestic Midwife or the best means of preventing danger in childbirth considered* (1795), pp. 4, 104–5.

NURSES' DUTIES AT THE MINERAL WATER HOSPITAL, BATH, c. 1835

Famous from at least Roman times for its waters, by the early eighteenth century Bath had become a hydropathic centre that attracted sufferers from all parts of England. Many grand practitioners, such as William Oliver, lived there and hardly any Georgian diaries or letters fail to mention visiting the city. Well-known sufferers included Alexander Pope, Samuel Johnson and John Wesley, as well as many members of the royal family. However, for poorer patients, the Mineral Water Hospital was opened in Bath on the site of the old playhouse in 1742, designed by John Wood. It took three years to build and the funds stood at £9,000 when it first took in patients, who were not admitted by their place of residence but by their need for medical treatment. It was, in fact, a national hospital and many eminent people became governors, including the actor David Garrick, Clive of India and the artist, William Hoare. In the early nineteenth century, nurses were paid £15 a year, had to be literate, unmarried, aged between 30 and 45 and fit enough to pass a medical. Beer money was paid until 1903. Until 1829 nurses slept on the wards and their diet was meagre, often less than the patients'.

Duties of the Nurses

1. The Nurses shall do their duty under the immediate direction of the Apothecary and Matron.
2. They shall enter upon their duty at Six o'Clock in the Morning, and be in Bed by Half-Past Ten; and shall, on no account, sleep out of the Hospital.
3. They shall take care that their Wards, Furniture, and Utensils, be cleaned and in good order, every Monday by Half-past Eight o'Clock; and that no Slops which may cause an offensive Smell, be emptied into the Troughs.
4. The Nurses are required to open the Windows upon every possible occasion for the purpose of ventilating the Wards.
5. They shall not leave the Hospital, without permission from the Apothecary or the Matron.
6. They shall not allow Spirituous Liquors, Beer, or Provisions of any kind, to be brought to the Patients, by their Friends or others.
7. They shall take especial care to keep the Beds of the Patients clean and decent; and that every Patient be washed regularly in the Morning, before Breakfast. Such as may not be able to wash themselves shall be washed by the Nurses.
8. They shall take the greatest care to enforce the Rules and Orders relating to the Patients, particularly those which regard the administration of Medicines, and the observance of the directions of the Physicians, Surgeons and Apothecary.
9. They shall take care that no Patient, who has been to the Bath, shall go out of the Hospital on that day, and they shall report to the Apothecary if any Patient break the Rules.
10. They shall be obedient and submissive to their superiors, and kind and attentive to the Patients.
11. They shall not receive any Present, Acknowledgement, or Gratuity, either in money or treat, or in any other way, from any of the Patients or their Friends.
12. Any Nurse, neglecting to attend to these Rules, will be discharged.

Roger Rolls, *The Hospital of the Nation* (1988), p. 71.

NOTES

1. Talbot Williamson was buried at St Mary's, Husborne Crawley, in 1765.
2. Mrs Townsend, the wet nurse, was the wife of James, joiner, of Deenethorpe.
3. Mr Fryer has not been identified as medically qualified; he may have been a bone setter. His bill for setting the nurse's arm and also 'a poor man's back' came to £4 13s.
4. Sarah Bradshaw, wife of William of Deene, was housekeeper at Deene Park.
5. Lady Frances Brudenell was Lord Cardigan's elder daughter; she and her sister, Mary, had been ill in April.

III
PATIENTS' OWN ACCOUNTS
OF ILLNESS

❖   ❖   ❖

Most family letters, diaries and journals recorded illness and medical attention, sometimes also fees and practitioners' comments or advice. Some of the medical responses and treatments were severe and harsh in the extreme, greatly adding to the patient's suffering. However, because medical attention, especially from a physician, was costly, it seems that many sufferers put off seeking medical advice in the early stages of an illness, often being treated only when incurable. Most patients' descriptions of illness show a high level of confidence in their treatments, even though fees were frequently a source of annoyance. Medical fees can often be traced in the estate or personal papers of a family and 'long-distance' prescribing was commonplace for patients who lived outside London.

SIR JOHN MORDAUNT'S LETTER TO HIS WIFE, 1701

The Mordaunt family had lived at Walton Hall, Warwickshire from the early seventeenth century and Sir John, 5th Baronet (1650–1721), corresponded regularly with his wife, Penelope. They were often apart, for he was an MP with estates in Norfolk and she would often be in London to be attended by John Radcliffe MD, the royal physician, in her many pregnancies. In early September 1701 Sir John was badly bruised when his coach overturned in Warwickshire and from London Penelope wrote him advice about alleviating his injuries. In response to her suggestions Sir John wrote of his symptoms and treatment later in the month.

> I did take ye Powders last night, & ye twitching or rather convulsion in my right hand I writ to you about, returning in ye night & this morning, haveing ordred Mr Bradshaw[1] to come over, he tooke away seven ounces of blood from me which makes me begin my Letter ye sooner, to give you an Account how I am after these remidies, it is now four of ye Clock, my Powders have wrought three times & I believe have done working, ye first cups of my blood appeare foule & discolour'd, the last is clear & of good colour; I did feare that twitching upon my Nerves & the tingling in my hands & numness in my Fingers, might proceed from want of A due circulacion in my blood, & am now confirm'd in it, for I have had nothing of them since an houre after I was blooded, & thanks be to God find myself very well & write all this that you may be sattisfied I conceal nothing from you but give you a true Account of myselfe. . . . I think I have, by Gods assistance, taken ye best course myselfe & hope it will continue to prove so.

> Warwickshire County Record Office, CR 1368/vol. 1.

THE GREAT DIURNAL OF NICHOLAS BLUNDELL OF LITTLE CROSBY, 1725–8

Nicholas Blundell (1669–1737), a Lancashire Catholic gentleman, kept a diary from 27 July 1702 until 4 April 1728 and during nearly twenty-six years he failed to make an entry on only one day. The journal noted activities on his estate near Liverpool, his amusements, his visits and local events, but also, with great regularity, family health and sickness. He consulted a wide variety of medical practitioners and in addition kept his own prescription book. However, his concern for the health of his younger daughter, Fanny (1706–72), is a constant theme throughout the three volumes of the diary.

1725

3 February Dr Bromfield[2] dined here, he Cooped Fanny between the Shoulders.
12 February Fanny being extreamly ill Mrs Blundell came againe to see her.
13 February Fanny was so ill of the Convultion Fits that Mr Aldred gave her the Holy Oyles. Dr Ferniho[3] of Chester met Dr Dickens[4] here, they had a Consult and lodged here.

14 February Dr Dickens went hence . . . Pothecary Livesley[5] came this Morning before day, he dres'd some of Fannys Blisters & lay'd on more Blistering plaisters.
15 February Dr Fernihough went hence.
18 February Chirurgeon Livlesley[6] dresed Fannys Blisters. Dr Dickens was here.
27 February Fanny took a Vomit by Orders of Dr Dickens.
11 March Apothecary Livlesley sent his Brother[6] to see Fanny.
4 April Fanny went to Lodg at More-hall for a change of Aire (there until 19 April).
26 April . . . at Dr Lancasters[7] in Ormschurch and gave him Account how Fanny did
6 June Fanny had one of her Violent Convultion Fits, such as she has not had of severall Weeks, it was Occasion'd by seeing a Mous in her Roome.
7 July Doctor Bromfield blooddied Fanny. Dr Lancaster made a Viset here.
5 August [at Ormskirk] Dr Lancaster gave us a Bowl of Punsh, I pay'd him all I ought for Phisick.
12 August Appothecary Livlesey came both in the Morning & Evening to give Fanny a Vomit but not being in Order eather time to take it, he stayed here all Night.
13 August Mr. Livlesley gave Fanny a Vomit in the Morning, she now begins with Mr Gelders Receipt for the Ague Fits.
18 August I pay'd Apothecary Livlesey a long Bill off, 'tis chiefly upon Fannys Account.

In his accounts ledger for the third quarter of 1725 Blundell noted:

Expences by Men and Horses when we went to Wigen, when Servants &c came to see us & whilst Fanny was at Leverpoole	£5	9	5
Meat, drink Lodging, Fire & Vailes for us two & a Maid	5	3	0
Washing & Candles for us three		11	3
Wine, Biskets, Sugar Candy & some such things for Fanny	2	10	8
Coffy, Tea & Sugar		15	5
Doctor Phees	19	12	6
Phisick for Fanny	13	4	6
Messinger to Fetch Doctor Fenihough from Chester		10	6

1728

12 March Dr Bromfield was here he let Fanny Bloode in the Arme. Cozen Butler sent to see Fanny and me & to let me know when Mr Chiselton[8] would be at Chester.
17 March Fanny went to bed very ill.
19 March Cozen Butler sent me an Express to let me know when Mr Chisleton would be at Chester.
23 March [at the Golden Talbot, Chester] Mr Chisleton, Dr Ferniough &c: came to my Lodging I advised with him about Mallys Eyes and mine & about Fannys Laimness [he paid £3 3*s* as 'Phees at Chester to Doctors' in the early 1728 accounts].

The Diurnal ended two weeks later. In 1733 Fanny married an Irish Liverpool merchant and succeeded to the Crosby estates. She lived to be sixty-six.

The Great Diurnal of Nicholas Blundell of Little Crosby, Lancashire, 1702–1728,
ed. Frank Tyrer, 3 vols (The Record Society of Lancashire and Cheshire, n.d.).

THE DIARY OF THE REVD BENJAMIN ROGERS OF CARLTON, 1730–9

Benjamin Rogers (1686–1771) was Rector of Carlton, Bedfordshire for half a century from 1720 until his death. His diary covers the period 1727–40, but later becomes a commonplace book. He went to Sidney Sussex College, Cambridge, was briefly a schoolmaster and was ordained in 1712. He and his wife, Jane, had twelve children, four of whom died as infants. Rogers recorded his own illnesses and also those of his parishioners, for some of whom he himself provided medical treatment.

8 September 1730 I was Seiz'd with a violent shivering about 3 in the Afternoon, which continu'd about 4 hours, after which follow'd great Sweating which lasted all night. In the Morning I took a vomit and went to Bed again and took the Bark, which purg'd me (I Suppos'd by taking it too soon after the Vomit); and so the fever began. On the 10th I was very Restless all night, but my Wife having some papers of Mr. Whitworth's Sweating powders I took them, which at last procur'd an Intermission; so I took the Bark again (I thank God) with good success on the 11th, and have had no more of it since.

2 January 1731 Yesterday I expected my fever, which for 2 Months last past Left me 10 days and was upon me 5; and before that it used to leave me 7 days and continued upon me about 3 or 4 days; I say, I expected it Yesterday, being the 11th day, but it did not come. I had indeed for a fortnight or more before taken Rhubarb infus'd in Ale every day except Sundays etc., And during this purging (which was about 2 stools a day) I had several Bloody stools, which made me afraid of a Dysentery, and so I took Eaton's stypticonce; but perceiving it to be no more than the febrile matter falling upon the parts I took no more of the Styptic, but continued to take Rhubarb, which I hope by the Blessing of God has purg'd my fever.

Note: neither vomiting, Sweating or the Bark did (as far as I cou'd see) me the least Good. So that my fever, which began the 8th of September, did not leave me till the 2nd of January, if it has now left me.

23 January 1739 Now since my Rheumatism was manifestly occasion'd by a sudden Stoppage of the Piles about a Year and a half before (For which I had been blooded several Times, but, I believe, not so often as I should; and not long before I was taken with the Rheumatism I was prick'd, but my blood was grown so viscid that I did not bleed) I say, Since the Rheumatism was thus occasion'd, no Doubt it required a great deal of Blood to be taken away. I remember too what Sydenham[9] says as to the Cure of this distemper, and that Mrs. Mead told me that Dr. Mead[10] took away no less in the like Illness from himself; no less than 60 Oz. of Blood in a little Time. And I believed that If I had been let blood once more I had been perfectly cured. Whereas for want of that I have had many Returns of it, and when I shal be intirely rid of it I know not.

The Diary of Benjamin Rogers, Rector of Carlton, 1720–71, ed. C.D. Linnell
(Bedfordshire Historical Record Society, XXX, 1949), pp. 21, 23, 88.

THE MEMOIRS OF JOHN JORDAN OF STRATFORD-UPON-AVON, 1756, 1787

John Jordan (1746–1809) was a rural poet and wheelwright, born in Tiddington, who lived and worked in nearby Stratford-upon-Avon, Warwickshire. He was apparently inspired by the jubilee that David Garrick arranged in 1769 in honour of Shakespeare to undertake research into the poet's life, corresponding with Edmond Malone, the collector, who was preparing a new edition of Shakespeare's works. Jordan also acted as a guide to some of the town's visitors, as in 1794 to Samuel Ireland, then gathering material for his topographical work on the River Avon. Described by one modern scholar as a 'doubtful repository of Stratford lore', in 1777, although self-educated, Jordan published a poem about the surrounding countryside, *Welcombe Hills*. He left two manuscript pages of memoirs, written towards the end of his life. The 1787 illness to which he referred appears to be a local outbreak of a serious national epidemic of influenza.

> In the Autumn of that year [1756] I was afflicted with a Dropsy and was under the Care of Sr Charles Shugburgh the Physician[11] and one Carruthers a Surgeon and Apothecary[12] a native of Scotland who then lived at Stratford. By undergoing a Course of Blistering Scarifying Cathartics Diuretics and Emitics I was contrary to the expectation of every body who saw me in my afflictions restored to health about the month of May . . . I was now got into the tenth year of my Age . . .

> . . . in the year 1787, August 22[d] to compleat my ruin I was seized with an Epidemic fever, which then raged in this Town with great Violence and I was reduced to the brink of the grave . . . and that and other disorders that succeeded continued on me 8 months out of the 12, and I was once given over by the faculty, and in short I have enjoyed but a very indifferent state of health ever since, for my occupation is so Laborious that it overpowers me, and I am apt to take cold, which often makes me ill . . . during my long illness in 1787 & 1788 I lost all my business, because I was not able to do it . . .

Shakespeare Birthplace Trust Records Office, ER1/122.

THE DIARY OF THOMAS TURNER OF EAST HOATHLEY, 1756, 1764

Thomas Turner (1729–93) was a village shopkeeper in East Hoathley, Sussex and his diary covers the years 1756–65. He held various parish offices, including serving as overseer of the poor, and was also the local schoolmaster. His diary is full of local and national events, but he was clearly fascinated by and quite well read in science and medicine. He remarried four years after the death of his first wife, Peggy, in 1761. He was buried in East Hoathley churchyard to the north of the chancel; his second wife, Molly, did not die until 1807.

> *Wednesday, 14 July 1756* About 4 o'clock Mr. Porter[13] came to me and told me he thought it was the parish's duty to examine into the death of this poor creature

who died yesterday, and have her opened. For there was, according to all circumstances, room to suspect she or some other person had administered something to deprive herself or child of life. For they had agreed with a nurse to come a-Monday, which she accordingly did, and was agreed with for only a week, and a person an entire stranger. Now this creature was very well all the day a-Monday and baked. And after she had taken the bread out of the oven, she took a walk and returned about 8 o'clock. And about 10 o'clock, or between 9 and 10, she was taken with a violent vomiting and purging and continued so all night until Tuesday, 5 o'clock, at which time she expired. And the latter part of her time she was convulsed, and if asked where in pain, she would answer 'All over'. Now what was very remarkable, she had not above 2 or 3 days more but her time as to child-bearing was expired. And during all the time of her sickness she never had any pangs or throes like labour, nor no external symptoms whatever, and complained of great heat, and was afflicted with an uncommon drought. [The local womaniser, a labourer named Peter Adams, was thought responsible for her death.] . . . And we all agreed to have her opened in order if possible to discover whether she or anyone else had administered anything to deprive her or the child of life. . . . I went forward to John Bridger Esq.[14] and . . . he told me he thought it was our duty and also very proper to have her opened, and as she was an inhabitant of the parish, her friends nor no other person could prevent our doing it. I then went to Lewes to get Dr. Snelling[15] to perform the operation. . . . But he told me if there should be anything found in the midwifery, he could not report it; so it would be proper to have a man midwife to assist him. . . . We agreed that I should set out early tomorrow morning in order to get Snelling and Davy[16] both to come along with me as early as possible.

Thursday, 15 July 1756 I got to Lewes about 6.20 where I called up Mr. Davy as also Mr. Snelling . . . We came up to my house where we provided ourselves with all the things necessary for the operation, to wit, a bottle of wine and another of brandy and aprons and napkins, together with a quantity of fragrant herbs such as mint, savory, marjoram, balm, pennyroyal, roses etc., and threaded all the needles. We then proceeded to the house when we duly examined the nurse, who confirmed all we had heard before, with the addition that it was such a case as she never saw before and that she was fearful all was not right. The doctors then proceeded to the operation after they had dressed themselves and opened their instruments. They first made a big cut from the bottom of the thorax to the os pubis and then two more across at the top of the abdomen as:

The operation was performed in mine and the nurse's presence. They also opened the uterus where they found a perfect fine female child, which lay in the right position and would, as they imagined, have been born in about 48 hours. And as the membranes were all entirely whole, and the womb full of the water common on such occasions there was convincing proof she never were in travail.

The ilea were all very much inflamed, as was also the duodenum, but they both declared they could see no room to suspect poison. But if anything else had been administered, it had been carried off by her violent vomiting and purging (though they said circumstances looked very dark and all corroborated together to give room for suspicion). We came back to my house about 1 o'clock . . . The doctors both allowed this poor unhappy creature's death to proceed from a bilious colic (so far as they could judge) . . . [I] gave each of the gentlemen one guinea for their trouble.

Friday, 13 January 1764 In the forenoon walked down to the Nursery where the body of Will. Lidlow was, who was found dead in our parish the 11th instant, the coroner's inquest being to sit touching the same. Accordingly Mr. Attree, one of the coroners of this county, came and swore the jury, *viz.*, myself the foreman of the jury and the other 12 . . . The verdict brought in, as it appeared plain by the examination of the people who found him, that he was in liquor and laid himself down on the ground and perished through the inclemency of the weather.

> The manuscript diary is in the Thomas Turner Papers in the library of Yale University. *The Diary of Thomas Turner, 1754–1765*, ed. David Vaisey (1984), pp. 51, 53, 284.

SOPHIA CURZON'S LETTERS TO HER AUNT, MARY NOEL, 1781–2

Sophia Curzon (1758–82) was the youngest child of Sir Edward Noel, later Viscount Wentworth, of Kirkby Mallory, Leicestershire. Her elder sister, Judith, was later Lord Byron's detested mother-in-law. In 1777 Sophia married Nathaniel Curzon (1751–1837), who became the 2nd Lord Scarsdale on his father's death in 1804. They had two children, Sophia Caroline, born in 1779, and Nathaniel, the heir, born on 3 January 1781. Especially after her marriage, Sophia wrote often and at length to her aunt in London, Miss Mary Noel, who had brought up the three Noel girls after their mother's death in 1761. In spite of making such a brilliant match, Sophia was often desperately short of money, for her husband gambled heavily and Lord Scarsdale was unwilling to help. The Curzons had recently been forced to sell the contents of their house for the benefit of creditors and they went to live with Sophia's sister and brother-in-law, the Milbankes, in London. Sophia miscarried in the interval between her two children's births and rarely seems to have enjoyed good health.

On 30 November 1781 she wrote to Mary Noel:

> I can now inform you of Dr. Ford's[17] opinion about me . . . He has been with me this morning & he almost confirms my suspicions which were that the child has been dead some time. He won't say that he is certain of it but that it is *most* probable. But he assures me that I shall continue very well till the time & then he says I shall be in no more danger than if the child was alive & shall recover afterwards faster than usual. I told him that if he apprehended I should be particularly ill I beg'd he would say so, as I should let you know as I was certain

you would come to me, but he said I had nothing to alarm me or fret me but the not having a live child. He desires I will go on just as usual & said he would call on me to see how I went on . . . I confess it has been much on my mind lately & I cannot help feeling more frighten'd than usual. Thank God I did not stay to be confin'd in the Country. I hope with a proper trust in God I shall be able to go through this affair.

1 January 1782: Sophia Curzon to Mary Noel

I think you would have wrote to me if you had known what I have suffer'd for this last 3 weeks. I have been attack'd with the most violent pains all on one side of my Body, which has entirely hindered my Sleeping of nights & has taken my Stomach away. I have been in a Fever with the torturing pain; it was thought Rheumatic for which I have try'd many things. Ford has given me James powders which have had a violent effect without doing me good. At last I was oblig'd to have my Nurse sit up with me every night & I got so much worse in every respect – my Legs swell greatly, my breath is now so bad – that I can't walk or go up & down stairs without resting three or 4 times, that Ford thought it proper to propose making a *certain enquirie* whether I was with Child or not. As I apprehended it to be *absolutely* necessary I consented to the *very disagreable* operation. I consider'd that through modesty I was not to give up my life. This morning he has made the examination & declares me not with Child. He has desired more advice immediately so I have fix'd upon Turton.[18] They are to meet here tomorrow morning.

After they have consulted I will for your further satisfaction desire one of them to write to you, as I wish you to know in what state I am, as possibly I may represent things wrong. My spirits are very bad; I cannot help being alarm'd at my complaints & my Size. Possibly they may think Bath necessary for me. How am I to find the money to go or indeed to pay my Doctors here God knows, & I am oblig'd to be at the expense of having Horses as I am *quite* unable to walk. Ford talks of my riding at Emerson's as being a very good thing for me; if I do that I shall give up the Coach Horses. I shall be ashamed to shew my face now as every body has talk'd so much of my being to Lay-in . . . It is a shocking thing to be with only servants when so ill. As for Curzon he don't know what it is to be ill therefore he can't believe I am so bad or suffer so much as I really do. I am not angry with him for I am sure he loves me & would be really concern'd if he had the smallest idea of what I feel.

8 January 1782: Sophia Curzon to Mary Noel

If you was to see me you would not think my chief complaint lowness of spirits. I am indeed very, very ill & have undergone a vast deal & have no prospect of getting better. Consider a stoppage of now near 9 months, my body very hard & large, my legs swell'd exceedingly, no breath, *violent sharp* pains all about me, but mostly in my breast & side – am oblig'd to be lifted up in Bed, hardly any sleepp & very little appetite & my Bowels in so dreadful a state that I almost faint away myself at the smell of my Stools.

The Medicines Turton have given me as yet have been merely to clear my bowels & take away my Fever which indeed are both so far better. To day he changes my medicines for something more strengthening but he does not seem to understand that my chief complaint is the Stoppage. I am certain all my other complaints *proceed intirely from that*. He mention'd a thing which appears to me in my present situation to be the very worst thing in the world & which I will never consent to, which is having an Issue. It would be a constant drain & would prevent the other . . . I think it would hasten a Dropsy which I fear will End my disorder.

Sophia died in London, having quarrelled with Dr Turton, on 28 June 1782 and was buried at Kedleston, Derbyshire, the Curzon family home, on 8 July 1782. She was twenty-four years old. Her husband fled abroad to escape his debts and in 1798 married a Flemish woman who bore him ten children, six of whom were born out of wedlock.

Malcolm Elwin, *The Noels and the Milbankes* (1967), pp. 185, 187–8.

THE DIARY OF THE REVD JAMES WOODFORDE, 1784–91

One of the best known of English diarists, James Woodforde (1758–1803), was the son of a cleric in Somerset and, after leaving Oxford in 1763, he held his father's living of Ansford for ten years. From 1776 to 1803 Woodforde was Rector of Weston Longeville, Norfolk. He regularly recorded national, parish and family events and had a considerable interest in medicine, reporting his own and others' symptoms and treatments.

13 March 1784 Nancy brave to day (tho' this Day is the Day for the intermitting Fever to visit her) but the Bark has prevented its return – continued brave all day. Dr. Thorne[19] and Betsy Davy with him on a little Hobby called on us this morning and stayed with us about half an Hour, but could not prevail upon them to dine. Sent Ben early this morning to sell a Cow and Calf for me which he did and returned home to dinner. Ben sold the Cow and Callf, and which I recd. of him [£]6.0.0. Dr. Thorne's Method of treating the Ague and Fever or intermitting Fever is thus – To take a Vomit in the Evening not to drink more than 3 half Pints of Warm Water after it as it operates. The Morn' following a Rhubarb Draught – and then as soon as the Fever has left the Patient about an Hour or more, begin with the Bark taking it every two Hours till you have taken 12 Papers which contains one Ounce. The next oz. &c. you take it 6. Powders the ensuing Day, 5 Powders the Day after, 4 Ditto the Day after, then 3 Powders the Day after that till the 3rd oz. is all taken, then 2 Powders the Day till the 4th. oz: is all taken and then leave of. If at the Beginning of taking the Bark it should happen to purge, put ten Dropps of Laudanum into the Bark you take next, if that dont stop it put 10. drops more of Do. in the next Bark you take – then 5 Drops in the next, then 4, then 3, then 2, then 1 and so leave of by degrees. Nancy continued brave but seemed Light in her head. The Bark at first taking it, rather purged her and she took 10 Drops of Laudanum which stopped it.
7 March 1791 Washing-Week at our House and a fine Day. The small-Pox spreads much in the Parish. Abigail Roberts's Husband was very bad in it in the natural

way, who was supposed to have had it before and which he thought also. His Children are inoculated by Johnny Reeve,[20] as are also Richmond's Children near me. It is a pity that all the Poor in the Parish were not inoculated also. I am entirely for it.

8 March 1791 Gave poor Roberts one of my old Shirts to put on in the small-Pox – His, poor Fellow, being so extremely coarse and rough, that his having the small-pox so very full, his coarse Shirt makes it very painful to him. I sent his Family a Basket of Apples and some black Currant Robb. There are many, many People in the Parish yet [who] have never had the Small-pox. Pray God all may do well that have it or shall have it. Went this Afternoon and saw poor old John Peachman Who is very lame, found him unable to walk and having no relief from the Parish gave him money. Called also at Tom Carys Shop and left some money for Roberts's Familys Use for such useful things as they might want and they have [?not]. Recd. for 4 Pints ½ Butter, at 9d., 0. 3. 4. Lady Durrant at Weston House.[21]

11 March 1791 Mem. The Stiony on my right Eye-lid still swelled and inflamed very much. As it is commonly said that the Eye-lid being rubbed by the tail of a black cat would do it much good if not entirely cure it, and having a black Cat, a little before dinner I made a trial of it, and very soon after dinner I found my Eye-lid much abated of the swelling and almost free from Pain. I cannot therefore but conclude it to be of the greatest service to a Stiony on the Eye-lid. Any other Cats Tail may have the above effect in all probability – but I did my Eye-lid with my own black Tom Cat's Tail . . .

15 March 1791 My right Eye again, that is, its Eye-lid much inflamed again and rather painful. I put a plaistor to it this morning, but in the Aft. took it of again, as I perceived no good from it. I buried poor John Roberts this Afternoon about 5. o'clock, aged about 35. Yrs.

16 March 1791 My Eye-lid is I think rather better than it was, I bathed it with warm milk and Water last Night. I took a little Rhubarb going to bed to night. My Eye-lid about Noon rather worse owing perhaps to warm Milk and Water, therefore just before Dinner I washed it well with cold Water and in the Evening appeared much better for it. Recd. for Butter this Evening at 9d per Pint 0. 2. 7¼. Mr. Custance came (walking) to my House about six o'clock this Evening, he found us walking in the Garden, he drank Tea with us and left us about 7. o'clock. He gave me a Guinea to pay for the Inoculation of Harry Dunnells Children 6. in Number, which was extremely kind and good of him – The Parish refusing to pay for the same, tho' at the same they agreed to the inoculating Case's Family and have had it done, tho' a Farmer and better off. All Mr. Custances Actions to the poor assimulate with the above, every one of them generous and charitable to the highest. Mrs. Custance just the same. Pray God! they may both long enjoy Health and Life, and blessings from above daily attend them. I wrote a Note this Evening to Mr. Thorne to desire that he would come to Weston to Morrow and inoculate Harry Dunnells 6. Children. I gave the Note to Harry Dunnell for one of his Children to carry it very early to Morrow to Mattishall to Mr. Thorne before he goes out.

20 March 1791 The first thing almost that I heard this Morn' was the Death of John Greaves, my Carpenter, a very inoffensive good-kind of a young Man as any in my Parish, married about 2. Years or more ago to a Servant Maid of Mrs. Lombe's, a good kind of young Woman, and lived very happy together and daily getting up in the World. Pray God comfort her and assist her in this Day of her great distress, and may thy good Providence protect her and her fatherless Child, and likewise give her a safe and happy deliverance of another Child with which she expects to be brought to bed almost every hour. Defend her O Lord from the small-Pox in this time of her great necessity and trouble if it be thy good pleasure. The small-Pox being almost at present in every part of the Parish by inoculation etc – Poor John Greaves was very suddenly taken of. He had been ill but a few Days, but in a very dangerous Disorder, called the Peripneumony. Mr. Thorne was sent for and attended him, but I am afraid he was not sent for soon enough. I had not the most distant Idea that he was in such danger as it turned out. He was a Man well respected by all that knew him.

James Woodforde, *the diary of a country parson, 1758–1802*, ed. John Beresford (1978), pp. 222–3, 395–7.

THE DIARY OF MRS FAITH GRAY, 1794

William and Faith Gray had married in 1777; they were a prosperous legal family who lived in The Treasurer's House, York from 1788. Frances Gray had been born in the city on 5 March 1793 into a large family. When Faith Gray's son, Robert, died in 1794 of a 'decline' following scarlet fever, she 'felt this stroke a punishment for my great grief for the loss of my dearest Frances' a year earlier. Her son, Jonathan, wrote of his visit to Nottingham Asylum in 1814 (p. 140).

24 January Frances ill with smallpox.
2 May Frances taken to Fulford to be weaned.
18 May She came back from Fulford.
22 May Frances, having a cold, was kept in the house. On returning from drinking Tea with Mrs Thompson I found her worse and sent for Dr Mather[22] who ordered her a blister and an emetic.
23 May Frances something better but a bad night.
24 May She was very ill this Day. Dr Hunter[23] was called in; he ordered bleeding with Leeches which relieved her a little but she had a relapse in the night.
25 May Frances suffered severely from 5 to 7 in the morning when she expired . . . Frances was one year 2 months and 3 days old. She was a fine child and very engaging. The stroke was the more afflicting to me having so lately suckled and nursed her through the smallpox, and only weaned her three weeks before her death.

A. Gray, *Papers and Diaries of a York family, 1764–1839* (1927), pp. 80–1.

HORACE WALPOLE'S LETTERS TO MARY BERRY, 1791

Horace Walpole (1717–97) was the fourth son of Sir Robert Walpole; he became the 4th Earl of Orford in 1791, the year of these letters. He is perhaps best known for his architectural work at Strawberry Hill, where he lived from 1747, and his voluminous correspondence during his long life. He was the author of the gothic novel, *The Castle of Otranto* (1764) and came to know the Berry family when they moved into Twickenham in 1788.

Mary Berry (1763–1852) was the elder of Robert Berry's two daughters; the family lived in Chiswick from 1770 until 1783 and then began their European travels. Mary was recognised as a beauty, with 'fine dark eyes . . . very lively when she speaks'. Horace Walpole considered her 'an angel inside and out'; there were contemporary rumours that their marriage was discussed. Mary Berry kept extensive diaries of her travels, including accounts of Paris at the time of the Revolution, and on the family's return to England in 1791 Walpole installed them in Cliveden, a house near to his own, known as Little Strawberry Hill. At his death he bequeathed the property to the Berry family and also Box O of his manuscripts and printed works 'to be published at their own discretion and for their own emolument'. Mary Berry noted in her diary how she worked almost non-stop on the project and in 1798 produced a handsome five-volume publication of Walpole's *Works*, which sold well. Mary Berry died on 20 November 1852 and was buried at Petersham, Surrey.

Berkeley Square, Sat. Jan. 22, 1791
I have been most unwilling to send you such bad accounts of myself by my last two letters, but as I could not conceal all, it was best to tell you the whole truth. Tho' I did not know that there was any real danger, I could not be so blind to my own age and weakness, as not to think with so much gout and fever the conclusion might very probably be fatal, and therefore it was better you should be prepared for what might happen. The danger appears to be entirely over; there seems no more gout to come; I have no fever, have a very good appetite, and sleep well. Mr Watson,[24] who is all tenderness and attention, is persuaded to-day that I shall recover the use of my left hand, of which I despaired much more than of the right, as having been seized three weeks earlier. Emaciated and altered I am incredibly, as you would find were you ever to see me again. But this illness has dispelled all visions! And as I have so little prospect of passing another happy autumn, I must wean myself from whatever would embitter my remaining time by disappointments.

Berkeley Square, Feb. 12, 1791.
Y^r other letter talks as kindly as possible on my illness, on which I am sure I have not deceived you, tho' I have talked too much on it; and on which, to satisfy you, I will still be particular. A fortnight ago I had every reason to think myself quite recovering, but in my left hand; then my pains returned for a week: they are again gone but in my left wrist, which to-day is uneasy enough. One comfort, however, I have, which is the conviction that all my pains have been and are gouty, not rheumatic, which I dread much more as less likely to leave me. The moment I lie down in bed, I go to sleep, and often sleep five, nay, seven hours together without waking. But there lies my whole strength.

Strawberry Hill, Tuesday night, July 12, 1791.
Now I must say a syllable about myself – but don't be alarmed! it is not the gout; it is worse, it is the rheumatism, which I have had in my shoulder ever since it attended the gout last December. It was almost gone till last Sunday, when the

Bishop of London[25] preaching a charity sermon in our church, whither I very, very seldom venture to hobble, I would go to hear him, both out of civility, and as I am very intimate with him. The church was crammed, and tho' it rained, every window was open. However, I went to bed and to sleep; but waked with such exquisite pain in my rheumatic right shoulder, that I think I scarce ever felt greater torture from the gout. It was so grievous, that I considered whether I should not get out of bed – but the thought that I might kill myself, and consequently not live to Cliveden-tide checked me – upon my honour this is true – I lay – not still, but writhing about, till about five o'clock, when I fell asleep. I have had but very moderate pain since. I own I did tremble at night, but I had my usual comfortable night composed of one whole dose of sleep, and could not be very bad yesterday . . . not worse to-day, when I have been writing this prolix syllable to you . . . Tho' the gout could never subdue my courage, not make me take any precaution against catching cold, the rheumatism and Cliveden have made a coward of me. I now draw up my coach glasses [windows], button my breast, and put a hat on the back of my head, for I cannot yet bear to touch my forehead, when I go into the garden. You charged me to be circumstantial when I am not well – I think I have been circumstantial enough!

Strawberry Hill, Sunday night, July 17, 1791.
Next to being better, I am rather glad I am a little worse, i.e., the gout is come to assert his priority of right to me, and when he has expelled the usurper, I trust he will retire quietly too; in the meantime, my case is party per pale good and bad: I slept last night without waking, but if I want still more gout, I think I can draw upon my right knee, where there seems to be a little in store for me. In good earnest, the rapid shifting of my complaint makes me flatter myself that it will not be permanent.

Strawberry Hill, Wednesday evening, July 20th, 1791.
. . . First, I am sure you will be glad to hear that I am much better, tho' an accident that happened to me on Monday night might have had ugly circumstances. Having had a good deal of fever, I take saline draughts: a fresh parcel came on Sunday night, with a bottle in a separate paper, which I concluded was hartshorn, which I had wanted. They were laid on the window, and next morning I bade James give me one of the draughts: he thinking it one of the former parcel, gave me the separate draught, and I swallowed it directly, but instantly found it was something very different, and sent for the apothecary to know what I had taken; yet before he could arrive, I found upon enquiry, and by the effects, that it was a vomit designed for one of the maids – to be sure, in pain and immoveable all down my right side, it was not a pleasant adventure, but it had not the least bad effect, and I dictated the conclusion of my letter to you that very night, tho' I would not then mention the accident, lest you might suspect me poisoned before this could arrive to convince you of the contrary. I was very well yesterday, and so I am to-day, and should have walk'd about the house but have had company the whole of the day.

Berkeley Square, Oct. 20, 1791.
I have had for some time a very troublesome erysipelas on my left arm. Mr. Gilchrist, my apothecary at Twickenham,[26] is dangerously ill at Tunbridge. Dreading to be laid up where I had no assistance nor advice, I determined to

come away – and did – which has proved fortunate. Mr. Watson, my oracle, attends my arm, and it is so much better that I passed the evening yesterday at Mrs. Damer's.[27]

Straw.-hill, July 26, 1796.
I have not writ to you till to-day that I was sure I was well enough; for two days I was in a strange way, yet said nothing of it. On Friday I came down to breakfast, and then attempting to dictate . . . , Kirgate[28] perceived that I neither articulated, nor used right words, and advised me to leave off. I did, and sent for the apothecary, who found my pulse low and quick, and would have had me take æther, but I would take nothing without Hewetson. Your father and sister were with me looking over prints in the evening, but thought I was very low, tho' I complained of nothing: but at one I was waked with a great palpitation, I was forced to call up my servants, and really thought I was going; but about three I felt sleepy, and did not wake till seven o'clock, since when I have been perfectly well, – such a strange constitution I have!

Mary Berry's account of Walpole's death

Very soon after . . . [15 December] the gout, the attacks of which were every day becoming more frequent and longer, made those with whom Lord Orford had been living at Strawberry Hill very anxious that he should return to Berkeley Square, to be nearer assistance in case of any sudden seizure. As his correspondents, soon after his removal, were likewise established in London, no more letters passed between them. When not immediately suffering from pain, his mind was tranquil and cheerful. He was still capable of being amused, and of taking some part in conversation; but during the last weeks of his life, when fever was superadded to his other ills, his mind became subject to the cruel hallucination of supposing himself neglected and abandoned by the only persons to whom his memory clung, and whom he always desired to see. In vain they recalled to his memory how recently they had left him, and how short had been their absence; it satisfied him for the moment, but the same idea recurred as soon as he had lost sight of them. At last nature, sinking under the exhaustion of weakness, obliterated all ideas but those of mere existence, which ended without a struggle, on the 2nd of March, 1797.

Extracts from the Journals and Correspondence of Miss Berry from the year 1783 to 1852, ed. Lady Theresa Lewis, 3 vols (1865), I, pp. 279–80, 283, 314, 315, 316–17, 371; II, pp. 10, 19.

THE DIARY OF ABIGAIL GAWTHERN, 1803

Abigail Gawthern (1757–1822) was the widow of Francis Gawthern (1750–1791), a wealthy white-lead manufacturer of Nottingham and her cousin, whom she married in 1783. She was the daughter of Thomas Frost, a local grocer, and a great-niece of Thomas Secker, who became Archbishop of Canterbury in 1758. She came from Holme Hall, near Newark and she lived at Low Pavement, Nottingham, after her marriage. She ran her late husband's lead works after his death until 1807 when the heir, Francis junior, came of age. Her diary covers most of her life until 1810. It is full of references to local marriages and deaths; she was greatly interested in the establishment of the Nottingham Infirmary, opened in 1782, and had many medical practitioners as her friends and acquaintances. She regularly noted her own family's ill-health and local deaths of all kinds. The diary seems to have been written in the years 1808–13 and much of it is therefore retrospective, but compiled from pocket books that she wrote up as events occurred. The entries end abruptly, suggesting that subsequent volumes, now lost, may have existed. The original diary consists of 181 folios. Abigail and Francis Gawthern had three daughters, two of whom died young, and one son. Her husband died after only eight years of marriage at the age of forty-one.

17 October I felt very unwell this day, having taken for the first time of some years 20 drops of laudanum last night, having had indifferent nights and a bad cold; feel a great pulsation from my heart to my head.
18. Extremely cold and windy, and I took cold.
19. . . . I at home reading psalms and lessons.
20. I increased my cold with getting seeds in the garden; I began from this day to be extremely unwell with a pulsation in my head and violent beating and palpitation in my heart.
21. . . . I was making saline draughts for my cold.
22. Extreme restless night.
23. Breakfasted in bed, felt very ill all over, told Mrs Brough[29] I wished to go to Nottingham tomorrow and we prepared accordingly.
29. Better of the pulsation of my head and beating at my heart.
Nov. 2. Dr Marsden[30] called and I took the opportunity of asking his opinion; he wrote me a prescription.
21. A restless night; the complaint in my head returned with pulsations and beating at my heart.
7 Dec. I had only one hour's sleep, Dr Marsden wrote me another prescription; much agitated, Hind[31] sat up all the night; took an opium pill, violent pain in my head 8th, 9th, 10th, 11th, 12th no better, had a new bed for a servant to sleep in my room; 14th, the best night I have had of a month.
25. Extremely unwell from taking a draught last night; too much laudanum and ether, 60 drops ordered by Dr Marsden.

The Diary of Abigail Gawthern of Nottingham, 1751–1810, ed. Adrian Henstock
(The Thoroton Society, XXXIII, 1980), pp. 103–4.

NOTES

1. John Bradshaw, an apothecary, lived in a large new house at 1 Jury Street, Warwick, built after the town was ravaged by fire in 1694.
2. James Bromfield, surgeon of Liverpool.
3. Philip Fernihough MD, physician of Chester.
4. George Dickins MD of Liverpool.
5. Edward Livesey, apothecary of Ormskirk.
6. Edmund Livesey, surgeon of Liverpool.
7. William Lancaster of Ormskirk.
8. William Cheselden MD (1688–1752), an eminent London practitioner.
9. Thomas Sydenham MD (1626–89), the most famous physician of his day, pioneered the use of bark for treating fevers.
10. Richard Mead MD (1673–1754), a celebrated royal physician, lived part of the year at Harrold Hall, near Carlton, and had earlier treated Lady Joliffe locally.
11. Sir Charles Shuckburgh MD (1722–73), 5th Baronet, inherited his family's Warwickshire estate of Shuckburgh in 1759 on the death of his cousin. He was the author of a treatise on inoculation.
12. Robert Carruthers (1718–99), a surgeon, left Stratford-upon-Avon to serve on the *Burford*, a man-of-war, in 1757; by 1779 he was in practice in Wareham, Dorset, where he died.
13. Revd Thomas Porter was rector of East Hoathley from 1752 until his death in 1794.
14. John Bridger of Offham was a local magistrate.
15. John Snelling, a surgeon-apothecary at Alfriston, was godfather to one of Turner's sons in 1773.
16. Thomas Davey was a surgeon at Lewes.
17. James Ford MD (1718–95), a well-known gynaecologist, was appointed as physician-extraordinary to Queen Charlotte.
18. John Turton MD (1735–1806), a fashionable London practitioner, was physician to the Queen's household.
19. Robert Thorne (b. 1745) was a surgeon-apothecary with five apprentices.
20. John Reeve does not appear to have been medically qualified, although a man of that name was licensed by the Bishop of Norwich in the seventeenth century.
21. Weston House was the home of the Custance family, built in 1781 for John Custance; it was demolished in 1926. Lady Durrant was presumably a guest there.
22. Alexander Mather was a surgeon-apothecary of Minster Yard, York.
23. Alexander Hunter MD (1729–1809), one of the most senior of the six physicians in the city, lived in Low Petergate. His monument is in the church of St Michael-le-Belfry, York.
24. Watson seems to be Henry Watson, surgeon of Westminster.
25. Dr Beilby Porteous, Bishop of London.
26. Sterling Gilchrist, an ex-army surgeon, lived at Twickenham and died in 1792.
27. Anne Damer (née Conway) was a well-known sculptor.
28. Thomas Kirgate was Walpole's printer.
29. Mrs Brough was a family friend who lived at Newark.
30. William Marsden MD (1767–1850) of Nottingham was formerly an army surgeon.
31. Hind was a female servant in the Gawthern household.

IV
EXPECTATION OF LIFE

❖   ❖   ❖

The fatalistic concept of life as 'nasty, brutish and short' before the present century is difficult to dismiss for the majority of English people. Childbirth was hazardous and life expectancy low, even for the well-to-do. Undoubtedly the many thousands of English parish registers are the most substantial source available to us. They were not, of course, kept for modern statistical analysis and incumbents had different ways of recording the basic information. Occasionally an epidemic would be noted, but usually we have to deduce this by the increased numbers of burials in a fairly short period.

As these extracts illustrate, by the eighteenth century as the birth rate rose there was considerable interest in infant mortality. Also by this period the investigation of the causes of death became far more uniform as the coroner's role developed; from the mid-eighteenth century he was paid for attending inquests and conducting post-mortem examinations, regularly reporting to Quarter Sessions. From 1801, national censuses were made every decade; they recorded all inhabitants in an individual dwelling, their ages and occupations, increasing the information available as the century progessed. The Cumberland survey and the coroner's report suggest that sudden death was experienced by all social classes, although occupational health risks were a major factor in life expectancy until the twentieth century.

BAPTISMS, MARRIAGES AND BURIALS IN THE PARISH REGISTER

Anglican parish registers unquestionably contain the most detailed and widespread data from the mid-sixteenth century onwards to show patterns of life and death in English communities. Every parish, urban or rural, was obliged to record such details and although baptism and marriage might escape the diocesan authorities, burial could not. Some registers are faulty or have disappeared, but the parish was required to make copies annually for the diocese, and these bishop's transcripts usually survive in the diocesan record office. During the English Civil War registration was erratic as it was no longer the task of the incumbent, usually ejected, but of a civil official, the registrar.

St Alban's, Worcester, is the second oldest parish in the city; in 1779 its population was 124. The Norman church has been heavily restored and in 1882 the living was joined with that of St Helen's into one benefice. St Helen's is now deconsecrated and is used as a branch of the Worcestershire Record Office. St Alban's registers date from 1630 and are in three volumes up to 1812. In the first volume, up to 1726, entries of baptism, marriage and burial were not divided, but entered chronologically. In the second volume these three categories were entered separately – marriages only until 1754 – and the third volume has marriages only up to 1812. Unusually, there is no break in the register for the Civil War years. Parish registers rarely gave the cause of death, although occasionally, as when plague broke out at Worcester in 1637 and 1644, this was noted. Occupations were normally not entered, but status was indicated. Thus 'Mr' or 'Mrs' suggests gentry parishioners; paupers were sometimes noted. Some entries recorded bastards as such, but not always. If a parishioner were a widow or widower, this fact was invariably added. Strangers who were married or buried in St Alban's had their home parish included in the entry.

From registers, therefore, it is possible to trace trends in pre-nuptial conceptions, illegitimacy, infant and maternal mortality, remarriages and social mobility, as well as age at marriage and life expectancy if parishioners remained in the locality.

Of the following twelve St Alban's baptisms, seven infants were to die, including one set of twins, and the one illegitimate child was buried aged only a year. The one gentry marriage, of George Abney to Anne Brodribb, was by licence rather than the more public banns, perhaps because she had married her first husband, Richard Brodribb, only six years before.

1737 Baptisms

July 8 Thomas, Son of John & Anne Evans, pr[ivate]ly: July 31 Cert.
— 10 William, Son of Samuel & Mary Carter.
— 19 Benjamin, Son of John & Mary Karver prly: Augt 8 Cert.

Sep: 18 Mary, Dau^r: of Thomas & Eleanor Farret.
— 20 Richard, Son of Richard & Elizth: Peart.
Oct: – Alice, Dau^r: of Ambrose & Elizth: Jones pr^{ly}: Nov: 6 Cert.
— 20 Thomas, Son of ye Rev^d: Mr. Samuel Nott & Elizabeth his Wife, privately. Nov: 6. Certified.
— Thomas, Son of Thomas & Elizth: Powel, privately.
Feb: 16 John, Son of George & Eliz^h: Roe, pr^{ly}. Mar: 12. Cert.
— Thomas, Son of Thomas & Milborough Harper, privately. Mar: 19. Cert.
— 19 Thomas & George, Sons of Thos: & Elizth: Sterry, pr^{ly}.

Marriages

Aug: 14 William Rowley, of Gt. Malvern, & Anne Fansons, of St. Alban's, Worc., P. Banns.
Sep^r: 30 Mr George Abney, of Birmingham & Mrs Anne Brodribb, St. Swit[hins], Worc., P. Lic.
Oct. 3 George Downes & Elizabeth King, Wid, P. Bans.

Burials

Mar: 30 Joseph, Son of Thomas & Eleanor Farret.
June 28 Thomas, Son of Thomas & Anne Crooke.
July 17 Elizabeth, Wife of George Downes.
Oct^r: 17 Mary, Dau^r: of Thomas & Eleanor Farret.
— 23 Alice, Dau^r: of Charles & Mary Graves.
Nov^r: 6 Thomas, Son of Thomas and Elisabeth Powel.
— John Williams, junr.
— 8 John Addenbrooke.
— 21 Richard, Bastard Son of Mary Britt alias Mason
Feb: 20 Thomas & George, Sons of Thomas & Elizth: Sterry.

E. Oldnall, Min[iste]^r.

The Registers of St Alban's, City of Worcester, Parish Register Society, 1896, p. 53.
The original register is in Worcestershire Record Office, BA 2335/13b(v).

THE AUTOBIOGRAPHY OF WILLIAM STOUT OF LANCASTER, 1736, 1742

William Stout (1665–1752) wrote his autobiography late in life, probably in 1742, when he was aged seventy-seven. His family were not Quakers but he joined the Society of Friends in 1686. Having been apprenticed, Stout kept an ironmonger's shop in Lancaster from 1688. He never married and his nephew, William, became his heir. His longevity was exceptional and, having survived a broken leg in 1743, he was obviously aware of his physical condition at such a great age.

In 1736

Upon the 10th day of the 2^d month this year, I tooke a jurney to Whitehaven, to the generall meeting of our Friends there, which I performed with as much ease as when I was about 20 years of age – although I was now entred into the seventy second year of my age. And I had hitherto had my health very well, and have not been at 1ˢ expence to doctor, apothycary, or physik or surgery, for therty years last past. And I have hitherto accustomed myselfe to rise at the sun rise in summer, and walke a round of two miles in the morning, in difrent ways each day of the weeke, and in my gardin an hower or more in the evning. I began to use spectakles at 50 years of age, and could not see to write or read without them till I was 70 years old; but since then my eyesight had recovered gradualy, so that I can now see to write or read without them. Yet when I write or read much I use them to preserve my sight.

1742

I have had my health very well hitherto, and continue to rise at sunrising in spring and summer, and walke a mile out of town, and, in the evning, an hower or more in my gardin. And in the winter evnings, if fair and clear, I choose to walke an hower or two in the gardin in the night, if it be frost and light moone, rather than to sit by the fire. Otherways, if confined to the house, I choose to walke upon the floor, rather than sit by the fire, or to walke one hower and sit another. And in the late great frost, I kept walking very much night and day, which got me a good appatite to my victualls, and to rest in the night and to go thinn of cloth[e]s. It was the midle of the 10th month this year befor I added any thing to my summer habit of cloth[e]s. My eye sight encreased yearly for seven years last past. Betwixt my age of 50 and 70 years, I could not see to read or write without spectacles, but now I can write tolarably well without them. But yet when I write or read much, I use them, but do not cary them about with me.

> *The Autobiography of William Stout of Lancaster, 1665–1752*, ed. J.D. Marshall
> (The Chetham Society, vol. 14, 3rd series, 1967), pp. 219, 231–2.

PARISH NURSES AND PAUPER CHILDREN

The problem of pauper births and children remained acute for the overseers of the poor in all parts of the country and increased as the population rose during the eighteenth century. In smaller rural parishes, the labourer 'overburdened with children' would be paid a larger weekly cash sum as his family increased, but in towns and cities many infants were farmed out to parish nurses or deposited in local workhouses, with equally low survival rates. Contemporary writers such as William Cadogan MD (1711–97) and Jonas Hanway (1712–86) severely criticised such practices, but also condemned the universal fashion among affluent mothers of putting their infants out to wet nurses rather than breast-feeding the babies themselves.

INFANT DEATHS IN LONDON IN 1766

Many children born of poor, idle or unfortunate parents, though they should have the best constitutions, yet die in great numbers under five years old. Many children instead of being nourished with care, by the fostering hand of a wholesome country nurse, are thrust into the impure air of a work-house, into the hands of some careless, worthless young female or decrepit old woman, and inevitably lost . . .

As far as I can trace the evil, there has been such a devastation within the bills of mortality, for half a century past, that at a moderate computation 1,000 or 1,200 children have annually perished under the direction of parish officers. I say under their direction, not that they ordered them to be *killed*, but that they *did not order* such means to be used as are necessary to keep them *alive*.

An acquaintance of mine once solicited a parish officer for 2s. a week for a servant while she was nursing her child; alleging that a common parish nurse had at least that sum, if not 2s. 6d. 'Yes', says the officer, 'it is very true; but the young women in question will most probably preserve her child, whereas in the hands of our nurses, after 5 or 6 weeks we hear no more of them.'

There is no wonder in this, when it is considered, that these children were put into the hands of indigent, filthy or decrepit women, three or four to one woman, and sometimes sleeping with them. The allowance of these women being scanty, they are tempted to take part of the bread and milk intended for the poor infants. The child cries for food, and the nurse beats it because it cries. Thus with blows, starving and putrid air, with the additions of lice, itch, and filthiness, he soon receives his *quietus*.

Mrs Poole [a nurse] had, in . . . 1765, the nursing of 23 children belonging to St. Clement Danes . . . The account of the 23 children stands thus:

Discharged at the age of 2 years	1
Discharged at the age of 5 months	1
Remaining alive	3
Departed out of this transitory life, in her hands after breathing the vital air about one month	18

For this piece of service to the parish, Mrs Poole has been paid 2s. each per week, which, considering the importance of the enterprise, must be deemed a very moderate price.

> Jonas Hanway, *An Earnest Appeal for Mercy to the Children of the Poor* (1766), pp. 4, 8, 39–42, 138.

FOUNDLINGS AND INFANTICIDE

A woman who became pregnant and could neither obtain an abortion nor marry the child's father might resort to murdering the infant if it were born alive. Some women chose to 'abandon' their babies and to help such orphans, the London Foundling Hospital was established in 1742. For domestic servants, especially, dismissal was usual in pregnancy and parish support was then their only future. As a result, bastardy remained a pressing, costly problem for the parish officers. Infanticide became an increasingly common crime in the eighteenth century, and newspapers regularly reported it. As a deterrent, many women found guilty of infanticide were sentenced to be anatomised after execution. Court cases suggest that the guilty woman often had help in her crime, especially from her family. Of the women hanged at Tyburn in the eighteenth century, 12 per cent were guilty of infanticide. However, some idea of compassion towards disturbed women who murdered their children can be seen when a capital sentence was commuted to transportation. Many medical authorities, including John Hunter, were interested in infanticide, which remained a capital charge until the twentieth century.

Foundlings

[London] On Monday night last, a male child about three or four days old, was dropped at a nobleman's door in Grosvenor Square, with an inscription on a paper pinned to his breast; the infant was sent to the workhouse of St George's Hanover Square. And on Thursday night another male child about a month old in a basket was laid at a clergyman's door near St James; the infant was neatly dressed, bearing a direction for the clergyman. It was sent to St James's workhouse.

Daily Post-Boy, 3 October 1735.

Cases of Infanticide

[London] The young Woman committed to Newgate for the Murder of her Child, (a girl about a Month old) was Servant to a Tallow Chandler in Cheshunt Street, from which Service she was dismissed on the Discovery of her being with Child by the Apprentice; and though the Officers of that Parish had obliged him to give Security to indemnify them, yet no Care was taken of her; and the Extremity she was reduced to, 'tis thought, deprived her of her Senses. It is said, that after she had cut off the Child's Head, she buried the Body in a Field near Dunance in Endfield Highway, but took it up again, and shewed it about, telling everyone what she had done, and being carry'd before Justice Marsh of Green-Street, she signed to a Confession of the Murder: the Child's Head is not yet found, and she being examined about it, said she *saw the Devil fly away with it.*

Ipswich Journal, 15 August 1730.

Last Thursday the Bodies of two new-born Children, supposed to be Twins, were plow'd up in a Field near Warwick: They were wrapt in a Piece of an old Blanket, and one seem'd to have been scorch'd with Fire, the other had an Orifice under its Ear, suppos'd to have been made with a Penknife. 'Tis thought they had not been long buried, for one of 'em voided its Excrements after it was taken up. Several Persons have been taken up on Suspicion, but as yet the real inhuman Perpetrator of this horrid Fact is not discover'd. The Children were Male and Female.

Worcester Journal, 20 April 1748.

Newcastle, Sept. 29. Last Monday Night, about 8 o'Clock, Eleanor Bennet bore a Bastard Child on the Rocks near Tinmouth, without any Assistance; immediately after she was delivered she strangled it, and threw it over the Rocks into the Sea, and on Wednesday Morning it was found by a Person belonging to the Fort. She was apprenhended as she was carrying Sand between Tinmouth and Shields, and examined by a Midwife, to whom she confess'd the Murder. She is now in the Custody of two Constables but will soon be sent to Gaol.

Aris's Gazette, 8 October 1750.

On Monday se'nnight Thomas Baker, upwards of Seventy Years of Age, and Anne Baker, his Daughter, of Great Houghton, near Northampton, were committed to the County Gaol, for the Murder of a Child which the said Anne Baker had by her father. It appeared that the old Man had debauch'd his Daughter when she was 18 Years old, and lived in a continual State of Incest with her for about 14 Years, till within six Weeks past; and soon after the Child above-mentioned was born, which was about four Years ago, he murder'd it, as his Daughter has confess'd, and buried it in a neighbouring Field. And last Friday Morning, the said Thomas Baker, who has been ill for some time past, died in the said Gaol.

Aris's Gazette, 25 May 1752.

A Mercer's apprentice in Knaresborough having had Carnal Dealings with a young Woman in that Neighbourhood of bad Character lately received a Letter from her to the following Purport, viz. "I am with Child by you, and have consulted the Midwife, who tells me it will cost 5s 6d to procure an Abortion; and I insist on 5s more, or depend upon it, I will expose you to your Father, Master &c." After the Receipt of the Letter he appointed to meet her in private in order to make up Matters; but wanting [lacking] the Cash, &c, Words arose, which were soon followed by Blows; and being much enraged, he murdered her in the most cruel Manner, by cutting her Neck near round &c. He has since confessed the Fact, and is committed to York Gaol. Two Persons are taken into Custody for being concerned and privy to the said Murder.

Aris's Gazette, 19 February 1753.

Bristol April 21. Tuesday Morning last Jane Williams, about 36 Years of Age, born in Caermarthenshire, and who lived in Stapleton, but since in Milk-Street in this City, secreted herself in a necessary House in the great Coach Yard there, where she was delivered of a Male Bastard Child and which she afterwards threw into the Soil. This being discovered, and the Mother found in a Privy adjoining in a very weak Condition, she was taken to a Neighbour's House, and a Midwife sent for, who found that she had been just delivered, upon which she was immediately carried to St Peter's Hospital, in order to be taken proper Care of. The Coroner's Inquest have brought in their Verdict Wilful Murder.

Aris's Gazette, 30 April 1753.

Whereas a new-born Female Child (supposed to have been born alive) was found in a Pool, call'd the Swan Pool, in the Parish of St John, in the City of Worcester, on Sunday Morning last, the 21st of this Instant April, and whereas one MARY HIDE, Single Woman, a Pauper of the said Parish (who has since absconded) is suspected to be the Mother of the said Child; Whoever shall apprehend her, (so that she may be brought to Justice) shall have HALF A GUINEA Reward of the proper Officers of the said Parish.

Worcester Journal, 25 April 1754.

Newcastle 24 August. Last Week the Assizes ended here, when Dorothy Catinby, for murdering her Bastard Child . . . [was] capitally convicted. [She] was executed on Monday about Ten o'Clock: She persisted to the last she did not murder her Child. Her body was given to the Surgeons to be anatomized. She left three Children by her late lawful Husband, two Sons and a Daughter; 'tis said the Sons have both drown'd themselves, and the Daughter, a Servant in this Town, has left her Service, and is gone to some remote Part of the Kingdom, where she may live without Reproach.

Aris's Gazette, 2 September 1754.

[Devon] On Saturday last was brought to the high gaol for the county of Devon, Mary Light, for that too common and most unnatural crime of murdering her own illegitimate infant. She is about 21 years of age, and lived as servant to one farmer Kerswell at a village near Modbury in this county, where, she says, a young fellow servant, also in the same house, courted her, to whose importunities she yielded, and became pregnant by him. Her condition was suspected by her mother, who charged her strictly with it, but she still denied it, concealing it also from all except her seducer, who on her acquainting him with it, left her and his service. About five weeks ago she was in bed seized with great pains, and was delivered of a living female child, without the knowledge of two girls who lay in the same room. She gathered up her infant, and got again into bed, wrapping the babe in one corner of the rug, and rising at her wonted hour, went about her household work. Her mistress going into her chamber, found the child stifled.

Northampton Mercury, 8 March 1756.

[Birmingham] On Friday last the Body of a Female infant was found in a Garden the Back of Edgbaston-Street; as was that of a Male one in New Hall Pool; on which the Coroner's Jury sat the same Day, and brought in their Verdict, that the Female Child died a natural Death, and was supposed to be buried in the Garden to save Funeral Expences; but adjourned to another Time regarding the other.

Aris's Gazette, 28 February 1757.

[London] Monday a servant girl belonging to a Merchant in Great Winchester-Street was delivered of a bastard child in her own room, when she cut the child's head entirely off from its body; she was carried to Alhallows workhouse to be taken care of till she is able to be removed to Newgate. The jury met on Tuesday evening, at the Crown at Little Moregate, and found her guilty of wilful murder.

Coventry Mercury, 4 March 1771.

CHRISTENINGS AND BURIALS IN LONDON, 1784, FROM *THE GENTLEMAN'S MAGAZINE*

The Gentleman's Magazine, a monthly publication, lasted for nearly 200 years from 1731 to 1907. It was founded by Edward Cave (1691–1754) who was the son of a Rugby cobbler and had been apprenticed to a London printer. *The Gentleman's Magazine* was a wide-ranging collection of up-to-date information, including book reviews, births, marriages and burials, international news and descriptions of the state of the economy. Its wide distribution enabled country readers to keep abreast of international events, London fashions, literary criticism, weather and commodity prices. It always had a keen interest in the statistics of life and death and these were frequently included, as for 1784.

The London general bill of christenings and burials, from 16 December 1783 to 14 December 1784

| Christened | Males | 8778 | Buried Males | | 9229 | Decreased in the | | |
| | Females | 8401 | | Females | 8599 | burials this year 1201 | | |

Died under	2 Years	5729	between 50 and 60	1523	aged	101	1
Between	2 and 5	1711	60 and 70	1359		102	0
	5 and 10	683	70 and 80	917		103	1
	10 and 20	636	80 and 90	391		104	0
	20 and 30	1417	90 and 100	48		105	0
	40 and 50	1781					

DISEASES

Abortive and stillborn	528	Fever, malignant, spotted, scarlet	1973
Abscess	1	Fistula	4
Aged	1240	Flux	9
Ague	8	French pox	32
Apoplexy and sudden death	207	Gout	63
Asthma and phthysic	337	Gravel, strangury, stone	35
Bedridden	12	Grief	3
Bleeding	4	Head ache	1
Bloody flux	1	Headmouldshot, water in the head	15
Bursten [hernia] and rupture	17	Imposthume	4
Cancer	43	Inflammation	198
Canker	2	Itch	0
Chicken pox	3	Jaundice	62
Childbed	133	[King's] Evil	13
Cholic, gripes, twisting of guts	8	Leprosy	0
Cold	3	Lethargy	0
Consumption	4540	Livergrown	4
Convulsions	4219	Lunatick	46
Cough and whooping cough	467	Measles	29
Diabetes	0	Miscarriage	3
Dropsy	830	Mortification	136

Palsy	66	Sores and ulcers	13
Pleurisy	15	St Anthony's Fire [erisypelas]	0
Quinsy	4	Stoppage in the stomach	10
Rash	0	Surfeit	1
Rheumatism	8	Swelling	1
Rickets	0	Teeth	369
Rising of the Lights	0	Thrush	6
Scald head [ringworm]	0	Tympany	1
Scurvy	4	Vomiting and looseness	2
Small pox	1759	Worms	11
Sore throat	6		

CASUALTIES

Bit by a mad dog	2	Killed by falls, other accidents	39
Broken limbs	3	Killed themselves	23
Bruised	2	Murdered	4
Burnt	14	Overlaid	0
Choked	1	Poisoned	2
Drowned	97	Scalded	5
Excessive drinking	8	Smothered	0
Executed	11	Starved	1
Found dead	5	Suffocated	3
Frighted	0		

Total 220

The Gentleman's Magazine, vol. 2 (LIV), 1784.

THE CORONER

There were two coroners active in Coventry in the mid-eighteenth century, James Birch and James Hewitt, both city attorneys. Coroners' records could include jury summonses and lists, witness statements, inquest reports and medical evidence. The case of the murder of Alice Gibbs, an eleven-year-old pauper apprentice, by her master, John Green, a weaver, in 1746 is an example of how the system would seek to explain a sudden or unexpected death.

James Hewitt (1709–89), the son of a city alderman, had a distinguished legal career, becoming a judge of the King's Bench and Lord Chancellor of Ireland; he was created Baron Lifford in 1768. James Birch was coroner for the years 1728–51 and acted in the murder of Alice Gibbs in 1746. He kept a memorandum book of inquests during these years, covering violent deaths (in mining and from contemporary traffic), drownings and suicides. There was also a small group of infant deaths in his records that required medical evidence.

Documents relating to Alice Gibbs's death

1. *Committal order to have John Green held in Coventry prison, 13 March 1746*
   To the Keeper of His Majesty's Prison
   City of Coventry to wit I send you herewith the Body of John Green of this City

Sappinlace weaver brought before me, and charged upon the Examination of Sarah Chaplin Joseph Waite & others with beating abusing & correcting one Alice Gibbs hiss Apprentice now dead with such Cruelty & Barbarity as to occasion a violent Suspicion that he was thereby the Cause of her Death. These are therefore, in His Majesty's Name, to Will and Require you to receive the said John Green into your Custody, and him safely there keep, until he be discharg'd by due Course of Law. Given under my Hand and Seal, this 13th Day of March in the 19th Year of the Reign of our Sovereign Lord George the 2, by the Grace of God of Great Britain, France, and Ireland, King, Defender of the Faith, and in the Year of Our Lord 1745/6.
James Towers

2. *Expenses of disinterring the body, summoning a jury and arranging the inquest.*
   1745/6 March 13, 15 & 17th
   Coventry D^r On acct of John Green's murdering his apprentice Alice Gibbs

	s	d
A Mittimus Paid Mr Towers for John Green on Suspicion	1s	0
Pd the Sexton of Trin: Pish for taking up the Corps of Alice Gibbs, & burying it again, & his attending ye Jury, & cleaning the Church	5	0
Pd Mr Wall the High Constable for Sumoning the Jury & bringing in at Severall times above a dozen Witnesses	5	0
Pd the Jury for their Trouble & attendances 2 days	6	0
For a Mittimus upon the Verdict ag^t J Green for Murder	1	0
For my Trouble & attendance 2 days 5 or 6 hours each day & taking many Sheets of examinations & binding the Witnesses to the Assizes Also for making fair Copies of the Examinations, Sent to the Judge of Assize to Leicester Drawing up the Recognizances & Attending the Clerk of Assize & Indictm^{ts}, Mr Serj^t Willes of the Court the	1 1	0
Pd the C^h of Indictmen^{ts} for the Inquisition & Indictm^{ts}	9	0

3. *Bill for disinterring and reburying Alice Gibbs*
   March 17th 1745/6

	s	d
for Digging up the Girl	1s	0
for tending on ye Jury	1s	0
for ye use of ye Beer and putting her in again	1s	0
for Cleaning ye Church	2s	0
£0	5	0

4. *Surgeon's post mortem report*
   City of Coventry William Steel[1] of this City Surgeon upon his Oath saith he hath carefully viewed & examined the dead body of one Alice Gibbs Saith there appears upon her right Thigh a wound about an Inch long which seems to have proceeded from a kick or Stroke lately given and that the skin is also off upon the Rump bone & the blood settled round it which seems to have been done a considerable time neither of which wounds as he apprehends could be the Cause of her death; further saith that the little Toe of her right foot is entirely rotted off & that the little Toe of her left foot is mortified which he apprehends to be owing to extreme Cold, also saith that the body of the deceased is so extremely emaciated that nothing remains but Skin & bone. Wm Steel
   Sworn 15 March 1745/6

5. *Witnesses' statements*

There were eleven witnesses, all from Coventry, three men and eight women, of whom five spoke on John Green's behalf. The prosecution witnesses all made virtually the same claims, with some variations on the forms of physical abuse, while those for the defence depicted Alice Gibbs as troublesome but adequately fed, clothed and housed. The first statement was sworn on 13 March 1746:

> Sarah Chaplin, Singlewoman Daughter of Geo Chaplin in New Street Silkweaver upon her Examination on Oath Saith that one Alice Gibbs an apprentice to John Green Sappinlaceweaver died last Saturday Evening about Eight of the Clock and this Examt Saith she hath great reason to believe the said Alice Gibbs's death was owing to the severe treatment & cruel usage she received from the said John Green for the said Alice Gibs was a fresh healthful girl about Eleven years old when she first came apprentice to her said Master about last Whitsuntide, but that she has looked miserably for a considerable time past and particularly this Examinant Saith she hath of late seen the sd John Green Strike & pinch & kick his s[d] apprentice with great violence, also Saith that within about a month last past She saw the said John Green take hold of the back part of the sd Alice Gibbs's head & obliged he to open her mouth and then put into her mouth some of her own Dung & obliged her to swallow it Also Saith the said Alice was obliged to lie in a damp place (where pigs had been kept, upon wet Straw & allowed her no other covering but her own Cloathes, in which place the said Alice lay all winter & till a day or two before her death as this Examinant verily believes The Mark X of Sarah Chaplin.

> Coventry City Archives, BA/E/D/2/2, 15, 16, 7, 4.

THE CAUSES OF WIDOWHOOD, *c.* 1840

These statistics on the causes of premature death among working men are from the parish of Alston and Garrigill, Cumberland, where lead-mining was the predominant occupation. The average age at death of these men was forty-five, although twenty-nine were younger. Several left families of seven or eight children orphaned. Of the eighty-nine men who died, sixty-eight (76 per cent) were miners and of these twenty-three died from asthma and a further twelve from consumption related to their employment; twelve also died in mine accidents. Surprisingly, there was one man aged eighty-three and five in their seventies. The figures on the following two pages were collected by Dr James Mitchell and published as an Appendix to the *First Report of Children's Employment Commission*, Parliamentary Papers, 1842, XVII.

Initials of Widows	Number of Children dependent at the time of Husband's Death	Occupation of deceased Husband	Age at Death	Years' loss by premature Death	Alleged Cause of Death
R. W.	—	Miner	83	—	Decay of nature.
M. S.	—	Tailor	78	—	Natural decay.
M. B.	—	Miner	73	—	Not stated.
M. R.	—	Miner	72	—	Decay of nature.
S. M.	—	Miner	72	—	Decay of nature.
M. T.	—	Mason	72	—	Asthma produced from age.
A. V.	—	Miner	67	—	Asthma produced from working in mines.
M. L.	—	Miner	64	—	Influenza.
A. M.	—	Miner	63	—	Asthma produced from working in the lead-mines.
M. S.	—	Miner	63	—	Natural decline.
J. P.	—	Labourer	62	—	Consumption.
H. T.	2	Mason	62	—	Asthma.
S. H.	2	Miner	60	—	Rupture of blood-vessel.
J. R.	—	Miner	60	—	Asthma produced from working in the mines.
H. L.	—	Miner	60	—	Asthma.
J. P.	—	Miner	60	—	Consumption.
M. T.	2	Miner	60	—	Bursting blood-vessel.
A. C.	—	Joiner	60	—	Jaundice.
E. K.	—	Miner	60	—	Asthma produced from working in the mines.
E. H.	—	Miner	60	—	Cholera.
D. J.	—	Glazier	59	1	Affection of the liver.
N. D.	4	Butcher	59	1	Apoplexy.
M. T.	—	Miner	59	1	Inflammation of the lungs.
H. A.	—	Miner	59	1	Asthma produced from working in the lead-mines, which terminated in consumption.
J. B.	—	Miner	59	1	Asthma ditto.
E. T.	—	Labourer	58	2	Accident by a coal-waggon.
M. P.	—	Miner	58	2	Asthma produced from working in the lead-mines, which terminated in consumption.
H. T.	—	Miner	57	3	Consumption accelerated by working in the lead-mines.
M. P.	1	Turner	57	3	Consumption.
H. S.	3	Miner	57	3	Influenza, terminating in dropsy.
M. J.	3	Blacksmith	55	5	Asthma.
S. M.	—	Miner	55	5	Inflammation of lungs from cold.
R. W.	—	Miner	55	5	Asthma produced from working in lead-mines.
M. R.	—	Miner	55	5	Asthma from working in the mines.
J. W.	2	Miner	54	6	Pleurisy.
A. F.	—	Miner	54	6	Asthma and rupture of blood-vessel.
J. L.	2	Miner	53	7	Chronic disease of rheumatism.
N. H.	2	Miner	53	7	Asthma produced from working in the lead-mines.
A. S.	—	Miner	52	8	Asthma and bursting blood-vessel.
M. W.	6	Miner	52	8	Asthma produced from working in the mines.
E. W.	5	Miner	52	8	Asthma produced from working in the mines, which terminated in consumption.
J. S.	6	Miner	51	9	Paralysis.
H. P.	9	Quarry-man	49	11	Asthma by working in the lead-mines.
H. P.	5	Miner	48	12	Typhus fever.
E. H.	6	Miner	48	12	Killed in lead-mines.
M. A.	7	Miner	48	12	Consumption by bad air in the pit.
J. C.	8	Miner	47	13	Asthma produced by working in the lead-mines.

Initials of Widows	Number of Children dependent at the time of Husband's Death	Occupation of deceased Husband	Age at Death	Years' loss by premature Death	Alleged Cause of Death
S. E.	6	Miner	47	13	Consumption produced from a continuance of influenza.
M. T.	8	Miner	47	13	Consumption and asthma.
E. B.	3	Miner	47	13	Affection of the head, caused from an accident received in the mine.
D. R.	—	Miner	46	14	Asthma produced from working in the lead-mines.
E. B.	5	Miner	46	14	Rheumatic fever, which produced inflammation of the brain.
M. S.	5	Miner	46	14	Killed in lead-mine.
M. R.	1	Joiner	46	14	Dropsy.
M. F.	7	Coal Miner	46	14	Explosion of fire-damp in a coal-mine.
L. T.	3	Miner	45	15	Asthma, which terminated with dropsy.
H. P.	3	Miner	45	15	Scarlet fever.
H. Y.	5	Miner	45	15	Consumption, accelerated by working in the lead-mines.
M. S.	2	Miner	45	15	Inflammation of bowels.
M. S.	5	Joiner	45	15	Consumption.
A. S.	6	Miner	44	16	Dropsy.
A. B.	6	Miner	44	16	Asthma from working in lead-mines.
F. C.	5	Miner	43	17	Asthma produced from working in the lead-mines.
M. D.	4	Miner	43	17	Consumption produced from asthma, caused by working in the mines.
H. M.	7	Miner	43	17	Asthma, which terminated in consumption.
A. P.	7	Superintendent	43	17	A fall from the 'horse' in the engine shaft.
P. W.	4	Miner	43	17	Pleurisy.
E. W.	8	Miner	42	18	Consumption and asthma produced from working in the lead-mines.
J. H.	4	Miner	42	18	Consumption.
J. J.	5	Miner	42	18	Pleurisy.
A. J.	2	Miller	42	18	Found drowned.
M. R.	—	Shoemaker	40	20	Injury from fall of a cart.
E. R.	7	Joiner	38	22	Affection of the liver.
J. B.	5	Miner	38	22	Consumption.
A. P.	7	Miner	37	21	Asthma.
E. W.	3	Miner	36	24	Accident in mine, which terminated in consumption.
E. H.	3	Miner	35	25	Killed in coal-pit.
M. L.	2	Miner	35	25	Water of the head.
A. S.	4	Miner	35	25	Income on leg.
S. H.	7	Miner	34	26	Accident in coal-mine.
J. H.	4	Cordwainer	30	30	Typhus Fever.
S. H.	3	Cartman	30	30	Accidental.
E. A.	2	Miner	30	30	Consumption.
M. J.	3	Teacher	29	31	Consumption.
M. R.	3	Miner	29	31	Affection of urinary organs.
A. W.	2	Miner	28	32	Cholera.
M. W.	3	Miner	27	33	Inflammation of bowels.
A. H.	1	Pitman	25	35	Accident at colliery.
J. M.	2	Miner	21	39	Small-pox.
89	242	—	4418	—	
		Average age at death of each below 60 years of age.	45		Total No. of orphans by deaths caused below 60 years of age. 236

A CORONER'S INQUESTS, 1875

Sources for coroner's inquests are relatively rare, but for the South Warwickshire district inquest records have survived from 1865. The coroner submitted his accounts to the county council every quarter and in 1875 he travelled 522 miles to conduct inquests, his longest a journey of 50 miles, usually spending three or four hours on each occasion. During 1875 he investigated transport accidents, seven drownings, three deaths from excessive drinking, an infanticide, a premature birth, a suicide and a murder – a total of thirty-three deaths. Three were declared to be from natural causes. The majority of inquests were held at local inns, but occasionally at an institution such as a hospital or workhouse. The coroner in these cases was Thomas Barnes Couchman, JP (1858–1932), a solicitor, who lived at Henley-in-Arden.

Date	Name	Occupation	Age	Inquest Held	Verdict of Inquest	miles	hrs	£	s	d
2 Jan	Eliza Collins	wife of Stratford pedlar	67	Hampton Lucy	'cold & exposure'	20	5	2	6	6
7 Jan	James E. Hawkes	carpenter of Henley	26	Ullenhall Henley	fall from church tower	–	1	3	13	6
18 Feb	Mary Jobson	inmate of workhouse	50	Alcester workhouse	burning & suffocation	16	4	2	8	6
1 Mar	Elizabeth Russell	wife of labourer	28	Kingswood Boot Inn, Lapworth	died in childbirth	10	4	3	12	6
7 Mar	Henry Roberts	labourer of Redditch	56	Warwick Arms, Ipsley	found dead/ natural causes	16	4	3	16	6
8 Mar	John Aubrey	labourer of Old Stratford	63	Stratford police station	sudden death/ natural causes	16	4	2	13	0
8 Mar	female infant	Tiddington	14 days	Crown Inn, Tiddington	found dead/ suffocated in bed	20	4	2	13	6
31 Mar	John Ball	farmer of Nuthurst	58	at Mr Ball's house	'apoplexy from excessive drinking'	6	2	3	6	6
31 Mar	George Waters	labourer of Aston Cantlow	29	Beaudesert Bird in Hand	run over by waggon	4	2	2	18	6
5 Apr	Charles Cale	licensee of Forshaw Heath	41	Horse and Jockey	apoplexy from excessive drinking	20	5	3	18	0
27 May	John Batchelor	farm labourer of Loxley	28	Stratford Infirmary	accident/run over by waggon	16	4	3	15	6

Warwickshire County Record Office, CR 1399/Box 1, ff. 89–99.

NOTE

1. Little is known about William Steel, but he was paid for his professional services to the sick poor in the 1750s by the Overseers of Baginton, a neighbouring parish.

Page from a coroner's casebook, 1875.

No.	Date of Information	Name (Surname) of Deceased	Trade or profession	Age	Date & place of death	Cause of death	Date of Inquest, action and active fees	Verdict	Miles employed	Hours employed	Expenses £ s. d.
3	17 August 1875	Robert Saunder of Somerset	—	58 Years	16 August 1875 Somerset	Seat Anatomy	18 Aug 1875 at Maidstone Fieldgate at W Cooper	Bought Journey apoplexy Anxiety occasion drowning	34	9	1 6 8
4	1st Sept 1875	Harriet Collins of Shutford on Avon	Domestic Servant	15 Years	15 Sept 1875 Shutford on Avon	Found drowned in River at Shutford on Avon at 10 oclock a.m.	17 Sept 1875 Shutford on Avon	Found Drowned	16	12 Hours	4 18 6
5	16 Sept 1875	Ann Tennant of Long Compton	Wife of John Tennant Labourer	80 Years	16 Sept 1875 at Long Compton	Stabbed by James Hayward with a hay fork	17 Sept 1875 Railway Long Compton at W Cooper	Wilful Murder	50		3 4 6
6	4 October 1875	Maria Court of Alcester	Wife of Thos Court Innkeeper	51 Years	3 October 1875 at Alcester	Fell down stairs	5 Oct 1875 at Lamb Inn Alcester at W Carlson	Anxiety of Railway	16	4	2 17 9
7	5th Oct 1875	Ann Clarke of Crafton	Wife of William Clarke Labourer	28 Years	5 October 1875	Died suddenly after eating Mushrooms	6 Oct 1875 at Warwickshire Army Anglers at work	Natural Causes	18	5 Hours	3 18 .

14 October 1875 Quarterly Return sent with Vouchers to Finance Committee, Warwick — Poisoning of Alexander Fry & Jessie Hayward by Ann Tennant etc.

| | | | | | | | | | Total | 166 | 36 £25 6 11 |

V
DISEASES

❖   ❖   ❖

Of all the great epidemics of the eighteenth and nineteenth centuries, only smallpox was effectively reduced as a result of medical intervention, first by inoculation and later by Edward Jenner's method of vaccination. The other great scourges, typhus, typhoid and cholera, were really affected only by better living conditions and public health measures. Many childhood diseases continued to take their dreadful toll into the twentieth century. The death rates from sexually transmitted diseases are impossible to estimate; while clearly different from other fatal infections, they were seen as self-inflicted, for example, by the friendly societies.

However, apart from infections, it is clear that many people were ill as a result of their work, either through the dangerous raw materials they used, the physical environment or after industrial accidents. Many parliamentary reports from the nineteenth century concentrated on the working conditions in different occupations, often in considerable detail.

OCCUPATIONAL HEALTH RISKS

The first medical publication to deal with the health risks associated with an occupation was Bernard Ramazzini's *A Treatise on the Diseases of Tradesmen* (1706), which was translated from Latin into English in 1726 by Robert James MD (1705–76) of Lichfield. It went into several editions and sold very widely indeed. Ramazzini (1633–1714) covered forty-three dangerous occupations from the traditional crafts (carpenter, saddler, blacksmith) to the professions (apothecary, surgeon). Other early writers on occupational health were Thomas Tomlinson (1734–*c*. 1783) and William Richardson (1766–91), both eighteenth-century Birmingham surgeons. However, their writings were superseded by the work of a Leeds surgeon, Charles Turner Thackrah (1795–1833), whose *The Effects of the Principal Arts, Trades and Professions . . . on Health and Longevity* (1831) covered about 177 trades. All writers advocated some form of protective clothing and washing before eating. However, neither safety measure was widely followed until well into the nineteenth century. Most workers, once apprenticed, remained at the same job for life, with a normal working day of fourteen hours for six days a week.

In 1747 R. Campbell wrote to advise intending apprentices and their parents about the choice of over 300 suitable careers in London, indicating what the premium, status, profits and career prospects would be; he also pointed out occupations with health risks, including those where heavy drinking was normal and where dangerous substances, such as lead, were a hazard.

HEALTH RISKS TO THE LONDON TRADESMAN, 1747

The Plumber

He requires a tolerable Genius, but no very nice Hand; but a moderate Share of Strength, yet a strong and healthy Constitution, to withstand the Effects of the Lead, which is apt to unbend his Nerves and render him paralytic. The Trade of the Plumber is abundantly profitable.

The Engraver

They must have a delicate and steady Hand, and a clear strong Sight, for their Work is very trying to the Eyes. There is little Strength required for this Branch of

Business; but, like all other sedentry Occupations, it requires a sound Constitution. All Businesses, however, trifling, that require Application, poring and sitting, are bad for Persons inclined to Consumptions: Employments that admit of moderate, but not severe Exercise, are fitter for Persons of that Habit of Body.

The Gilder

Gilding is a very profitable Business, but dangerous to the Constitution; few of them live long, the Fumes of the Quicksilver affect their Nerves, and render their Lives a Burthen to them. The Trade is but in few Hands; some of them Women. A quick Hand may earn from Fifteen Shillings to a Guinea a Week.

The Tailor

It is a mistaken Notion, that a Boy of a sickly weak Constitution is fittest for a Taylor; it is true it does not require a robust Body, or much muscular Strength; but the Custom of sitting cross-legged, always in one Posture, bending their Body, makes them liable to Coughs and Consumptions, more than any other Trade I know. You rarely see a Taylor live to a great Age; therefore I think a sickly tender Constitution, or a Habit the least inclinable to a Consumption, is very unfit for a Taylor; he ought to have a strong sharp Sight, which is much tryed by working at Candle-light.

R. Campbell, *The London Tradesman* (1747), pp. 190, 114, 145, 193.

A SMALLPOX AND POPULATION SURVEY OF STRATFORD-UPON-AVON, 1765

Although inoculation was commonplace by the 1760s, outbreaks of smallpox occurred regularly, a great burden to the parish overseers of the poor, particularly if they had to care for paupers whose settlement rights were elsewhere. Presumably for this reason a household survey was conducted in Stratford-upon-Avon on 19 April 1765 by George Beauchamp, a town ironmonger, to ascertain how many people lived in each house, their place of settlement and how many had had smallpox. He recorded the results in tabular form. Of the total population of 2,287, 44.9 per cent (1,027) had not had smallpox. At least 72 families came from 35 other communities in Warwickshire and a further 49 from 37 places beyond the county. There were 461 recent immigrants in the town. The total number of households was 512 and there were 21 inhabitants in the almshouses, 30 in the workhouse (of whom 9 had never had smallpox) and 39 residents in the White Lion inn. Domestic households ranged downwards from 11, with 51 in single occupancy. The original survey of eighteen pages has now been lost, but a local antiquarian, R.B. Wheler, made a copy of it in about 1800.

High Street Ward

No. 1	2	3	4	5	6	7	8	9
Mr Hucknalls Corner House void SW								
victualler Mr George Garwood	5	3	Borough of Stratford	3	–	–	–	–
bookseller Mr Salisbury Goode	7	5	Do	5				
mercer Mr Samuel Jarvis	7	–	Do	–				
widow of the Rev Gabriel Barodale								
curate & schoolmr Mrs Barodale	4	–	Do	–				
Apothecary & Surgeon Mr John								
Meacham	7	1	Do Mayor of the Jubilee in 1769	1				
Mrs Sarah Higgins	2	2	Do	2				
Mrs Baylis	7	5	Do	5				
Richard Hiron	5	5	Butlers Marston, Warws	–	–	–	5	5
Mercer Mr William Burbage	8	2	Borough of Stratford	2				
Sadlers Ironmonger Mr William Eaves	7	1	Do	1				
Butcher Mr Samuel Heritage	4	1	Do	1				
Sadler Mr John Tissell	8	4	Do	4				
Milliners Misses Mary & . . Jarrett	5	–	Do	–				
Bookseller Mr James Keating	4	–	Do	–				
Mercer Mr Nathaniel Cookes NE	4	1	Do	1				
Apothecary & Surgeon Mr Thomas Nott	4	–	Do	–				
Currier Mr Francis Parsons	9	7	Do	7				
Brazier Mr Levi Stickley	10	4	Do	4				
Innkeeper Mr William Judd	10	8	Do	8				
Barber John Satchwell	7	5	Do	5				
Brazier &c Mr . . . . . . Persehouse	4	–	Do	–				
Glover Mr . . . . . . Webb	5	2	Banbury, Oxfordshire	–	–	–	5	2
Shoemaker Mr . . . Edwards	6	1	Borough of Stratford	1				
Maltster Mr Charles Weston	1	–	Weston upon Avon, Glos	–				
Plumber & Glazier Mr John Izod	9	3	Borough of Stratford	3				
Butcher Mr Martin Bagg	6	2	Wellesbourne Mountford	–	–	–	6	2
Apothecry & Surgeon Mr Richard Walls	3	–	Borough of Stratford	–				
Barber Mr William Lees	10	2	Do	2				
Inholder Mr William Gurney	2	–	Do	–				
Chandler & Grocer Mrs Widow								
Jeacocks	4	1	Do	1	–			
	174	65		56	–	–	16	9

Columns
1. Names of the householders.
2. Number of persons in each house.
3. Number that have not had smallpox.
4. Where householder has legal settlement.
5. Number that have had smallpox.
6. Old Stratford parishioners in Stratford.
7. Number of those that have not had smallpox.
8. Number of residents in Stratford belonging to any other place except Old Stratford.
9. Number of them as are to have smallpox.
When no place of settlement stated (col. 4) it is unknown or dubious.

Shakespeare Birthplace Trust Records Office, ER1/8.

THE SUTTONIAN METHOD OF INOCULATION AGAINST SMALLPOX, 1767

Since the late sixth century smallpox had been the most feared disease in Western Europe and even the greatest were not immune. In London some 2,000 a year died from the infection in the seventeenth century. Even if not fatal, smallpox caused facial scarring – hence the expression 'pockmarked' – and could also result in blindness and male infertility. When Lady Mary Wortley Montagu returned to England in 1718 from Constantinople, she brought with her an account of how inoculation was carried out in Turkey and the technique became widely used in Britain. It involved giving a healthy patient a mild attack of smallpox, using the 'matter' or pus from a sufferer who had a light form of the disease.

In its early decades inoculation was an expensive process taking a considerable time, involving isolation and a controlled diet, exactly as described by Radcliffe below. However, this strict regime was later considered unnecessary for inoculation, which increasingly became available to the poor, either from their parish overseers or through local charities. Inoculation was superseded by Edward Jenner's discovery of vaccination, a much safer technique that did not use live smallpox matter; inoculation became illegal in 1840.

Richard Radcliffe (1727–93) attended Queen's College, Oxford, before holding the livings of Colsterworth, Lincolnshire, and Holwell, Devon; in 1776 he became Bursar of Queen's College. John James (1729–85) was at Queen's College with Radcliffe and was head of St Bees School, Cumberland, for seventeen years; he then held a country living until his death.

Richard Radcliffe to John James, senior, of Queen's College, Oxford

26 August 1767

Dear James,

Your letter arrived at the proper time, and gave me a pleasure greater than usual. I was sorry however to hear, that mine had had such an effect upon my sister. I thought it might possibly occasion a surprise, but I never dreamt of its being attended with serious consequences. Inoculation has been practised in this country so much and with so great success, that it seems to have lost all its terrors. I am willing to flatter myself, that I was not presumptuous or confident upon the occasion; though certain it is, that I was never more happy and chearful in any part of my life. On Sunday, July 12, I received my instructions from Mr. Sutton;[1] by which I was ordered to abstain from butter, cheese, spices, animal food of every kind, and from all vinous, spiritous, and malt liquors. Most luckily he does not forbid the use of tobacco, so that I indulged myself freely in my old custom, and drank thy health in water, whey, milk well-skimmed, or lemonade. On the same Sunday evening at bed time, I took a paper of his powders, supposed to be a preparation for the mercury, and in quantity not exceeding a good large pinch of snuff. The next morning I had the pleasure of swallowing about an ounce of Glaubar salts, and I dare say you will vastly rejoice to hear that they operated very briskly and plentifully. These powders and salts were repeated twice afterwards, resting two or three days between each dose. Being thus reduced and prepared I set out with six of my neighbours for Newark, on Tuesday July the 21st. The doctor attended us instantly, and performed the operation upon us, which was done by dipping the point of his lancet in a pustule of one of his patients, and lightly piercing the outer skin in two different places on each arm, a little above the elbow. No blood was drawn, nor was the puncture hardly perceptible, so that there was no occasion for any plaister or bandage. On Wednesday we had the curiosity to examine our arms, and could perceive little red spots at the places of incision, exactly resembling a flea-bite. These spots continued to inflame every day and ripened at last into fine pustules, and then died away with the rest. On Thursday the doctor came again, and after due inspection, pronounced that we had all received the infection. This piece of intelligence pleased me most wonderfully, as it had been a matter of dispute among my friends, whether or no I had had the distemper. On Friday I was ordered to eat a little meat, and on Saturday to drink a little ale; an indulgence not allowed to any one else in the company. On Sunday I had, or fancied I had, a little touch of the head-ach; which, fortunately, was all the illness that fell to my share. On Monday evening or Tuesday morning an eruption appeared on that part of my body, which gentlemen of the birch are often indulged with a sight of; and this, with the pustules at the places of incision, was all I had to shew for my money. I am however assured by Mr. Sutton, and two other sensible and experienced gentlemen, that I have had the distemper very effectually, and that I never had it before. From that time I was allowed to eat, drink, and live as I pleased; and after paying the doctor five guineas, and expending about four pounds upon other occasions, I returned to Colsterworth the Tuesday following, with great satisfaction of mind, and (I trust) with a proper gratitude to the Great Disposer of all things.

The Letters of Richard Radcliffe and John James of Queen's College, Oxford, 1755–83,
ed. Margaret Evans (Oxford Historical Society, IX, 1888), pp. 25–6.

AN AGREEMENT TO INOCULATE THE PARISH POOR IN SHIPSTON-ON-STOUR, 1772

The parish of Shipston-on-Stour, formerly in Worcestershire, now in Warwickshire, experienced various smallpox epidemics in the early part of the eighteenth century. That of 1744 had an 11.8 per cent death rate and was sufficiently serious for Richard Mead MD to include an account of it in his *Discourse on the plague*. Shipston was a substantial market town in the area, with some 200 households, and was served by two families of surgeon-apothecaries, the Misters and the Horniblows. The 157 inhabitants to be inoculated constituted 17.4 per cent of the population. At 6s each the total cost would be £47 2s. William Horniblow, a surgeon-apothecary in the town, who worked regularly for the overseers of the poor, carrried out the mass inoculation.

April 26th 1772 at a Vestry then held twas agreed To Inoculate all the poor Inhabitants [being Parishioners] that are willing to be done by a subscription for that purpose to be Collected. But if the said Subscription should not be sufficient for that Purpose the overseers shall pay the defficiancy out of the poors Levys and the poor to be Inoculated according to this Agreement shall be Given the Apothecarys In a List for that Purpose to the Number of 157 Persons and that the said Apothecarys do [?perform] for Six Shillings p^r Head.

May 3rd 1772 At a Vestry then Held twas agreed to allow the overseers of the poor their Noat Disbursements to this Day being £37 12s 6d. At the same [time] agreed to allow the overseers of the poor a Levy of twelve Pence in the Pound. At the same time it was agreed that it is the sense of the Vestry that no Person shall be admitted into this Town by way of Inoculation for the small Pox after Thursday next.

Warwickshire County Record Office, DR 446/50.

SEXUALLY TRANSMITTED DISEASES

Two venereal diseases were common in Western Europe from at least the fifteenth century – gonorrhoea and syphilis. Gonorrhoea was non-fatal, but was then considered to be an early stage of syphilis and the diseases were not differentiated until 1879. Syphilis, 'the great Pox' or 'the clap', was undoubtedly the scourge of fashionable, urban eighteenth-century England, recorded in poems, plays and art. Cures for sexually transmitted diseases were the commonest advertisements in the Georgian press; many were expensive – for example, Lisbon Diet Drink cost 10s 6d a bottle. The standard treatment was mercury, itself a dangerous substance, because it reduced the obvious external symptoms of syphilis, which was, until the coming of antibiotics, incurable and fatal. Charitable Lock Hospitals for sufferers were opened from 1747, as patients were usually excluded from county infirmaries. The Contagious Diseases Act of 1864 obliged prostitutes to be medically examined and treated, but the problem was not satisfactorily tackled until the twentieth century following the discovery of Salvarsan, penicillin and the coming of local VD clinics.

JAMES BOSWELL IN LONDON, 1763

Boswell was aged twenty-three when he arrived in London in 1763 from Edinburgh; a solicitor by training, he hoped to enter the army, and was obliged to live on a modest allowance from his father, also a lawyer. He is now best known as Samuel Johnson's biographer, but he also kept substantial personal diaries all his life. He regularly patronised prostitutes and in January 1763 he contracted the third of his eighteen venereal infections; on this occasion he was attended by Andrew Douglas MD. Occasionally Boswell used a condom, his 'armour', to reduce the risk of infection. Condoms, usually expensive French imports, were sold in London by a Mrs Philips. Standard treatment for sexual infections was isolation while salivation took place and Boswell found a solitary existence unbearable; during it he regularly wrote his diary, on the occasion below noting that 'the evening was passed most cheerfully. When I got home, though, then came the sorrow. Too, too plain was Signor Gonorrhoea.'

Thursday, 20 January

I rose very disconsolate, having rested very ill by the poisonous infection raging in my veins and anxiety and vexation boiling in my breast. . . . I have just got a gleet [discharge] by irritating the parts too much with excessive venery. And yet these damned twinges, that scalding heat, and that deep-tinged loathsome matter are the strongest proofs of an infection. . . . I thought of applying to a quack who would cure me quickly and cheaply. But then the horrors of being imperfectly cured and having the distemper thrown into my blood terrified me exceedingly. I therefore pursued my resolution of last night to go to my friend Douglas,[2] whom I knew to be skillfull and careful; and although I knew it should cost me more, yet to get sound health was a matter of great importance, and I might save on other articles.

Sunday, 30 January

I regretted much my being kept from divine service. I was not so well. I had more inflammation, so I caused Douglas to blood me, which gave me relief. I now began to take a little better diet. I had a pound of veal made into a bowl of weak broth. This gave me better spirits, and cherished my nerves.

Friday, 4 February

I had been very bad all night, I lay in direful apprehension that my testicle, which formerly was ill, was again swelled. I dreamt that Douglas stood by me and said, "This is a damned difficult case". I got up today still in terror. Indeed, there was a little return of inflammation. I had catched some cold. However, before night I was pretty easy again.

Boswell's London Journal, 1762–1763, ed. Frederick A. Pottle (1991),
pp. 155–6, 173, 178.

WILLIAM HICKEY'S *MEMOIRS*

The eighth child of an Irish lawyer, William Hickey was born in Westminster in 1749; as a legal apprentice he was an unmanageable youth and after he embezzled from his employers, his father sent him abroad in the service of the East India Company. But he had not reformed and was subsequently sent to practise law in the West Indies. Hickey has been described as 'an unscrupulous amorist' and he certainly consorted with prostitutes regularly, drank excessively and gambled. His manuscript *Memoirs* cover the years up to 1810 and consist of 742 pages, including his accounts of his 'venereal taints' and his 'endless course of folly'. He had a further infection when in Paris some years later and treated this outbreak himself with two quarts of Velno's Vegetable Syrup. However, Hickey lived to be eighty-one.

During the last two years, I had never been entirely free from venereal taints, sometimes extremely ill and constantly using that powerful medicine mercury; nor did I ever give myself fair play – in the worst stages of the disorder, if I could move at all, frequenting my noctural haunts, sitting up whole nights committing every degree of folly and excess. Mr Hayes,[3] the surgeon who attended me, frequently remonstrated, observing that death and destruction must inevitably be the consequence of the life I led, and never shall I forget a speech he once made me. I had, as was often the case, by inattention, late hour and intoxication, whilst using mercury, thrown myself into a salivation; my head suddenly swelled to an enormous size; my tongue and mouth became so inflamed I could take no other nourishment than liquids; in which forlorn state he found me; when, instead of the pity and condolence I expected, he, in a great rage, swore he had a strong inclination to leave me to die as I richly deserved. His passion having vented itself, he with more temper said, "Indeed, indeed, William you are playing the devil with a very fine constitution, for which folly, should you ever reach the age of forty, which I think impossible, your unfortunate body and bones will pay most severely". He proved a false prophet as to the length of my life, but I have often, when agonized with spasm and pain, thought of his prediction.

Memoirs of William Hickey, ed. Peter Quennell (1984), p. 160.
The original manuscripts are in private hands.

CHARLES TURNER THACKRAH OF LEEDS

Thackrah, the only child of a chemist, was born in Leeds on 22 May 1795. He was apprenticed in 1811 for five years to a local surgeon-apothecary, Obadiah Brooke, whose partner he became in 1820. In 1815 he spent a year as a pupil at Guy's Hospital, London, in company with the poet John Keats. There he was taught by Astley Cooper, who remained a dominant influence on his career. Thackrah returned to Leeds, where he served as town surgeon. As well as indenturing six apprentices, he set up a private anatomy school in the city in 1826, with its own medical museum. The Leeds Medical School was founded in 1831, following those already established at Bristol (1818), Manchester (1824), Birmingham and Sheffield (1828). Thackrah's The Effects of the Principal Arts, Trades and Professions . . . on Health and Longevity appeared in an expanded second edition in 1831. It was noted in the local press and favourably reviewed in medical journals. Although other treatises had been written at this period about single occupational diseases (John Darwall MD on grinders' asthma, Charles Hastings MD on bronchitis in the yellow leather and china workers of Worcester), Thackrah's was innovative as a wide-ranging survey. He discussed some 177 occupations, grouped by risk-factors (odours, dust, temperatures, harmful agents), but he also considered the mental stress of professional men. He was clearly aware of wider dangers, such as poor housing, town pollution and even the dangers to females of wearing tight stays. Thackrah died, aged only thirty-eight, from pulmonary tuberculosis on 23 May 1833.

Dangerous occupations described in The Effects of Arts, Trades and Professions . . .

BRICKLAYERS, and particularly their Labourers, are exposed to lime-dust. This frequently excites ophthalmia, and cutaneous eruptions, but not internal disease.*
The remark applies also to LIME-WORKERS AND LEADERS OF LIME.

PLASTERERS AND WHITE-WASHERS, who are also of course exposed to lime-dust, suffer from it no sensible injury. They are however more pallid and less robust, than the men last noticed. They complain of the ammoniacal gas evolved from the glue; but I doubt its injurious effects. STENCILLERS do not appear to suffer from the currents of cold air to which they are exposed by their employ.

WOOLSORTERS are occasionally annoyed with dust from the lime, which in some kinds of wool is used for separating the fleece from the skin. No sensible effect is produced on health.

TURNERS, when employed on the bone, receive into the throat and air passages, considerable portion of dust. This, however, is said to be rather grateful than noxious.

THE EFFECTS

OF

ARTS, TRADES, AND PROFESSIONS,

AND OF CIVIC STATES

AND

HABITS OF LIVING,

ON HEALTH AND LONGEVITY:

WITH

SUGGESTIONS

FOR THE

REMOVAL OF MANY OF THE AGENTS WHICH PRODUCE DISEASE, AND SHORTEN THE DURATION OF LIFE.

By C. TURNER THACKRAH, Esq.

SECOND EDITION, GREATLY ENLARGED.

LONDON:
LONGMAN, REES, ORME, BROWN, GREEN, & LONGMAN;
SIMPKIN & MARSHALL.
LEEDS: BAINES AND NEWSOME.

1832.

Title page from Charles Turner Thackrah's work on occupational health, 1832.

The MAKERS OF BONE BUTTONS are subjected to some dust, but this is not sufficient to produce sensible disorder. The MAKERS OF PEARL BUTTONS appear to suffer more. The pearl-dust produces often bronchial irritation, and this excites pulmonary consumption in individuals predisposed to the disease. Both classes of button makers are, in Birmingham at least, generally intemperate, devoting two days a week to the impairment of their health.

BLEACHERS are exposed to chlorine both in inhalation, and by often standing for the whole day in water strongly impregnated with this gas. They work in open sheds, and are occasionally employed in the field, spreading out the yarn. They are healthy and strong. None are affected with rheumatism. They live to a good age.

* We hear an adage in the mouth of the workmen, that "Bricklayers and Plasterers' Labourers, like asses, never die" (Ramazzini).

Review of The Effects . . . in The Edinburgh Medical and Surgical Journal, 1831

There is, we will venture to say, no country in the world where the effects of trades on the health, and longevity of the workmen who follow them, are so excessively pernicious as in Great Britain. For there is none where the proportion of the people employed in hurtful trades is so great, none where the workmen are congregated so much in towns, and large manufactures, . . . where the working hours occupy so large a part of the day. It is then melancholy to reflect how little has been done in this country by medical men or philanthropists out of the profession, towards ascertaining the nature and extent of these effects, as well as the means of correcting them, and how little encouragement has been held out by our government for such investigations. English medical literature has been till now destitute of a single general treatise on the disease of trades and professions . . . on one occasion only has this government interested itself in the fate of the sickly and short-lived citizen. No one will feel surprised at the apathy of a government, which has long been notorious for indifference to scientific inquiries.

A SURGEON'S REPORT ON A MILLINERY APPRENTICE AT MOORFIELD'S HOSPITAL, 1843

A delicate and beautiful young woman, an orphan, applied at the hospital for very defective vision . . . she had been apprenticed to a milliner, and was in the last year of her indentureship. Her work-hours were 18 in the day, occasionally even more; her meals snatched with scarcely an interval of a few minutes from work, and her general health evidently assuming a tendency to consumption. An application was made, by my direction, to the mistress for relaxation: but the reply was, that in this last year of her apprenticeship her labours had become valuable, and that her mistress was entitled to them, as recompense for teaching. Subsequently, a threat of appeal to the Lord Mayor, and a belief that a continuance of the occupation would soon render the apprentice incapable of labour, induced the mistress to cancel the indentures, and the victim was saved. It was not until many months afterwards that her health was re-established.

Evidence from John Dalrymple, assistant surgeon at the Royal London Ophthalmic Hospital, Moorfields, Parliamentary Papers, 1843, XIV.

WORKERS' HEALTH, 1833, 1840

Evidence for the working conditions in many nineteenth-century occupations was presented to a variety of Select Committees, to most of whom medical evidence was submitted. The details about the health and deaths of climbing boys given to a parliamentary Select Committee in 1816 was undoubtedly the most shocking and eventually that particular form of child employment was abolished. However, many occupations brought health risks and in 1833 depositions were made about the workers' health in Kidderminster's carpet trade, the town's main manufacture, by four local Worcestershire medical practitioners. In 1840 the report of Joseph Fletcher, an Assistant Commissioner in the Midlands, addressed the whole problem of weavers' health, their 'feebler constitutions' and the 'injurious trade influences' they experienced, especially in comparison with the local watchmakers'.

The Factory Commission, 1833 – depositions taken before Mr Horner

7. DEPOSITION of THOMAS THURSFIELD, Surgeon, sworn to before Leonard Horner and S. Woolriche, Esquires, 6th May 1833.

You are a general medical practitioner? – Yes.

What is your age? – Twenty-eight.

How long have you been in practice in Kidderminster? – Two years and four months.

I understand you are surgeon to the Borough Dispensary and Lying-in Society of Kidderminster? – I am.

What is your opinion as to the general state of health of the persons employed in the manufactories of the place? – They labour under the usual diseases consequent upon confinement and a comparatively bad air, such as irregular visceral action, producing indigestion, constipation, &c. Weavers are particularly subject to hernia.

Have you observed any marked difference between the health of the children employed in the spinning-mills and those engaged in the carpet manufactory? – I have not.

What is your opinion of the state of the health of the persons employed in the manufactures of the place, as compared with carpenters, smiths, bricklayers, gardeners, and other artizans? – They are less healthy than other artizans, inasmuch as they live in a more confined air, and have usually more debauched habits; but notwithstanding the confined air and their debauched habits their general health is better, in consequence of being able to obtain a regular supply of good food, than the health of persons of the same class of the people less regularly employed.

Are accidents of frequent occurrence at the spinning-mills? – They are rare. During the time I have resided in Kidderminster I only recollect two or three slight ones, and one extensive laceration of the hand occurring on a boy not employed on the premises.

Have you visited the spinning-mills of this neighbourhood? – I have, frequently.

Do you consider the dangerous parts of the machinery sufficiently protected against the occurrence of accidents? – As far as I am able to judge, they are.

10. DEPOSITION of GEORGE WILLIAM JOTHAM, Surgeon, &c., confirmed by Thomas Lukis, another Surgeon, before Leonard Horner and T. Woolriche, Esquires, 7th May 1833.

You are a surgeon and general practitioner in this town, I believe? – Yes.

How long have you been in practice? – Five years.

Is the work of the drawers productive of any peculiar disease or injury to the health of the children? – I have frequently seen distortions of the ankle-joints, apparently produced by standing at their work a number of hours, and also yielding of the knee-joints.

Is it your opinion that the children are frequently worked a number of hours beyond their strength? – Unquestionably. I believe it is the common practice for idle weavers to place their draw-boys in the loom, and to employ younger boys or girls as drawers, to make up for their own laziness or dissipation. The weavers are in general idle the early part of the week, and they afterwards work from eighteen to twenty hours to make up their lost time, during which the draw-boy or draw-girl must attend them. I have known frequent instances of their commencing work at two or three o'clock in the morning.

What is your opinion of the state of health of the persons employed in the carpet manufactory, as compared with that of those engaged in the spinning-mills? – The comparison can hardly be made, as in the spinning-mills they are chiefly girls, and drawers are chiefly boys.

What is your opinion of the state of the health of the persons employed in the manufactories of the place, as compared with that of carpenters, smiths, bricklayers, and other artizans? – Certainly not so good. Diseases are much more easily excited amongst the manufacturers; the weavers are decidedly inferior in strength and fulness of growth to the rural population around Kidderminster.

Are accidents of frequent occurrence in the spinning-mills? – Very rare.

Are the persons employed in the spinning-mills subject to diseases in consequence of the nature of their employment? – Yes; the females are frequently afflicted with dyspepsia, frequently connected with hysteria and spinal irritation, most probably produced by working a number of hours in an erect posture, and in an elevated temperature. I have known frequent instances of themselves and their mothers complaining of their suffering from excessive pains in the back.

What is your opinion of the general state of the dwellings of the working classes in point of healthiness and comfort? – They vary. There are many very bad, but many also that are good.

The preceding deposition of Mr. Jotham was taken in the presence of Thomas Lukis, Esq., surgeon and general practitioner, who states that he has resided twelve years in this town, and concurs in all the answers which Mr. Jotham has given in the course of his examination.

15. DEPOSITION of THOMAS BRADLEY, Esq., Surgeon, and a magistrate for the Borough of Kidderminster, sworn to before S. Woolriche and Leonard Horner, Esquires, 7th May 1833.

You are, I believe, a surgeon and a general practitioner in this place, and also a magistrate? – I am.

How long have you resided here? – All my life: I am thirty-nine years of age.

What is your opinion of the general state of health of the persons employed in the manufactures of the place? – I consider them on the whole tolerably healthy. I have found more illness among the carpet weavers than those employed in mills.

Is there any complaint to which the persons employed in the carpet trade are peculiarly liable? – The men are very subject to hernia and to haemorrhoids, also to disorders of the digestive organs, arising from their sedentary and irregular habits. With regard to the joints; they are also frequently the subject of scrofula.

Do you consider that the drawers are generally over-worked? – Not generally; if their masters went on regularly with their work they would go through with it; they are very often exposed to unnecessary and over-fatigue by their masters working extra hours to make up time lost by dissipation.

Have you remarked any difference in the general state of health of the children employed in carpet factories and those employed in the spinning-mills? – I certainly think that those employed in the spinning-mills are healthier than those in the carpet factories.

Are the persons employed in the spinning-mills subject to any particular diseases? – I am not aware of any. Girls are generally employed there.

Have you compared the state of the health of the children employed in the manufactures with those not so employed? – I have found the health of those not employed in manufactures to be better than those employed in the carpet trade and spinning-mills.

Have complaints come before you, as a magistrate, of the children having been maltreated in the carpet trade? – Very frequently; few weeks elapse without cases of that sort coming before us.

Have complaints come before you with regard to children employed in spinning-mills? – During nearly two years which I have been a magistrate I scarcely remember a complaint being made, and believe that they very rarely are made, which arises from the better management of the mills; whereas the drawers in factories are immediately under the control of the weavers, their masters.

Are serious accidents of frequent occurrence in the mills or factories? – No; they are very rare.

Then you consider the dangerous parts of the machinery to be well protected? – I do.

Report of the Factory Commission, Parliamentary Papers, 1833, XXI.

Report on the handloom weavers by Joseph Fletcher, 1840

The weavers are, as compared with the dyers, for instance, persons of much inferior physical character, smaller in stature, of less muscular development, and enjoying lower animal spirits. They are, in fact, small in size, not averaging perhaps more than five feet six inches, and pale and phlegmatic in countenance. They are, however, more intelligent, and any of them can explain the nature of their machines. They have courage and activity with their intelligence, and the difference between them and a body of navigators was seen most conspicuously in a mob-fight at an election not long ago. The navigators expected to fight a pitched battle with fists, but the weavers broke their ranks, closed in upon them, and completely beat them by numbers. The town-born women are small, being early confined to winding, filling, or some part of the business. There is an attraction in the trade which brings into it women from the surrounding country in preference to going to service, and this accounts for some of the women being much larger; but the Coventry-bred weavers of both sexes are small. The indoors and shop habits of the weavers are certainly such as to induce an early development of the sexual passions, and, whatever may be the amount of illicit intercourse, marriages generally are very early.

The character of diseases among the weavers differs very materially from that of the diseases affecting such operatives as the dyers; being chiefly diseases of the digestive organs and of the lungs, indigestion and its consequences in various forms, and consumption. Of the weavers in the self-supporting dispensary it is the experience of Mr. Nankivell, that about two in every five that are attended are labouring under diseases of the digestive organs, while among the watchmakers, dyers, labourers, and those of other occupations who have required aid, the proportion affected by such diseases is only about two in seven. Scrofula is very frequent among the weaving population. They are less liable to acute diseases, and the town appears to be particularly free from fever generally. The cholera was by no means severely felt. In acute diseases they have to be much more cautiously dealt with than the dyers, who are a fair specimen of the hardier class of artisans. There is also in Coventry an intermediate class as to health – that of the watchmakers. The weaver is very much more frequently indisposed than the dyer or the watchmaker; but he is much less liable to acute disease. Cannot say what is the state of longevity among the weavers, but does not see many old men amongst them. Not many now enlist as soldiers, but many old weavers have been soldiers. The physical depression of the weavers shows itself in their mental character. Anxiety as to the circumstances of their families and their trade is very conspicuous, and insanity is most frequent among them. The anxiety is greatly aggravated by the fluctuating nature of the trade. When work is pretty constant, they have to labour, if possible, to clear off the debt incurred in a previous bad time; and even badness of material much harasses them.

'In the institution to which I am attached as a medical officer,' states Mr. Nankivell, surgeon to the self-supporting dispensary, in a lecture addressed to the members of the Mechanics' Institute, 'it frequently falls to my lot to witness the effect of anxiety and depression of mind on the public health, consequent on the fluctuating trade of this city. No sooner does a bad state of trade occur than there is generally an immediate increase in the number of dispensary patients, and this takes place long before the physical causes of disease – the privation of food and of the comforts of life – have had time to operate. In individual cases, the influence of the same cause is still more painfully evident – often leading, by long-continued care and mental distress, to the complete destruction of health and to death itself. Did time permit, I could relate many instances of this kind, in which poor industrious men have fallen sacrifices in their struggles to supply their own wants by their own means rather than suffer the degradation of begging charitable or parochial assistance.'

The weavers generally are a moral set of men, exceedingly attached to their homes, their families, and their domestic duties. The period of life when they encounter the greatest difficulties is in the first years after marriage, when the wife is bearing a family of children, who are yet too young to earn anything at winding, filling, or the other branches of the trade.

The resting of the breast against the loom, the constrained position, the want of air, and the frequent over-exhaustion, are the chief bad influences in the trade-occupations of the weaver; these are very serious in their effects. There is another injurious circumstance which affects also the watchmakers, viz., that they make supper, with beer, their principal meal, because to make a hearty meal in the earlier part of the day they find to make the sight rather less acute for their business, and they therefore continue their labour on insufficient nourishment to the end of the day, when a hearty meal is injurious. Such is the effect of all these influences that, without any influx of country population, the race of weavers would assuredly terminate. But a fact, proving that the weaving is to the young women of the surrounding country a seductive occupation which brings in a constant flood of superior health, is, that not only the inhabitants of the town, and those of the rural weaving districts, but the farmers of the neighbourhood, complain of their inability to get or to keep servants, who prefer the earnings and the independence of the ribbon-weaving. The physical inferiority which the trade gradually induces must obviously be to the great body of town weavers, an insurmountable obstacle to a resort to any other branch of labour with chance of reasonable success. With the great mass it is 'once weavers and always weavers', whatever may be the fate of their trade.

The homes of the best class of weavers, as compared with the cottages of agricultural labourers, are good, comfortable dwellings; some of them very well furnished; many have nice clocks, and beds, and drawers; are ornamented with prints; and some have comfortable parlours. These are the men who have looms of their own; cleanliness is the prevailing character, though some are slovenly, dirty, and without decent bed clothing; but these instances arise from the misconduct or mismanagement of the parties, unless in the instances of inferior workmen, who really cannot make decent earnings. There are instances of great poverty, in the cases especially of the few single-hand weavers in the city. The general habits of the first-hand journeymen are frugal, but knows many cases of great depression, anxiety, care, and consequent illness, because of the difficulty which they find to live in decency. The first-hand journeymen classes of weavers are generally well-clothed, and there is a great pride of appearance, which seeks to conceal the defects which may exist. They are also, the better classes of them, well fed, getting meat, potatoes, bread, and puddings of various sorts. But there is a grievously prevalent want of a knowledge of domestic appliances, and consequently of economy and management, resulting from the trade education in lieu of domestic education of the women. The latter are fond of finery; but generally, the cleanliness of the houses is remarkable.

Report on the Handloom Weavers, Parliamentary Papers, 1840, XXIV.

FARM WORKERS' DEATHS FROM TYPHUS, BERKSHIRE, 1846

Upton hamlet is adjacent to the village of Blewbury on the eastern edge of Berkshire and Wallingford is its nearest market town. There are eighteenth-century almshouses and a charity school in Blewbury and several ancient earthworks nearby. This report appeared in the Buckinghamshire rather than the Berkshire press. The unnamed fever was probably typhus, especially severe that year in London.

So destructive have been the ravages of fever in some parts of Berkshire that the parish of Upton, a hamlet adjoining Bluebery, in that county, the population of which was 142 seven weeks ago, is now reduced to 73, sixty-nine having died within that short period – many through want. Among the number are four children of the minister, who, on attending the dying beds of the victims, caught the infection and conveyed it to his dwelling, whereby he lost four of his offspring. According to the opinion of the physician of the place, the only alternative appears to be for every individual to quit the village, and for every dwelling to be destroyed, there being no other means left to stay the infection; such is therefore about to be done. Respecting the cause of this awful malady, the following facts are stated: That the labourers' wages are not half sufficient for the support of

their families; that the potatoes they had partly subsisted on for the last three
months were poisonous and infectious; that their food was bread alone – and of
that no sufficient; that meat or other substantial food they never tasted; that they
could not procure firing, hence their huts were always damp and unhealthy, nor
the soap necessary for common cleanliness. At length fever broke out, till none
remained unvisited by the calamity.

The Bucks Gazette, 19 December 1846.

NOTES

1. Robert Sutton (1707–88), a Suffolk surgeon, introduced his own system of inoculation for smallpox in 1757. He kept his methods a secret except for those practitioners who paid him to use his system. His six sons and two sons-in-law continued the arrangement. Robert Sutton boasted of the thousands he had inoculated and he certainly became very wealthy.
2. Andrew Douglas MD (1735–1806), a surgeon in Pall Mall, later treated Boswell again at his eleventh re-infection from a prostitute.
3. Samuel Hayes, surgeon, possibly of Hampstead, who had treated Hickey earlier.

VI
PRACTITIONERS' OWN RECORDS

❖ ❖ ❖

Like all other professionals, medical practitioners invariably kept records of their work, partly, in an age of long credit, to be able to submit accounts of medications and journeys, but also to know what illnesses their patients had suffered in the past. Thus a practitioner's records could comprise cash ledgers, case notes, correspondence with patients and, in fewer instances, a diary of his daily personal and professional life. Their records, especially bills and receipts, letters and prescriptions, also exist in patients' family papers and in the archives of institutions for which the practitioners worked, the parish, prison or workhouse. A minority of men, such as Percival Willoughby, published on their work, but these were usually the leaders of the profession rather than its general practitioners. The fact that medical records are now relatively scarce as archives, especially from before the mid-nineteenth century, suggests a high destruction rate, but such material could survive when a practice had functioned continuously over the centuries, as Thomas W. Jones's papers illustrate.

CASES FROM PERCIVAL WILLOUGHBY'S OBSERVATIONS IN MIDWIFERY

Percival Willoughby (1596–1685), the son of Sir Percival Willoughby, a local landowner, was born at Wollaton Hall, Nottinghamshire. He was apprenticed to a London surgeon in 1619 and from c. 1630 he practised in Derby, chiefly as an obstetrician. His case notes cover the years up to 1672 and describe over 200 female patients he attended, from paupers to aristocrats, across the Midlands. An edition of his Observations was published in Dutch in 1754 but did not appear in English until 1863, when 100 copies were printed. He was strongly opposed to midwives' interventionist practices and his book was intended to instruct them 'how to help poor suffering women in distresses'. He is buried at St Peter's, Derby.

Alice, the wife of Ralph Doxy, was delivered by mee of a dead child. The arme came first, and it was mortified by the midwives pullings. I slid up my hand, and, upon the child's belly I found the knees. I fetched down the feet, and quickly laid her at Snelton, Apr. 27 die Ois 1662.

I travelled all night in May 1631 and came to Nottingham by sun-rising to one Mrs. Reason. With her I found two midwives, and severall other women of good credit, and repute, all expecting my comming, and desiring my help. I found Mrs Reason weake, and, through her long sufferings, her countenance began to chang, and I perceived her nose half way palish. The birth came by the arme, the which the midwives endeavoured to reduce, but failed in the performance, and the child was dead by their operations.

I thought it not good with new strivings to disquiet her body, by turning the birth to the feet, but rather to take the arme off close to the shoulder, and, afterward, to draw forth the body of the dead child with the crotchet, following the counsell, and directions of Pareus.

All these operations were quickly performed, and the after-birth was soon obtained. So she was laid into her bed. Thus shee was eased of her tortures, after her delivery. I gave her an infusion of tin in white wine, which was made in a quart pewter pot, having the lid put down, and so the pot was kept warm by the fire, of which shee took every morning, and night, a wine glasse full.

This medicine kept her body in a gentle, breathing sweat, and shee was much refreshed by it. By degree shee recovered her health, with strength. Yet for some time, the neck of her bladder was so infeebled, that shee could not hold her water, but, as strength increased, this infirmity left her, and shee lived in good health, above 30 yeares after her sufferings.

When the child is great, an all the waters have issued, a hard and difficult labour usually followeth.

Anne Houghton of Darby, having been long in labour of a dead child, that was, for greatness, a little gyant, desired my help. And *although I knew that the child was dead*, yet I was desirous to hear what a grave Divine would say in a doubtfull case, and, in my proceedings, to have his approbation. This Divine thought it better to let the child perish, then to lose the mother's life with the child. Upon his words I did draw away the dead child with the crotchet, and shee hath had severall children since, and shee was there living in health Anno 1669.

Good wife Anne Barnet of Church Mayfield in Staffordshire, Anno 1663 had suffered much through a corrupted, dead child, for severall dayes. I had delivered her of a dead child, two yeares afore this time. I thought that I could have laid her again by the feet, but through the drines of the womb, the child would not move, and one of the legs separated at the knee, in the drawing by the child's foot. Seeing this, I used the crotchet to draw forth the head. Afterwards with much struggling, I brought forth the rest of the body. The child was great, and swel'd. It was rotten, and smelt unsavourly; upon the after-birth, nigh to the navel-string, was a gangrene, with blisters. Yet this woman recovered, and did well, and had a child since Anno 1668, and shee was living in Anno 1669.

Observations in Midwifery by Percival Willoughby, ed. Henry Blenkinsop
(Warwick, 1863), pp. 98–9, 105.

EDWARD SHIPPERY'S BILLS TO LORD FITZWILLIAM, 1698–9

Edward Shippery was a member of a London family of apothecaries, able to ask £60 as a premium with an apprentice. William, 1st Earl Fitzwilliam (1643–1719), was presumably in London when he was treated, although he was then living at Milton House, Northamptonshire. In 1669 he had married Anne Cremor, a Norfolk heiress; they had four sons and six daughters. The Earl and Countess have a magnificent monument by James Fisher of Camberwell in Marholm church.

1698

		£	s	d
11 November My Ldy	A box of purging pills for 4 Doses			10
12 November My Lord	Three blistering plasters		2	0
	Four melilot plasters			8
	A Cordial Apozem a quart		1	10
	A paper of Cordial powder with Bezoar		1	6
	A Cordial Julep a pint		2	0
13 November	An antifebritic bolus		1	0
	The Julep Repeated		2	0
	The Apozem Repeated		1	10
	A Compound Gargarism		1	3
	The bolus Repeated		1	0
	The same		1	0
	The same		1	0

		£	s	d
13 November	The same		1	0
	The same		1	0
	Four melilot plasters			8
14 November	The same			8
	A bolus as before		1	0
	A Cordial Julep		1	6
	The Apozem Repeated		1	10
	The Bolus Repeated		1	0
	The Julep Repeated half quantity		1	0
	melilot plasters			8
	The Bolus Repeated		1	0
	The same		1	0
15 November	Two plasters			4
	The Julep as before		1	0
	The Bolus Repeated		1	0
	The same		1	0
16 November	A melilot plaster			2
	A Cordial Apozem			11
	A melilot plaster			2
	melilot plasters			4
17 November	A Cordl Ptizan		1	6
	A Cerate for ye blisters			4
18 November	The Ptizan Repeated		1	6
		1	18	6

Decembʳ 7th 1698
Recd then of William Lord Fitzwilliam the full contents of this Bill, being One Pound Eighteen Shillings & Six pence By mee Edward Shippery (Endorsed: Mr Edwd Shippery Bill pd in full for my Physicke in my illness)

1699

29 April	A paper of purging powder			6
2 May	The same			6
5 May	A Chalibiat Electuary		4	0
	A Cordial Julep a pint		2	0
9 May	The same		2	0
12 May	The Electuary Repeated		4	0
13 May	The Julep Repeated		2	0
21 May	The Electuary as before		4	0
23 May	The Julep as before		2	0
		1	1	0

June the 3rd Recd the full Contents of this Bill

Northamptonshire Record Office, Fitzwilliam MSS, Misc. Box B. 4.

THE JOURNAL OF JAMES YONGE, SURGEON OF PLYMOUTH

James Yonge (1647–1721) became a naval surgeon's apprentice at the age of ten and spent his early years at sea. He began practice in Plymouth, where he served as mayor, and was appointed surgeon in charge of the first naval hospital there in 1671, the year of his marriage. He was later admitted to the College of Physicians in London and became a Fellow of the Royal Society. The diary records family births and illness, as well as the very substantial fees his important patients paid. His diary indicates that he also kept a casebook. Yonge lived on for another thirteen years after his journal ceased; the year 1708, when his only grandson, his daughter and his wife died, he noted as his '*Annus Tenebrosus*' (year of darkness).

1679 On the latter end of May, the smallpox being thick in Plymouth, my daughter Elisabeth was taken ill of them. They began with a convulsion fit, which had almost carried her off. Soon after, John Yonge had them, very thick, and little Johanna, so that 4 of my children were down at once and very ill of them, and on June 28 my daughter Jane died of them. She was now almost 5 years old, a handsome, brisk and good child. Her I buried on the foot of her Aunt Elizabeth Cramporn's grave . . . The rest, though very very ill in them, recovered, blessed be God. My poor Jinny that died had but a year before escaped death; a sled drawn by a horse having 5 barrels of beer on it was drawn over her forehead, tore off the scalp and made a desperate wound, which I cured. Also this year, I having many men used to come to shore on the king's account, did fit up the Hospital, where sometimes I had 36–38 men, by whom I usually got 20s. per diem. All the year I had a good number and I had also the best practice – especially for the pox – that ever I had. By that one disease I got this year above £120.

27 February 1680 . . . sent for to Stoke to Mr John Stones, whose son (being 4 years old) received by the fall of a gate two fractures in the skull of great bigness, one opposite to the other on each bregma. I took out a piece as big as a very large half–crown on the left side, which was wholly separate and had by one of its points run through the meninges and wounded the brain, a part of which as big as half a hazelnut shell would hold came out. I cured him in 10 or 12 weeks.

1701 August 3rd this year died my good friend Mr. Philip Andrews of Butshead . . . and soon after his lady removed to Exeter, by which I lost as much as the dock was worth, for I believe in 7 years that I was employed there I got besides presents and good treatment £60 or £70 per annum. January 30th died Mr. W. Addies, another good friend and profitable patient; he had an ulcer in the bladder 4 years, in which time I had of him near £200.

20 December 1704 I kept an account on my Almanack this year of all my patients, and had exactly the same number, viz. 444, and just 14 died as did last year.

The Journal of James Yonge (1647–1721), Plymouth Surgeon, ed. F.N.L. Poynter (1963), pp. 162, 163, 209, 227.

THE MEDICAL PRACTICE OF CLAVER MORRIS MD OF WELLS

Claver Morris (1659–1727), the son of a Dorset cleric, qualified at Oxford and practised as a physician in Salisbury until 1686 and at Wells, Somerset, for the rest of his life. His diaries survive for two periods, 1709–10 and 1718–26, and his cash books for the years 1712–23. He recorded family details, including household and clothing purchases, but also money spent on his 'Elaboratory', his music and entertainments. He had an extensive practice in Somerset within a 20–30 mile radius of Wells, but also covered considerable distances to his grander patients, Lord Conway at Sandywell, Gloucestershire, and Lady Davie beyond Exeter (75 miles). He travelled at about four miles an hour and must have spent over forty hours a week in the saddle. When more prosperous in 1722 he bought a calash from a London coachmaker. He noted his patients' symptoms in the diary, referring surgical cases to other practitioners. However, Morris was keenly interested in chemistry and scientific experiments, a facet of his character noted on his monument in Wells Cathedral. He was also actively musical; he sang and played seven instruments, as well as founding a music club at Wells.

In addition to his diaries, Claver Morris recorded his fees in cash books for many years. Until 1710 he earned £100 to £150 a year, which then increased to between £200 and £300 and in 1718 he noted 257 separate fees received. However, his expenses were considerable: between 1699 and 1702 he built himself a new house in East Liberty, Wells (now part of the Cathedral School), he married three times, his children went away to school, and he visited Bath and London. He also bought expensive, fashionable clothes, wine, books, paintings and musical instruments.

Claver Morris is commemorated with a portrait bust, his arms and a tablet in the east cloister of Wells Cathedral; he died on 19 March 1727 aged sixty-seven.

Charges at Oxford when he qualified as MD, 1691

June 30	To the Keeper of the Schools for signifying to the University that I would beginn to Read my Lectures on Friday following at 1 of yᵉ clock & at 3, & at 8 on Saturday in the morning		5s	0d
July 4	To yᵉ Congregation for obtaining their leave to be admitted to the Degree of Doctor		3s	0d
July 6	When I was Presented Doctor in Physick To the University for Fees	£56	12s	2d
	To the under Servants of the University		16s	0d
	For Gloves at my Presentation, to yᵉ Faculty	£5	7s	6d
	For Sweet-Meats at my Circuiting, & Biskets at my Presentation	£6	5s	0d
	For Wine at my Circuiting, & Presentation	£5	1s	0d
	To the Hall as a Due 4£ as a Gift towards their intended Building 6£	£10	0	0
	For a Dish of Scotch-Collops, a Hash & 2 Dishes of Fowle for yᵉ Hall	£1	6s	0d
July 14	For the Loane of a Scarlet Gowne 'till this day when I was admitted to Regency		10s	0d
	For adding velvet to my Gowne, & Tufts	£2	13s	0d
	For a Doctor's Capp		16s	0d

Examples of fees Claver Morris received, 1685–1723

		£	s	d
16 June 1685	Capt Piers of Wells	1	1	6
16 Oct 1690	Mr Grove of Zeales [Wilts]	1	1	6
17 Oct 1690	Lady Weymouth[1]	1	1	6
12 May 1691	Col St Loe, Little Fontmell, Dorset	3	4	6
6 June 1691	Of a Woman yt would not be known		10	0
23 May 1692	Bishop Kidder[2]	1	1	6
24 May 1692	Mr Gravener, Ubley		10	0
12 Sept 1692	Mine Heare Copeman	1	1	6
5 Jan 1694	Mrs Arnold in London	1	4	0
5 Jan 1694	Mrs Dorothy Cocks	2	8	0
5 Jan 1694	Earl of Roscommon in London	6	0	0
18 Feb 1694	Col Fust for his Lady, Port[i]shead	3	12	0
24 July 1695	Col Fust at Hull, Glos. [Hill]	4	0	0
27 July 1695	Frances Spencey, Dreycourt [Draycott]		2	6
5 Oct 1695	Mrs Porch, Glastonbury		2	6
5 Nov 1695	Of Mrs White a Half Carolus		17	0
21 Jan 1696	Mrs Fust, Morton, Glos 2G.	3	0	0
16 Jan 1716	Lady Phelips of Montacute[3]	2	3	0
14 Feb 1716	Lord Conway, Sandiwell, Glos[4]	12	18	0
1 Feb 1716	Geo Mattocks	1	1	6
28 June 1716	Col Hales, Cottle[s, Atworth] Wilts	2	15	0
20 Sept 1716	Mr Trevillian of Curry Reivil, now at Somerton	1	7	6
29 Nov 1722	Lady Davie at Sir Geo Chudley's	12	12	0
11 Oct 1723	Mr Harrison for his daughter Betty	8	8	0

Somerset Record Office, A/AHZ 1, 2, 3.

A LETTER FROM SIR HANS SLOANE TO LADY MORDAUNT, 1705

Hans Sloane MD (1660–1753), the seventh son of an Irish gentleman, received his medical education at Paris, Montpelier and Orange. In 1716 he became the first medical baronet. He was physician to George II and succeeded Sir Isaac Newton as president of the Royal Society in 1727. He was president of the Royal College of Physicians for a record length of time (1719–35). He was a wealthy man, for as well as his professional fees, he had income from patent medicines and he married an heiress. He bought the manor of Chelsea in 1712. Many aristocrats (Lady Newdigate, Lady Verney) were his patients and he advised them by letter when they returned to the country. Penelope, Lady Mordaunt (née Warburton), was the second wife of Sir John, 5th Baronet (1650–1721) of Walton Hall, near Wellesbourne, Warwickshire. Sir John had endured ill-health since a coach accident in 1701.

London July 12 1705

Madam,

I had the favour of Y[r] Lap[s] of the 9th yesterday and think Sr John cannot yet safely take the purging waters. I think he hazarded a little in taking of the rhubarb so soon after his feaver was cured by the bark. He ought not to purge after his feaver in lesse then two or three compleat months. For the pain & sowrenesse at his stomach he had better take some pearle, crabs eyes or crabs clawes powder about ½ a dram at a time twice or thrice a day w^h asses milk in the morning and a good large draught of Bathe waters warmed afternoon and at going to bed. If these Symptoms do not abate upon the use of these remedies he may with much more safety take an easy gentle vomit then purge any way. Perhaps bleeding (unless something I know not should forbidd it) would help him. I am glad to find Y^r Lap^p so well. I think you do well not to take medicines since you are so much mended. The pain in Y^r Lap's back seems to come from the kidneys & for that I know no properer remedy than a little syrup of marshmallows. Please to give my humble service to Sr John. Lady Thanett is extreamly well tho a good way gone with child which gives a great deal of joy to all that family & to those who have the happiness to be known to them. The first time I see them I will let them know the part Yo^r Lap takes in that matter. I am

> Yo^r Lap's most obedt & most humble Servt
> Hans Sloane

Warwickshire County Record Office, CR 1368, III, 73 and Elizabeth Hamilton, *The Mordaunts* (1965).

MEDICAL NOTES OF JAMES CLEGG OF CHAPEL EN LE FRITH, 1729

James Clegg (1679–1755), ordained in 1703, was a Dissenting minister in the Peak District of Derbyshire; he obtained a medical degree from Aberdeen in 1729. He also ran a small farm but was never affluent and seems to have taken up medicine to supplement his income. He was informally trained by Dr Adam Holland of Macclesfield (1666–1716), who bequeathed Clegg his medical books. Clegg travelled to preach and to practise; he had patients of all social classes in Manchester, Chesterfield and across the Midlands. His diary began in 1708, soon after his marriage, but it was not until 1727 that he made daily entries, which continued until his death; it is some 600 pages long, written in double columns. As well as noting patients and epidemics, Clegg also recorded family matters, especially illnesses, and events in the locality and beyond. He did not include the medical fees he received.

[October] Being this month created Doctor of Physick by a Diploma medicum from the University of Aberdeen in North Brittain, upon the Testimonials and recommendations of Dr. Nettleton[5] of Halifax, Dr. Dixon[6] of Bolton and Dr. Latham[7] of Findern, I think it now proper to keep a more exact account of my Patients, their diseases the Remedies prescribed, and the events. Desiring ever humbly and above all things to depend on the Divine blessing for success, which I most earnestly beg for the sake of his son Jesus Christ who when on earth went about preaching the Doctrine of the Kingdom and healing all manner of Diseases, Amen.

September 26th. 1729
I was calld to Mary, Daughter of John Fieldsend of Ford, she was seizd about 3 in the morning when the moon was at the Full with what I think may properly be calld the Hysteric apoplexy, she was about 20 years of age, never had the least menstrual evacuation; lookd pale was weak and short breathd and very thin, I found her layd along on a bed on the floor, her face deadly pale, the lips blue, the limbs stiff and to all appearance quite senceless and near dying.

Upon applying a bottle of c[ornu] c[ervi] to her nose she turnd it aside upon which I took about 3 ounces of blood from the left arm, and applied a Blistering plaister to each arm on the inside betwixt the elbow and armpit and bound em on. About 12 a clock at night when the Blisters begun to rise she began to move and speak but could remember nothing that had passd. Next day I sent Pill Ruffi i scruple to be taken with white wine posset drink which gave two stools and she was better. Two or three days after when the strength was a little recruited, I sent her Pil Cock Major I drachm in 10 pills for 2 doses which purgd her well and she recoverd.

October 1 or 2
Calld to Amos, son of Thomas Mellor of Town end, seizd with a continual fever of a Bad sort; about six days before, when he first begun to be indisposd I orderd Rad[ix] Ipecac[uanha] gr[ains] 10 in whey which workd well, I was then calld abroad and when I returnd found him delirious, exceeding hott, cheeks red, but yellow about the nose, his tongue white about the edges, yellow in the middle and very harsh and dry. He purgd violently and his stools came involuntarily as did his urine, all lookd on him as gone. I orderd a large blister to be raisd on his back forthwith, and 1 pint of the white decoction with Syrup of lemons, to drink of three or four times each day. The Blister evacuated a great quantity of thick white matter, the purging stayd well, and by slow degrees the child recoverd. I purgd him after with senna and prunes etc.

October 19
Thomas Mellor, Father to the Boy mentiond was siezd with the same Fever, Oct 21 I was calld to him and orderd him a Vomit viz Rad Ipec gr 15. Tart[ar] emet[ic] gr 2, this workd very well upwards and then downwards, after which the pain of his head abated, but a tickling cough came on which was troublesom, his pulse was quick but not full or high, and he was very thirsty. I orderd Powder of oyster shells 3 drachms sal Prunell[a] ½ drachm Gascoigne powder and lapis contrayerva ana Sal volat[ile] succin gr x, Camphor gr v misc f[iat] pulv in chartules ix distribuendus capt. unan quarta quaq[ue] hora, superbibend iv ounces vini als[a] aqua palustris. While he took this he spit abundance of a thick viscid flegm, his Fever abated and he continues to recover without any other sensible evacuation or the use of any other means but a proper regimen.

About the 10th of October Charles Lingard of Milton Junr was seizd with a Fever a violent pain in his head and back and the other usual symptoms. I orderd a vomit and it did well, his drink was at first small beer, Toat and water, and afterwards thin water grewel, small red spots appeard about the 11th day all over his body very thick, his drought very great, his tongue a dark yellow colour and very dry and hard, he slept little talkd wildly and lay singing in bed highly delirious. I applied a good large Blistering plaister about the 12 day to his neck which answerd well, he drank large quantities of thin grewle, and as the blister ran abundantly he came more to himselfe and rested better but was exceeding [gap]. On the 14th day he raved and begun to be restless again. I orderd two blisters more for his arms one of which did well. I then orderd the Powder of shells 2 drachms Sal prunell ½ drachm camphor ½ scruple mitte in 6 chartules dibidend, one to be taken in the forenoon another afternoon, after this his Fever abated, and he begins to recover.

October 22
I was calld to the wife of the above mentioned Charles Lingard big with child about 6 months gone and seizd with an tremor and shivering which returnd at first each day after which she had an hott fitt and was full of pain especially in her head, I was afraid a vomit might have occasiond a miscariage, therefore it was omitted and a blistering plaister applied to her neck, the pain of her head abated but she complained of her back and parted with little urine and that with pain which she thought owing to gravel, I suspected it might be occasiond by the cantharides, and orderd her Testaceous powders to be takn in milk and water boyld, but all on the sudden about the 7th day the pains of travel came on her, she earnestly desired me to bleed her. I was afraid of doing it on account of the state of the Fever, but after wishd I had done it. Before I saw her again a midwife was sent for, and she was deliverd but instead of the usual evacuations at that time she was seizd with vomiting great quantities of blood which she had been subject to sometimes in her pregnancy but had not told me of it, she was deliverd about midnight and died next morning before I could come to her. She was interrd at Chinley Chappel Nov. 1st 1729.

Vanessa S. Doe (ed.), *The Diary of James Clegg of Chapel en le Frith, 1708–55* (Derbyshire Record Society, vol. 5, 1981), pp. 923–5.

THE CASE NOTES OF RICHARD WILKES MD OF WILLENHALL, 1743

Richard Wilkes (1691–1760) practised medicine in Staffordshire after leaving Cambridge in 1720, although he originally intended to enter the church. From 1736 he kept detailed case notes on over 300 patients, as well as a private diary with some personal entries in Latin. He had considerable antiquarian and scientific interests. His patients ranged from the local gentry, such as the Vernons of Sudbury and the Leveson Gowers of Trentham, to the poorest, whom he treated free for the medical interest of their symptoms. He published works on smallpox, dropsy and cattle plague. A wealthy man, he died suddenly while visiting patients in Wolverhampton; he was buried at Willenhall, his family home.

8 January About a Month ago Mrs Catherine Walters, ye only surviving Child of 16 of Mr Walters of Rudge near Pattingham married Mr Wm Boycot of Uppington near Shresbury, one of ye Filisers. By this Match Rudge wch had been bought of Mr Creswel of Barnshurst, & several other Estates came to this Family, but she is in ill Health & not like to have Issue.

John Addis of Moor-Hall Com. Warwick Esqr.
Aged 67 never had any Illness to confine him
from the Time of his Infancy till March 1751.

18   He was out late at Night, the Air having
been long cold & wet. From this Time he felt,
as he said afterwards some Uneasiness in his
Bowels, but it was so little that he did nothing
for it, & so went about as usual till the

23 when he had a regular Fit of an Ague about Noon
25 Another such Fit about 8 in the Morning
27 Another Fit about 2 oclock in the Morning
29 A 4th Fit about 8 at Night, in wch he took the
Saline Draughts by his Apothys Direction.

30 He took a Purge.
31 A 5th Fit about the same Time of Night, after wch
he began to take the Bark, wch prevented the
next Return, but tho' he continued to take it

5 twice or thrice a Day on April 5 he had a
Shivering in the afternoon & another the next
Day about the same Time. He was always
of a very costive Habit, & it was found very
difficult to procure him Stools.

A page from the case notes kept by John Wilkes MD of Willenhall, 1731.

14 January Admiral Vernon & General Wentworth were recall'd from yᵉ W Indies
& this Day waited on ye King at St James's.

17 January Mr Altree⁸ told me & several others at Whampⁿ that some few Years
ago he was fetched to a Collier's Wife at yᵉ Lye between Dudley & Stourbridge,
who was in Labour but could not be deliver'd by the Midwife: that she never had
an open Passage for yᵉ Penis to yᵉ Uterus, but only a Small Hole, thro wch he
passed his Probe wth some Difficulty thro the Vagina: that he cut through this
outward Skin first, & then into ye Uterus through the Os Finea; yt he was all
Night in bringing away ye Foetus, wch was dead; & that the Midwife & many
Women now living can attest the Truth of it; & that the Woman did well. Query
How was it possible for this Woman to be gotten wth Child?
This Month flying, Rheumatic Pains were more frequent than usual, & many died
suddenly both in London & the Country.

16 February Mrs Stannier of Pepperhil told me she had cur'd many poor people of
ye Ague by giving them one Spoonful of good Mustard, prepar'd to eat wth Meat,
in a good Glass of Wine or Brandy, just before the Fit. In some it works by Vomit,
in others by Sweat. I believe it is very likely to do great Service in this Disorder. At
the same Time her Mother Mrs Bache told me yt formerly she was cur'd of the
Itch by anointing only once wth Glass very finely pounded & pass'd through a fine
Seive, mixt wth Butter; but that it made her very uneasy for some Time, when she
felt as if she had been rolled in Nettles.

[*March*] Rheumatic Pains, & Intermitting Fevers were very common, & Agues
among poor people; This whole Month [was] very dry, little or no Rain having
fallen hereabout.

2 March The Revd Mr. Wm Clievland of Worcester told me yᵗ some Years [ago]
he advised an old poor Woman of his Parish, who had long been terribly afflicted
wth the Stone, to drink Tea made of Marshmallows for her common Drink; wch
she did & sometime after voided a Stone yt weighed somewᵗ more yⁿ two Ounces
wⁿ she gave it him, wch was a good while after it came from her; wn we may
suppose it was become dryer, & lighter yn at first. His Brother, ye Revd. Mr Jon
Clievland said he had several Times seen ye Stone weighed, & that the Weight of
it was full 2 Ounces.

5 March By Accts from Rome a most terrible Distemper, called by yᵗ Physicians
Influenza raged there, wᶜʰ they say is not a Plague but a Forerunner of one. In
September last it begun in Saxony, & has visited Venice, Genoa, Milan, Florence,
Naples, & Rome, where tis said 500 at this Time dye in a Day. All Italy, & indeed
all Europe is greatly alarm'd at ye Destruction made by it, & most States are
endeavouring to prevent its coming among them by enjoining Quarentine to be
perform'd by all Travellers, as well by Land as Sea. God grant it may not visit this
Island; but if Providence ever designs to punish Iniquity in this World, we may
reasonably expect it to rage here wᵗʰ yᵉ utmost Violence.

Wellcome Library, London, MS 5005, pp. 160–2. Wilkes's earliest
diary (1736–8) is at Staffordshire Record Office, 5350.

THE DIARY OF RICHARD KAY OF BALDINGSTONE, 1744, 1749

Richard Kay (1716–51) was the son of a surgeon-apothecary at Baldingstone, 2 miles north of Bury, Lancashire. He was apprenticed to his father, Robert (1684–1750) and in 1743–4 spent a year training in London, where he had some very eminent teachers. Kay began keeping a diary in April 1737, noting patients, journeys and his religious life. After his return from London he joined his father in practice. The diary stops abruptly with an unfinished entry on 19 July 1751. Kay died on 2 October 1751 aged thirty-five, presumably in the typhus ('spotted fever') epidemic that was raging in the area. His mother and two of his sisters died in the same year. Richard Kay was buried in the graveyard of the Unitarian chapel, Bank Street, Bury.

May 1744
2. This Day I attended the Hospitals. Mr Sharp[9] lectur'd to us upon Midwifry. Lord, Help me to give proper Attention to, and make proper Improvment in every Thing that may be of Use and Service.
7. This Day I attended the Hospitals; we have seen as indeed we see every Day a deal of Affliction. In the Afternoon enter'd upon a Course of Midwifry with Mr. Smelley the Man Midwife[10] in Ferrard Street near Leicester Fields in Company with Mr. Stead,[11] Mr. Ellington[12] an Apothecary in the Borough and a young Physician belonging to St. Thos., he gave us our first Lecture. Lord, Qualify me for great Usefulness in my Day and Place, and if it be thy Will, grant that my Life may be long, easy and prosperous.
9. This Day in the Morning Mr. Smelley lectured to us; Mr. Girle[13] lectured to us at the Hospital afterwards. Spent the Evening with Mr. Stona[14] at his Lodgings one of the young Men, and some others. Lord, Do thou ever guide and direct my Thoughts, Words and Actions aright.

Monument to Richard Kay of Baldingstone, 1716–51, and his family in the graveyard of the Unitarian Chapel, Bank Street, Bury.

11. This Day I attended the Business of the Hospitals. In the Afternoon Mr. Smelley lectur'd to us upon Midwifry; after Lecture went with Mr. Stead to Ranelagh House to see the Evening Diversions there. Lord, suitably furnish and endow me with all useful Knowledge.

[In May and June Kay attended three more lectures from Smellie and one more from Sharp; he visited Bedlam, the Tower of London and saw a performance of *Richard III*. He also heard George Whitefield preach and attended a service at St Paul's.]

August 1744
25. This Day I attended at Guy's. Mr. Sharp Surgeon at Guy's signed my Certificate to day as I am now in a little Time to leave the Hospitals; I writ to Friends this Evening that I intended to leave London Monday Sev'night, and return amongst Friends . . .
28. This Day I attended the Hospitals. The Surgeon's signed me a Certificate to Day. Spent the Evening with Mr. Steade. Lord, I have been sent for Improvement, may I be well improved, and may my Life be long spared to be useful.
29. This Day I did not attend in the Hospitals; about Hospital Time went with Mr. Steade to see my new Chirurgic Instruments, before they were sent Home. Lord, Give me Success in my Undertaking . . .
31. This Day I were not in the Hospitals. Sent some Medicines and Instruments Home by the Carrier that I've bought here . . .

[Kay then joined his father's practice in Baldingstone.]

1 August 1749
This Day in the Morning I returned from Moston, called at Chesham where I dined, Coz. Richard Kay complains of not being well and has done so for some Time, tho' thinks himself worse at present; I advised him to acquaint his Brother Doctor Kay[15] in Manchester. I drank Tea in the Afternoon and spent the Evening with our Family and some others at Richard Kay's in Gooseford Lane. Lord, May we all answer the End of our Creation, obtain the Favour of our Creator, and behave so as we may make ourselves easy now, and happy for ever.

The Diary of Richard Kay, 1716–51, of Baldingstone, near Bury, Lancs,
eds W. Brockbank and F. Kenworthy (The Chetham Society, vol. 16, 1968),
pp. 83, 88, 143.

A LETTER FROM JOHN WALL MD TO SIR JOHN RUSHOUT, 1766

John Wall (1708–78) practised all his life in Worcester, married into a local gentry family and was instrumental in setting up the Worcester Porcelain Company in 1751. A talented artist, he exhibited at the Royal Academy in 1774. He also published widely on such topics as typhus, inoculation and angina, but also on hydrotherapy and lead-poisoning. His medical practice extended far beyond the city of Worcester, where he was honorary physician to the hospital for thirty-one years, and his patients included Lady Luxborough, Lord Dudley at Halesowen Grange and the Lytteltons at Hagley Hall. He reputedly suffered from gout and in 1774 left

Worcester for Bath, where he died on 27 June 1776. His white marble monument in Bath Abbey shows the palette of an artist and the caduceus of a medical practitioner.

Lady Anne was the daughter of the 4th Earl of Northampton; in 1729 she married Sir John Rushout (1685–1775) of Northwick Park, Gloucestershire (now Worcestershire). Wall travelled more than 25 miles from Worcester to attend her and stayed at Northwick overnight. Lady Anne had one son and two daughters. She died on 20 December 1766, aged seventy-one, only two months after Wall's visit. There is a fine collection of Rushout family tombs in the parish church of Blockley, Gloucestershire.

> Sunday, Oct.26. 1766
> S^r,
> I am very sorry to inform you that I have been called to Lady Ann Rushout & found her very ill; & I am not a little apprehensive of ye Consequence. I visited her Ladyship on Fryday last & lay at Northwick that Night. She had then a very troublesome & almost incessant Cough without Expectoration; which coming upon ye Difficulty of Breathing which She has so long laboured under, each increases the other. I shall not seal up this Letter till ye Post comes in the morrow, that if any new particulars should be sent me by Mr Johnson[16] I may communicate them to You. I apprehend her Ladyship caught some Cold by going to Church on Sunday last, & perhaps something of ye Gout may have concurred; for on Fryday Evening She found a sharp Pain in ye Ball of ye Great Toe which look'd a little Red & was somewhat swelled. I did not find her Pulse irregular, but it was too low to venture at Bleeding: I therefore applied a Blister betwixt ye Shoulders & gave her some Medicines to promote Expectoration; I have order'd her to bathe her Feet in a strong suspension of Mustard Seed & Horse Radish; & to apply Mustard to ye Foot if there should appear any gouty Symptoms. I fear She will not be able to meet you soon in London. Tho' I think Her Ladyship is evidently declining yet I am not apprehensive of any thing immediately dangerous unless a sudden fit of Suffocation should come on from ye Violence of ye Cough [join'd] with ye difficult Passage of ye Blood thro' ye Lungs which is evident from her Bad Breathing.
> I have the Hon^r to be
> Sr John
> Y^r most obliged & most obed Servt, J. Wall
>
> Worcestershire Record Office, BA 4221/26(ii) Ref: 705:66.

THE OBSTETRIC CASE NOTES OF THOMAS WOEN JONES OF HENLEY-IN-ARDEN, 1793–4

Thomas Woen Jones (1764–1846) was the son of a Warwickshire surgeon-apothecary, apprenticed in London in 1785 for seven years with £150 premium. In London he was taught by William Osborne MD and John Clarke, two noted obstetricians, and kept notes of their lectures. From 1791 Jones practised in Henley-in-Arden attending both poor law and prosperous patients. In this casebook he recorded a total of 422 deliveries, reaching a peak of 72 in 1798, with abnormal

A page from the obstetric casebook kept by Thomas Woen Jones of Henley-in-Arden, 1794.

presentations particularly noted and 10s 6d his usual fee. He attended five patients for no fee, but two paid him a guinea each. Almost all of his patients lived within 5 miles of Henley-in-Arden. The case book covers the period from 22 May 1791 to 7 August 1800 and is of exceptional interest because Jones included his fees for obstetric work.

1793

Case	Patient	Residence	Date	Child	Comments	£	s	d
17	Mrs Foxall	Lapworth	13 Jan	son	A remarkable quick good labor		10	6
18	Mrs Shaw	Henley	22 Aug	son	natural labor nothing particular occurred		10	6
19	Mrs Harris	the Turnpike	10 Feb	son	Natural labor the greatest quantity Lochial discharge which I ever knew which of course made her weak		10	6
20	Mrs Lane	Wilmcote	22 Feb	daur	natural labour nothing remarkable occurred		10	6
21	Mrs Joseph Price	Wilmcote	28 Feb	son	natural labor do		10	6
22	Mrs Cranmore	near Royal Oak, Wilmcote	6 Mar	son	natural labor do		10	6
23	Joseph Bishops wife	Wootton	7 Mar	son	natural labor do		10	6
24	Wm Wagstaffs wife	Henley	24 Apr	daur	natural labor do		10	6
25	Thomas Meads wife	Lapworth St	9 May	son	natural labor do		10	6
26	Seth .oys wife	Wilmcote	10 May	daur	natural labor, great looseness		10	6

Case	Patient	Residence	Date	Child	Comments	£	s	d
27	Mrs Jennings	Yarningale	17 May	son	natural labor nothing particular		10	6
28	John Joyces wife	—	26 May	son	natural labor nothing particular		10	6
29	Thos Shakespeares wife	Henley		son & daur	Complex Labour Pains had been strong upon the Patient for 26 hours at least, her labor was accomplished without much trouble and nothing particular occurred more than Natl Labr		10	6
30	Mrs Davis	near Liveridge Hill	22 June	son	natural labor nothing particular	10		6
31	Mrs Clarke	Rookery	7 July	son	Premature Labor having completed only 30 weeks of Gestation		10	6
32	Mrs Barret	Wilmcote	10 July	son	natural labor nothing particular occurred		–	–
33	Joseph Hopkins wife	Pinley Green	25 July	daur	natural labor do do		10	
34	Mrs Baylis	Liveridge Hill	6 Aug	son	natural labor do do		10	6
35	Mrs Hartley	Henley	7 Aug	son	natural labor the Child Still Born having a very large Hydrocephalus with scarcely any Ossification of the Bones of the Cranium		–	–
36	Mrs Kendal	Rookery	9 Aug	son	natural labor nothing particular	10		6
37	Mrs Brown	Lowsonford	11 Aug	son	Preternatural labor the Feet presenting accompanied with the Furniss She was soon & safely delivered and as good a time as any common labor		10	6
38	John Joiners wife	Henley	2 Sept	son	natural labor nothing particular	10		6
39	Mrs Rd Taylor	Preston Field	15 Sept	daur	natural labor do do		10	6
40	Mrs Grissel	Beaudesert	21 Oct	son	natural labor do do		–	–
41	Mrs Sharmon	Claverdon	28 Oct	son	Difficult Labor A case of arrest within the Pelvis owing to a small portion of deformity in the inferior Aperture delivered with the Crotchet the woman doing remarkably well		10	6
42	Mrs Bradbury	Lapworth	24 Nov	daur	natural labor nothing particular	10		6
43	Mrs Jackman	Kite Green	8 Dec	son	natural labor do do		10	6
44	Mrs Boney	Bearley	11 Dec	Daurs	Complex labor of both preter natural presentations delivery however decomp[os?]d	10		6
45	Mrs Brant	Bird in hand	23 Dec	daur	natural labor nothing particular	10		6

Year 1793 Women 29

1794

Case	Patient	Residence	Date	Child	Comments	£	s	d
46	Mrs Cashmore	Pinley Green	11 Jan	daur	do do do		10	6
47	Mrs Smith	Kite Green	11 Jan	daur	Preternatural Presentation the Breech presenting Patients Age 14 & 6 Months yet had a good Labor and the Child a proper size		10	6

Case	Patient	Residence	Date	Child	Comments	£	s	d
48	Mrs Wm Webb	—	26 Jan	daur	natural labor nothing particular		–	–
49	Mrs Wm King	Shelfield Green	13 Feb	boy	natural labor do		10	6
50	Mrs Alice	Print Bearley	25 Feb	son	do do		10	6
51	Mrs Richard Gibbs	at the Mill	5 Mar	son	do do		10	6
52	Mrs Hemming	Shelfield Green	9 Mar	son	do do		10	6
53	Mrs Clarke	Henley	23 Mar	son	Premature Labor the Patient wanting three Months of her time		10	6
54	Anne Baker	Beorley	12 Apr	daur	Difficult Labor having been kept by an Old Woman six days – the last 20 hours two violent floodings came on She was easily delivered by the Forceps and done well		10	6
55	Betty Headon	Finwood Green	21 Apr	daur	natural labor but attended with very violent pains	1	1	0
56	Mrs Findon	Walmsmore	11 May	son & daur	Complex Labor attended with Floodings		10	6
57	Mrs Palmer	Beorley	9 June	son	natural labor nothing particular		10	6
58	Mrs Baker	Beorley	15 June	daur	do do do		10	6
59	Mrs Foxall	Hole Houses	15 June	daur	do do do		10	6
60	Mrs Dawes	Wootton	29 June	son	do do do		10	6
61	Sarah Barford	Aston	5 July	son	do do do		10	6
62	Mrs Lane	Beoley	8 July	daur	Abortion having completed only 20 Weeks of Gestation		10	6
63	Mrs Sarah Douglas	Beorley	9 July	son	natural labor nothing particular		10	6
64	Mrs Higgins	bottom of Henley	6 Aug	son	do do do		10	6
65	Mrs Canning	Henley	15 Aug	son	do do do		10	6
66	Mrs Gardiner	Henley	16 Aug	son	do do do		10	6
67	Mrs Tandy	near Wootton Tollgate	21 Aug	son	Preternatural Labor; Foot Presentation Labor neither Long or difficult		10	6
68	Mrs Coxe	Aston	24 Aug	son	Difficult Labor a case of arrest within the Pelvis obliged to deliver with the Crotchet		10	6
69	Mrs Boney	Henley	7 Sept	son	natural labor nothing particular		–	–
70	Mrs Rabone	Nuneham	28 Sept	daur	do do do		10	6
71	Mrs Whitehouse	Earthen Ware Wm	2 Oct	son	Preternatural Labor Foot Presentation the Woman wanting two Months of her time		10	6
72	Mrs Sharman	Claverdon	6 Oct	son	natural labor		10	6
73	Mrs Duffin	Shelfield Green	9 Oct	son	An Abortion at 22 Weeks the Patient laboring under a Violent Hemorrhage for 12 days previous to the expulsion	1	1	0
74	Wm Madews wife	Henley	17 Oct	daur	natural labor nothing particular		–	–
75	Mrs Anthony	Edkins Aston	20 Oct	daur	do do do		10	6
76	Mrs Brown	Lowsonford	2 Oct	daur	do do do		10	6
77	Mrs Eborall	Lapworth Hill	23 Oct	son & daur	Complex Labor the first Child presented naturally, the second the Hand presented and was brought away with that Presentation with very little difficulty		10	6

Case	Patient	Residence	Date	Child	Comments	£	s	d
78	Mrs Day	Wilmcote	26 Oct	son	natural labor Face Presentation	10	6	
79	Mrs Canning	Partloe	18 Dec	daur	natural do do		10	6
80	Mrs Ingram	Wootton	20 Dec	daur	do do		10	6
81	Mrs Cranmores	Hockley	28 Dec	daur	do do		10	6

Year 1794 Women 36

Warwickshire County Record Office, CR 3019.

THE DIARY OF GIDEON MANTELL, SURGEON-APOTHECARY, 1818–47

Mantell was born in 1790 in Lewes, Sussex, the son of a shoemaker; after training in London, he practised in Lewes and Brighton. He was a noted geologist and his journal recorded the problems of medical practice, his scientific studies and friends, as well as details of his patients. The diary covers the period from March 1819 until June 1852, shortly before his death; the original manuscript is in New Zealand.

August 1818 An immense number of Persons in this Town and neighbourhood are ill with Typhus fever – I have visited upwards of 40 and 50 patients every day for some time: yesterday I visited 64. Our house is like a public office from the continual progress and egress of persons sending for their medicines.

December 1818 Mr Moore[17] had a most severe fit of Apoplexy; I was with him when it came on and immediately made a large orifice in a vein and took away forty ounces of blood: then I cupped him, had leeches applied etc. he had convulsions repeatedly for three days successively. Dr Blair[18] and Mr Hodson[19] thought his case hopeless. I left him one morning (the third after the fit) apparently dying. I wished to bleed him again, but Mr H. would not consent; he thought it useless and that he should be left to his fate. I was obliged to go into the country to visit a patient some distance from Lewes; upon my return in the evening, I found Mr Moore in the same state as I had left him; pulse slow and full; breathing stertorous; convulsions every half hour; he was entirely senseless. I resolved to bleed him again as the dernier resort. I took from him 20 ounces; whilst the blood was flowing he muttered out 'better Mantell, better': this induced to me not to stop the bleeding till his pulse faultered: he amended from that very minute; he had no return of the convulsions, his breathing became very calm and easy: I ordered 10 grains of Calomel every four hours, for three days; this produced ptyalism and the mercury was discontinued . . . he is so far recovered that he can converse rationally, can walk without assistance; his speech is not altered, except that he rather lisps from the loss of two front teeth.

5 November 1821 This afternoon was requested to attend an accident at Malling Mill; on my arrival I found a poor boy, who had accidentally called at the Mill, with his hand dreadfully lacerated; thought it necessary to remove the forefinger and thumb at the wrist joint.

12 November 1821 Accompanied Mr Hodson . . . and assisted him in the amputation of the thigh of a poor man, who had long suffered from a disease of the knee joint.

16 November 1821 Was called to a most distressing accident at Chailey Mill. A poor boy by some accident got his clothes entangled by an upright post that was rapidly revolving; the lad in consequence was whirled round with great velocity, and his legs were dashed against a beam; the consequence was a separation of the left tibia from its articulation at the knee joint and a laceration of the whole muscles of that leg: on the right side the femur was knocked away from its epiphysis, and projected between the muscles of the ham; but in both instances the joint of the knees remained perfect and uninjured. It was considered absolutely necessary to amputate the left leg above the knee: the right femur was reduced and kept in its place by appropriate compresses; but the constitutional shock was so great that the boy died the next day.

12 August 1829 Yesterday I wrote to Dr Babbington[20] respecting Mr Richardson, Linen Draper of the Cliff, and in the evening I attended the wife of one of the convicts who was taken in labour in the street: she was removed to St John's Poor House and I delivered her of a fine boy at eleven in the evening.

20 March 1830 Muddled away another week in doing nothing. The same dull round of visiting patients.

19 January 1831 My confounded bills so engross my time that I cannot, dare not, devote a moment to my pleasures; have sat up writing every morning till two or three, and yet have not got through two-thirds of my horrible task: neither Partner nor assistant affording me any effectual help!

1 May 1847 Went to Bartholomew's Hospital, and witnessed two operations under the influence of Ether: the first I have seen. The loss of sensibility in both instances was complete: no consciousness of the operation. But the effect on the system was appalling, though very transient.

The Journal of Gideon [Algernon] Mantell, surgeon and geologist, 1818–52,
ed. E. Cecil Curwen (1940), pp. 2, 42, 68, 75, 215.

THE JOURNAL OF JOHN SIMPSON MD OF BRADFORD, 1825

John Simpson (1793–1867) came from an established medical family in the Knaresborough area of Yorkshire. He took his MD at Edinburgh in 1821 and early in 1822 he began practice in Bradford, which he found most uncongenial. He was delighted to give up medicine and become a country gentleman on the death of his uncle, Dr John Simpson of Malton, Yorkshire, whose heir he was. In 1827 he married a wealthy heiress and took her family surname of Hudleston. The journal covers the period from 1 January to 25 July 1825. It describes his social life and his involvement with the Bradford Dispensary, as well as his part in the establishment of a local newspaper. He died in London on 8 October 1867.

1825
28 February I walked this morning to Heaton to see Mr. Field who has not yet got quit of his cold, in fact it has turned out to be the Whooping-Cough, and what is

very remarkable his mother who is upwards of seventy years of age has got the same complaint also, as well as both her grand-daughters.

1 March The medical profession is one of constant privation and unpleasant occurrences and the remuneration is never held adequate to the anxiety experienced. In the very room in which I now sit I witnessed the last moments of a friend, a man of uncommon talent (Mr. Crossley, Attorney), who died of Apoplexy. I believe I could have saved him if I had seen him at the commencement of the attack, but I was unfortunately from home and when I returned it was too late. I am very much afraid that I shall have to witness a similar scene. When I returned from Steeton Hall last Tuesday evening I was requested to see the younger brother of my old friend Thompson and found him attacked with typhus fever and that in a most severe form. He is sixteen years of age and a boy of considerable talent. Sharpe[21] and I have attended him regularly ever since and have done whatever lay in our power to relieve him, but after all I am very much afraid that we shall be beat, for he is this night in considerable danger.

4 April I went today with Mr. Illingworth[22] to see my young patient in Diabetes. I found that he had completely recovered, by adopting the mode of treatment I proposed. He now only parts with about two pints of urine in 24 hours and all the functions are natural. I therefore pronounced him well.

13 April There was a meeting this evening of the Dispensary Committee. It was agreed that the Dispensary should open for patients on Monday next. I and Mr. Sharpe, being the senior Physician and Surgeon shall have to attend on that day. I have no doubt but we shall be fully occupied and Mr. Roberts[23] the Apothecary is making preparations.

18 April On this day was opened our Dispensary for the admission of patients. I and Sharpe had to attend, but as Sharpe was engaged, Mr. Blakey[24] attended for him. We had I think about eight or ten patients. Within the last four months four people have been killed at the different mills by the same kind of machinery. On Saturday night last a young man was accidentally shot at one of the main mills, and today a manufacturer has taken a quantity of poison, which will kill him. Also a man has had his skull fractured by being struck at with an iron crow by one of his companions, and is I believe likely to die. The lower order of people here are such savages that they care very little for killing one another in their passions, or drunken feasts.

31 May I am very anxious to increase, if I could, my private income, for then I should be able to go and live where I liked best. If from one source or other I had an income of three hundred pounds per annum, independent of my profession, I would then leave Bradford and go to reside probably at Harrogate or some place or other that better suited my ideas and taste than this abominable manufacturing district.

29 June In the evening I attended the dissection of a poor Dispensary patient who had died. It was a very interesting case. He as a boy about fourteen and a patient of mine. I admitted him some time ago with a hopeless disease of the heart. I never in my life saw so well marked the efficacy of medicine in relieving sufferings. His time ever since he was admitted a patient has been comparatively easy. I foretold great enlargement of the heart and the dissection bore me out.

There were Drs. Outhwaite[25] and Macturk[26] and Mr. Thos. Cooper from Bingley, who happened to be in town. Mr. Roberts opened the body and the whole disease was found to be in the heart which was four or five times the natural size. We brought away the heart privately and have made a preparation of it for the Dispensary. Macturk, Cooper and myself went home with Outhwaite to supper. We remained with him until very late.

21 July A man has committed a rape on a child only eight years of age. Beaumont[27] was the surgeon who examined the child, but she was also sent to me for examination. I am very apprehensive that I shall have to give evidence in the case. I had much rather avoid it if possible. The man has been sent to York, but the Grand Jury having been dismissed, he will have to remain until the next Assizes.

The Journal of Dr. John Simpson of Bradford 1825 (Bradford City Libraries, 1981), pp. 16, 25, 26, 28, 48, 63, 72.

THE DIARY OF JONAS ASPLIN, SURGEON-APOTHECARY, 1826

Born in 1772, Asplin was apprenticed in 1786 to a surgeon-apothecary, William Miller, of Aveley, Essex, for six years with a premium of £90. In 1825 he returned to England from a long period of practice in Paris and, with his wife, Eliza, settled at Prittlewell. He later practised at Rayleigh, where he died and was buried in 1842. His diary covers the years 1825–8 and carries accounts of his social and personal life, as well as of his medical activities.

1826
2 March Visited a Mrs Harvey (bakers) a bad and desperate case of cancer. Mr Marsh[28] called and accompanied me to Mrs Harvey's, and, as she seems inclined to submit to an operation, agreed to see her on Saturday and decide upon its practicability.

12 March Eliza to Church. At 2½ was sent for to a case of Hernia. William drove me to Gt. Wakering, whence Miller[29] accompanied me to the workhouse at Little Wakering, where the subject of the case is. Operated on a strangulated femoral Hernia in the case of Mrs. Fletcher, formerly Germany, and then kept the Anchor at Great Wakering. Left her as well as possible.

14 March Rode to Lt. Wakering and visited Mrs. Fletcher, who is going on well.

27 March Rode to Little Wakering to see my patient, on whom I operated for Femoral Hernia; she is perfectly well recovered.

3 April Attended a Vestry meeting. They pay the medical men so badly in this Parish for attending the poor that no one will take the parish on the terms offered. £60 per annum is demanded, the parish offer £45 and have risen to £50. Mr Hardwick called in the evening; he tells me that someone from Rayleigh is about taking the parish.

13 April Am so ill today that I cannot go to Rochford.

14 April Being sent for to Little Wakering, I determined on going, though certainly not in a state to go out.

15 April In bed all day. Mr. Grabham called and bled me. Several kindly sent to make enquiries.

17 April Bled myself 22 ounces.

26 April Visited Mrs. Johnson, glazier; her husband is in prison and herself confined with her 4th child and in a most dangerous state. On my way home was called in to another patient of Miller's at Wren's old house at Southchurch, who was also confined; she is dying and not much above 19.

27 April At 11 drove to Wakering, called at Southchurch and found the poor young woman died about 2 in the morning. Her infant died just before I saw her last night. She appeared to be a very fine young woman.

3 June Went to Southend and set a broken collar bone for a son of Mr. Braybrooke, the consequence of the electioneering suppers given by . . . the candidates for the Borough of Maldon.

9 August Miller having mentioned the death of Jonas Thornborough in the Island and his being an interesting case of Angina pectoris, I determined on endeavouring to examine the body and accordingly rode this morning to the Hall to breakfast by 8, and Charles drove me over to Foulness. Found the body of Thornborough in such a state I could not inspect it.

13 August Visited Mrs. Nashe's little girl at the workhouse.

15 August Mrs. Cause called with a sick servant maid.

15 September Rode to S. End and operated for Hydrocele on Mr. D. Thomas' infant, the only case of the kind in an infant I ever saw.

21 September Clay from North Shoebury workhouse called for me to see his wife. Visited Mr. Harvey, the baker, and arranged for an amputation of part of the foot tomorrow.

22 September Rode to Rochford and performed an operation on Mr. Harvey's foot. Mr. Fairchild[30] and a Mr. Thos. Smith[31] of Nottingham present.

20 October Amputated a finger for Mr. Nunn from Eastwood. Mrs. Bennewith from Wakering called with an order from the parish of Foulness for me to attend her daughter with an old case of Fistula Lachrymalis.

25 October To Shopland and visited James Adams, who has a concussion of the brain and has been three weeks under the care of a medical man without being once bled!

27 December Sent for to Mrs. D'Aranda. Opened an abscess for her in the throat, brought on by her own bad treatment of herself.

A.F.J. Brown, *Essex People, 1750–1900* (1972), pp. 137–45. The original MS diary is at Colchester Central Library, reference E 029.6 (locked cabinet).

NOTES

1. Frances, wife of Thomas, 1st Viscount Weymouth, died 17 April 1712.
2. Bishop of Wells (died 1703), who has a monument in the cathedral's north transept.
3. Presumably Elizabeth, who died in 1728.
4. Lord Conway, Horace Walpole's cousin, bought Sandywell House in about 1712; his son, later Marquess of Hertford, sold it in 1748.
5. Thomas Nettleton MD (1683–1742) practised at York and Halifax; he had qualified at Utrecht.
6. Thomas Dixon MD (1680–1729) of Bolton and later of Whitehaven, had trained at Edinburgh; he was, like Clegg, a practising minister.
7. Ebenezer Latham MD (1688–1754) had earlier been master of an academy at Derby; also a Dissenting minister, he had qualified at Glasgow.
8. John Altree was a surgeon-apothecary at Wolverhampton.
9. Samuel Sharp FRS (1700–78), surgeon at Guy's Hospital.
10. William Smellie MD (1698–1763), surgeon and man-midwife, had moved from Lanark to London in 1739 and began teaching there in 1741.
11. Benjamin Stead MD (b. 1713), apothecary at Guy's Hospital, to whom Dr Samuel Kay sent Richard Kay's tuition fee.
12. This seems to be Joshua Ellington (b. 1722).
13. John Girle FRS (d. 1761), former army surgeon and surgeon at St Thomas's Hospital (1731–49).
14. Stona, from Whittlesea, Cambridgeshire, was Samuel Sharp's dresser.
15. Samuel Kay MD (1708–84), practised in Manchester and was the first physician when the infirmary opened there in 1752. He was Richard Kay's cousin, as their fathers were brothers.
16. Probably James Johns(t)on MD (1730–1802) of Worcester.
17. James Moore, apothecary, formerly Mantell's partner, died on 6 September 1820.
18. Dr Blair was one of the town's two physicians.
19. Thomas Hodson was a Lewes surgeon-apothecary.
20. William Babington MD (1756–1833) was a senior physician in London.
21. William Sharpe, senior, leading surgeon in Bradford until his death in 1833.
22. Jonathon Illingworth (c. 1793–1854) became a surgeon at Bradford Infirmary.
23. John Roberts (d. 1859) was later a consulting surgeon at the infirmary.
24. John Blakey (1784–1831), a Quaker surgeon, was a native of Bradford.
25. John Outhwaite (1792–1868), surgeon to Bradford Infirmary.
26. William Macturk (1795–1872) practised in Bradford from 1824.
27. Thomas Beaumont (1795–1859), a Wesleyan, practised in Bradford from 1822.
28. Thomas March was a surgeon at Rochford.
29. Charles Miller was a surgeon at Wakering.
30. Edmund Fairchild was a surgeon at Beccles.
31. Thomas Smith MD (1764–1848) later practised in Bury.

VII
Hospitals, Lunatic Asylums and Prisons

❖ ❖ ❖

HOSPITALS

Hospitals' records generally have a good rate of survival, although few institutions have every category of source represented. Thus Worcester Infirmary has lists of subscribers, but no patient admission registers, and many hospitals have gaps in such series; however, most infirmaries have surviving copies of their printed rules and their annual reports. As charitable organisations, with boards of governors and trustees, their financial records are often the best preserved of hospital records, while sources about patients are a rarer survival.

PATIENTS' DIETS AT WINCHESTER HOSPITAL, 1737

Winchester was the first provincial infirmary founded, for although London had five well-established hospitals by 1733 (St Bartholomew's, St Thomas's, Westminster, Guy's and St George's) none existed in the rest of England until Winchester was established in 1736. Alured Clarke, a Canon of Winchester Cathedral, was responsible for arousing interest and support for the charitable project. The clergy were later to do the same in other cathedral cities. Winchester Hospital occupied a former abbey when it first opened and then moved to a new building in 1759. Winchester's rules were widely used as a model for other eighteenth-century infirmaries, such as Worcester. At the end of the first year, the Governors noted that one of the reasons for the success of the hospital was the simplicity and regularity of the in-patients' diet, 'which contributes much more to their recovery than their own way of living'. The hospital had four main diets for patients, described as full, low, milk and dry. The diets were

A TABLE of DIET for PATIENTS

FULL DIET.	LOW DIET.
SUNDAY.	**SUNDAY.**
BREAKFAST. A Pint of Broth or Milk-Pottage.	BREAKFAST. A Pint of Water-Gruel or Milk-Pottage.
Dinner. Eight Ounces of boiled Mutton or Veal.	*Dinner.* Two Ounces of roasted Veal with a Pint of Broth.
Supper. A Pint of Broth.	*Supper.* A Pint of Water-Gruel or Milk-Pottage.
MONDAY.	**MONDAY.**
Breakfast. A Pint of Milk-Pottage.	*Breakfast.* A Pint of Water-Gruel or Milk-Pottage.
Dinner. A Pint of Rice-Milk.	*Dinner.* A Pint of Rice-Milk.
Supper. Two Ounces of Cheese or Butter.	*Supper.* A Pint of Water-Gruel or Milk-Pottage.
TUESDAY.	**TUESDAY.**
Breakfast. A Pint of Milk-Pottage.	*Breakfast.* A Pint of Water-Gruel or Milk-Pottage.
Dinner. Eight Ounces of boiled Mutton.	*Dinner.* Two Ounces of boiled Mutton with a Pint of Broth.
Supper. A Pint of Broth.	*Supper.* A Pint of Water-Gruel or Milk-Pottage.
WEDNESDAY.	**WEDNESDAY.**
Breakfast. A Pint of Broth or Milk-Pottage.	*Breakfast.* A Pint of Water-Gruel or Milk-Pottage.
Dinner. Baked Pudding.	*Dinner.* Baked Pudding.
Supper. A Pint of Milk-Pottage.	*Supper.* A Pint of Water-Gruel or Milk Pottage, or two Ounces of Cheese or Butter.
THURSDAY.	**THURSDAY.**
The same as on Sunday.	The same as on Sunday.
FRIDAY.	**FRIDAY.**
Breakfast. A Pint of Milk-Pottage.	*Breakfast.* A Pint of Water-Gruel or Milk-Pottage.
Dinner. A Pint of Barley-Broth.	*Dinner.* A Pint of Barley-Broth.
Supper. Two Ounces of Cheese or Butter.	*Supper.* A Pint of Water-Gruel or Milk-Pottage, or two Ounces of Cheese or Butter.
SATURDAY.	**SATURDAY.**
The same as on Tuesday.	The same as on Tuesday.
The Patients shall have Bread and Beer sufficient without Waste.	Bread sufficient without Waste.
N. B. Three Pound of additional Mutton or Veal, is allowed to every Gallon of Broth.	Small Beer but a Pint a Day. *N. B.* Patients on Low Diet are to be served first.

published in 1737 in *A Collection of Papers relating to the County-Hospital for Sick and Lame, &c. at Winchester.*

Hampshire Record Office, 169M84W/18.

THE FIRST SUBSCRIBERS TO NORTHAMPTON INFIRMARY, 1743

As early as 1731 a surgeon in Northampton, John Rushworth (1669–1736), wrote to his local newspaper, the *Northampton Mercury*, suggesting that the government should establish a hospital in every county centre. This was clearly a revolutionary idea, and Winchester Hospital was to be the first English provincial infirmary in 1736. However, nothing more was heard of the idea until, in 1743, James Stonhouse MD wrote to the press in similar vein, but with the powerful support of the Dissenter, Philip Doddridge DD, who preached a lengthy sermon to encourage subscribers. An inaugural meeting was held at the Red Lion, the rules of Winchester Hospital were adopted and the Northampton Infirmary opened – the second provincial establishment – in temporary premises in March 1744. Two physicians (including Stonhouse) and two surgeons served in an honorary capacity; an apothecary, secretary and matron were appointed. In addition to cash gifts and subscriptions, benefactions in kind were also made, including gifts of cutlery, furniture and kitchen equipment, by local traders.

The list of original subscribers predictably included the grandest aristocracy (the Earls of Northampton and of Halifax, Lady Betty Germain) and gentry (the Cartwrights of Aynho and the Ishams of Lamport), both from within the county and beyond, for many supported charities in the area where their family had historically had a presence even though they no longer lived there. Northampton Hospital has a remarkably long and unbroken association with the county's leading family from James, 5th Earl of Northampton, President in 1743, to the 7th Earl Spencer, who held office until the NHS took over in 1948.

Names	Place	Sums		
		£	s	d
Rt Hon Earl of Northampton	Castle Ashby			
Rt Hon Earl of Halifax	Horton			
Valentine Knightly Esqr	Fawsley	5	5	0
Sir Edward Isham Bart	Lamport	5	5	0
Thoms Cartwright Esqr	Aynho	5	5	0
Wm Cartwright Esqr	Do	5	5	0
Mrs Ward	Do	5	5	0
Miss Cartwright	Do	2	2	0
Miss Eliz Cartwright	Do	2	2	0
Sr Jno Dryden Bart	Cannons Ashby			
Sr Thoms Palmer	Carlton			
Mr Robinson Senr	Cransley	2	2	0
Sr Thoms Samwell Bart	Northampton	2	2	0
Edwd Clark Esqr	Watford	1	1	0

Names	Place	Sums		
		£	s	d
Ben: Allicock Esqr	Loddington			
Thoms Thornton Esqr	Brockhall	2	2	0
Revd Dr Isham	Rector Lincoln College	2	2	0
Revd Mr Allicock	Lamport	1	1	0
Thoms Ward Esqr	Houghton	1	1	0
Thoms Blencowe Esqr	Marston St Lawrence	1	1	0
Jos: Clarke Esqr	Nortoft	1	1	0
Jno Sheppard Esqr	Brockhall	1	1	0
Wm Hanbury Esqr	Kelmarsh	5	5	0
Wm Loveday esqr	Brackley	1	1	0
Wm Brooke Esqr	Great Oakley	1	1	0
Josh Jekyll Esqr	Dallington	5	5	0
Wm Dixey?	Northampton	2	2	0
Mr Jos: Snowdin	Do	1	1	0
Edwd Cave	Owner of Northton Mills	5	5	0
Mr Tho: Yeomans	Northampton	1	1	0
Mr Edwd Binyon	Do	2	2	0
Mr Thos Binyon	Do	1	11	6
N. Castleton Esq		2	2	0
Dr Kimberley[1]	Northampton			
Mr Lucas		1	1	0
Rd Jenins Esqr	Warton by Weedon	1	1	0
Mr Lucas	Northampton	1	1	0
Mr Wm Rose	Do	1	1	0
Revd Dr Doddridge	Do	2	2	0
Mr Jas W . . . foold	Do	2	2	0
Tho: Clendon Esqr	Meers Ashby	5	5	0
Mr Valentine Roberts	Northton	1	1	0
Dr Jas Stonhouse[2] his Attendance (if required) gratis				
Mr Jams Whiting	Harleston	2	2	0
Thos Samwell Esq	Upton	5	5	0
Grey Longueville Esqr	Shildlington	1	1	0
Sam Sheppard Esq	Brady	1	1	0
Jno Hervey Thursby	Abbington	5	5	0
Mr Frans Robinson	Wilby	2	2	0
Revd Mr Herrick	Lodington	1	1	0
Bart Tate Esqr	Delapre	2	2	0
John Lister Esqr	Floor	1	1	0
Dr Stratford[3]		5	5	0
Mr Jos Woolston	Northampton	2	2	0
Charlwood Lawton	Do	1	1	0
Revd Mr Horton	Guilsborough	1	1	0
Mr Edwd Litchfield[4] Surgeon his attendance gratis (if required)				
Mr Jno Murray[5] Surgeon his attendance gratis (if required)				
N. Pierce Esqr	Chap. Brampton	1	1	0
Mr Shipton[6] Surgeon	London			
Sr John Dolbin	Thingdon	5	5	0
Hon Coll. Whitworth		2	2	0
Revd Mr Payne	Horton	1	1	0

Names	Place	Sums		
		£	s	d
Revd Mr Tooly	Kelmarsh	1	1	0
Revd Docr Grey	Hinton	1	1	0
Revd Mr Holmes	Wellingbrow	1	1	0
Lady Betty Germain		5	5	0
Unknown hand by Dr Stonhouse		1	1	0
Mr Wm Hartly Gayton		1	1	0
Countess Halifax		10	10	0
Lady Ann Montague		2	2	0

Northamptonshire Record Office, IL 2826.

EXPENSES IN SETTING UP WORCESTER INFIRMARY, 1745–7

Following the lead of Northampton in 1743, Worcestershire was the second midland county to open an infirmary (in 1746), with Shropshire (1747), Gloucester (1755) and Stafford (1766) following suit soon afterwards. The Bishop of Worcester, Isaac Maddox, took the initiative in October 1745 by renting a house in Silver Street in the city and on 11 January 1746 patients were occupying its twenty-five beds. The governors considered new larger premises by the mid-1750s. In July 1764 a subcommittee was formed to plan a new hospital, which was designed by Anthony Keck and opened in 1766.

1745

		£	s	d
19 Oct	Robinson the Mason for putting Glass on the Wall		5	6
8 Nov	Mr Thos Corbyn for Medicines	11	3	0
	Jno Soule for a Lock		6	6
13 Nov	Saml Robinson for Masons work done in the Apothecarys Shop		19	11
21 Nov	Saml Smith for scales weights Bras pan & Mortar for the Apothecary	1	2	6
21 Nov	for Corks for the Apothecary		4	0
21 Nov	for Bottles for the Apothecary	3	17	0
30 Sep	Mr Stephens for several Standards in ye House	4	13	0
20 Sep	Mr Stephens as agreed for quitting ye House	2	2	0
28 Sep	Mr Garway for printing Advertisements		10	0
29 Aug	Mr Bryan for Advertisements		6	0
11 Oct	Do for inserting an Acct of the orders at ye General meeting		6	0
	the two Nurses & House mayd Earnest		3	0
	Mr Jackson for ye Rules of ye Bristol Infiry		1	0
27 Oct	for a Dresser for the Kitchen		14	0
4 Dec	Mr Salmon for 3 half Hog^d & 2 q^r Barrels	1	15	6
4 Dec	Jno Hill for 2 doz. Chairs	1	10	0
4 Dec	Do for 2 small Sways		1	8
4 Dec	Mrs White for 3w. board wages		12	0
11 Dec	Mr Stephen Bryan for printing 1200 Consid^n and 250 Letters	3	11	0
30 Nov	Ben Hill for cleansing ye Vault of ye N^y House	1	7	0

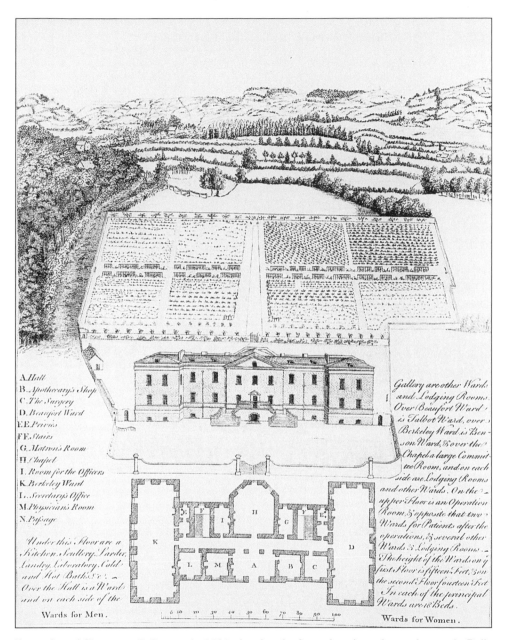

A. Hall
B. Apothecary's Shop
C. The Surgery
D. Beaufort Ward
E.E. Privies
F.F. Stairs
G. Matron's Room
H. Chapel
I. Room for the Officers
K. Berkeley Ward
L. Secretary's Office
M. Physician's Room
N. Passage

Under this Floor are a Kitchen, Scullery, Larder, Laundry, Laboratory, Cold and Hot Baths, &c. Over the Hall is a Ward and on each side of the

Wards for Men.

Gallery are other Wards and Lodging Rooms. Over Beaufort Ward is Talbot Ward, over Berkeley Ward is Benson Ward, & over the Chapel a large Committee Room, and on each side are Lodging Rooms and other Wards. On the upper Floor is an Operation Room, & opposite that two Wards for Patients after the operations, & several other Wards & Lodging Rooms. The height of the Wards on y first Floor is fifteen Feet, & on the second Floor fourteen Feet. In each of the principal Wards are 18 Beds.

Wards for Women.

Engraving of Gloucester Infirmary in 1764, showing the front elevation, plan and grounds. Built in 1755–61 and designed by Luke Singleton, the hospital was demolished in the 1980s.

		£	s	d
11 Dec	Willm Stephens the Mason for Brick and workmanship for building the Wall	8	8	0
12 Dec	Jno Callowhill for Tubs	2	2	0
	for 1 Tun of Coales		9	6
13 Dec	Mr Smith for a Copper Furnis	6	6	0
	Mr Wakeman		5	8
	Mr Hope		3	2½
18 Dec	Mr Sclater for Drugs	15	10	6
	Mr Davis for Furniture for the Apothecarys Shop and for Drugs	10	5	2
	Mr Ald: Garway for Sheeting Cloth	9	8	6

1746

		£	s	d
1 Jan	Mr White for sweeping ye Chimneys 1 Load of Dressg a Hatchet		2	8½
	Mr Taylor for a marble Pestil & Muller		5	0
	Mr Hope for 2 [?lb] of Cinamon		16	6
	Mr Stephens for Brick & Labour in Building the necessary House &c	4	9	0
	Mr Walker for 4 Bushl of Malt		10	0
11 Dec	Mr Hoskyns for a Sauspan Tundish &c for ye Apoʸ		3	10
2 Jan	Mr Smith for a Copper Pot, Ladle, Lanthorn		6	0
9 Jan	Mr Perkins for Spirits for ye Apothecary	1	3	0
11 Jan	Mrs White for Housekeeping	—	—	—
15 Jan	Mr Smith for a Stole pan and Bed pan		13	0
14 Jan	Mr Willoughby for Beesoms Mops Sope &c	1	6	0
13 Jan	Mr Cornwall for Carr. of Drugs		5	0
13 Jan	Mr Thos Corbyn for Medicines	4	7	6
15 Jan	Mr Blayney for Diaper Cloth	1	3	6
15 Jan	Mrs White for Six Weeks board Wages for her Self till the opening of the House	1	4	0
15 Jan	P. Perry for two weeks Do		5	0
16 Jan	Mr Smith for a Saus pan & Mortr for ye Apo:		8	1
	Mr Mountford for Books & Paper for ye Apo:		9	6
20 Jan	Mr Phil Tomlins for Spirits for ye Apo:		17	0
11 Jan	Wm Field for work done in ye Garden		14	9
20 Jan	Ann Dance for Sand	1	10	8
22 Jan	Mr Thos Bourne ye Apo:y for what he laid out for Medicine &c	5	13	0
11 Jan	the Matrons Bill for Houskeeping		9	1½
18 Jan	Do for Do		12	8¾
	Do for Sundry Pans Bowls &c		5	2¾
	for 2 Caps to Mr Russell			10
	Bad peice of Money		2	6
23 Jan	Thos Wythes ye Taylor for making Coates & Gowns for the use of ye Patients		13	3
22 Jan	Mr Saml Smith for a Kettle		8	0
22 Jan	for a peice of Marble for ye Apoʸ		3	6
23 Jan	Mr Wm Sextie for Oil for ye Apoʸ		15	0
29 Jan	Mrs White the Matron for Houskeeping		12	0¾
22 Jan	Jno Read for the use of Scaffold Poles		1	2
29 Jan	Mr Bourne [Apo] for wt he paid for Herbs		1	6½
25 Jan	Mr Hope for Almonds for ye Apoy		1	4
29 Jan	Thos Guest for Knives & Forks		8	0

		£	s	d
30 Jan	Mr Jno Craig for Flanell for Patients Coates		19	3
4 Feb	Jno Hill for two Chairs		2	4
	Mr Meredith for Sugar & Seeds for ye Apo		7	0
	Mrs White ye Matron Houskeeping Bill		12	9½
	Do for Water &c for Washing			6
6 Feb	Ed. Jackson for Lime used in Buildingg ye Wall	2	2	6
4 Feb	Russ. Laugher for Brass & Pewter for the use of the House and the Apothecary	7	14	0
12 Feb	Mr Kidley for 4 Bush. of Malt		10	0
12 Feb	Mrs White the Matron for Houskeeping		12	5
	Do for Combes Sissars &c		1	2½
15 Feb	for a Surgery Dressing Box	1	5	0
12 Feb	Mr Johnson for Cloth Shirts & Towells	2	3	6
19 Feb	Mr Soule for Sundry Utensils for the House and the Apothecary's Shop	3	9	0
	Mr Herbert for Brick		17	0
	Mrs White the Matron for Houskeeping		15	9
	Do for Basket & platters &c		1	5
18 Feb	Mr Brodribb for Cloth for Pats Coates	1	4	0
20 Feb	Mr Saml Andrews for Books, Quills & Ink		7	10
18 Feb	Mr Wm Freme for Locks nails &c	3	16	10½
21 Feb	Mr Saunders for Coales & Car'd	2	11	8
22 Feb	for Glasses for the Surgeons Box	1	7	0
24 Feb	Mr Lane for Trenchers Bowls & Pails	1	0	6
26 Feb	Mr Yarnold for glazeing Work & a led Pipe for ye Bath		11	0
26 Feb	Mrs White ye Matron for Houskeeping		15	4¼
26 Feb	Mr Bourn for Sundry Medicines		7	5½
3 Mar	Mr Jas Turner for wine for ye Apot		8	0
	Mrs Baylis for Sundry Medicines		13	0
5 Mar	Jno Hill for 12 Chairs		12	0
	Mrs White the Matron for Houskeeping		16	7¼
	Do for a Basket & a pan		4	2
10 Mar	Thos Guest for Surgeons Instruments		6	0
6 Mar	Mrs White ye Matron for Houskeeping		11	10½
13 Mar	Do for Do	1	2	10½
22 Mar	P. Robinson ye Mason for Ceiling ye Brewhouse		13	0
25 Mar	Thos Oliver for paper Books printing &c	1	6	6
20 Mar	Mrs White ye Matron Houskeeping		14	11½
27 Mar	Do Do		15	2½
2 Apr	Mr Bourn ye Apothecry for Medicines		15	8½
4 Apr	J King Secretary half a Years Salary due at Lady Day last	5	5	0
9 Apr	Mr Stephens for 4 Bushels Malt		10	8
	Mr Bourn ye Apoʸ for Herbs &c		16	11
	Mrs White ye Matron for Houskeeping	1	2	10½
16 Apr	Mr Fra Brook half a Years Rent for the House due at Lady Day last	5	5	0
	Mrs White ye Matron for Houskeeping	1	1	10
23 Apr	Mrs White ye Matron for Houskeeping	1	7	9
	Do for Flanell		4	2
	Mr Bourn for Sundry Medicines	2	3	10
25 Apr	Mr Tim: Edwards for sundrys for ye Apoʸ		16	9
30 Apr	Mrs White ye Matron for Houskeeping	1	1	9
	Mr Bourn the Apothecary for Sundrys		19	10

		£	s	d
29 Apr	Mr Stephen Bryan for printing Advertisements	1	1	6
5 May	Mr Bird for a Press for ye Apoth^y	2	5	6
7 May	Mrs White ye Matron for Houskeeping	1	2	9¾
14 May	Mrs White ye Matron for Houskeeping	1	7	9
	The Secretary for paper Books Ink &c		12	1
	Mr Sargent for Candles Earthen Ware &c		5	9
	Mr Bourn ye Apothecary for Herbs &c		9	8½
21 May	Mrs White ye Matron for Houskeeping	1	1	6½
	Mr Saunders's Bill		10	3
	Mr Cornwell for Carriage		5	0
2 May	Mr Ald. Martin for Honey &c		18	4
27 May	Millington ye Glazier		14	10
28 May	Mr Spilsbury for Candes Pots &c		1	0
	Mrs White ye Matron	1	7	10¼
4 June	Mrs White the Matron Houskeeping	1	4	7
	Dickens ye Carpenter for a Sweating Machine		15	4
28 May	Mr Bourn ye Apothecary for Sundry Medicines		13	2½
11 June	Mrs White ye Matron for Houskeeping	1	8	11¼
12 June	Mr Robt Taylor ye Upholsterer for 5 Beds	20	0	0
4 June	Mr Tho Dickens for Grocery	1	2	11
7 June	Mr Wm Ward for 5 Beds	20	0	0
30 May	John Saunders for Coales and Carriage	2	13	11

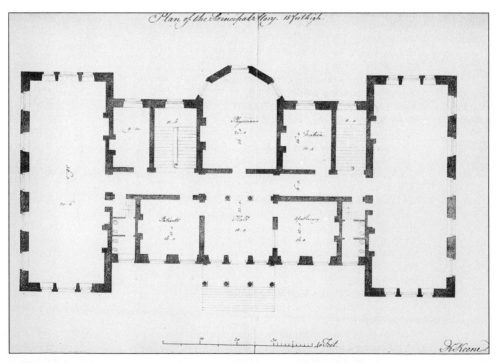

'A Plan of the Principal Storey' of Worcester Infirmary by Henry Keene.

Date	Description	£	s	d
14 June	Mr Bolus for 5 Beds for ye Sick & One for Servants	26	11	0
18 June	Mrs White ye Matron for Houskeeping	1	0	4
29 May	Mr Tim Edwards for Rozin		1	2
23 May	Saml Corbyn on Acc. of Clutton & Co. for Medicines	5	12	0
23 June	J. Vernon on Acc. of Sclaters for Drugs	18	3	0
	the Secretary for Paper &c		11	7
	Mr Smith the Tinman for Sundrys	1	10	8
10 June	Mr Ben. Perkins for Spirits		10	0
24 June	Mr J. Soul for Furniture for ye Surgeons Box		10	6
12 July	Mr Phil Tomlins for Spirits	2	8	0
25 July	Thos Bourn ye Apo^y for Medicines	1	7	6
28 July	Mrs White ye Matron for Houskeeping	1	3	8
25 July	Mr Saml Yardley for Malt		10	8
1 July	Jno Saunders for Coales & Carr^d		19	8
2 July	Mrs White ye Matron for Houskeeping		16	10½
5 July	Mr Brook for Malt		10	8
	Mr J. Corbyn for Do		10	8
7 July	Mr Hen. Hope for Sugar for ye Apo^y		5	0
	Gaskell for Car^d of Drugs		5	8
24 June	Sargeant for Honey		2	9
	Mr Wm Harris Oil for ye Apothecary		9	6
9 July	Mrs White ye Matron for Houskeeping	1	3	11¾
	Mr Bourn ye Apothy for Medicines	1	0	10½
12 Aug	Mr Willoughby for Soap		14	6
16 July	Patience Perry ye Servant half a Years Wages due at Midsummer last	1	10	0
16 July	Nurse Goslin half a Years Wages due at Midsummer last	1	15	0
16 July	Nurse Whetstone Do	1	15	0
	16 July Mrs White ye Matron Houskeeping		10	10¼
	Mrs White ye Matron half a Years Wages due the 5 May last	3	0	0
	Mrs White ye Matron it being Cash deposited to carry on ye Expense of Houskeeping	2	2	0
23 July	Mr Taylor for Malt		10	8
	Mrs White ye Matron Houskeeping	1	1	6
	Mr Bourn ye Apothecary for Medicines		6	3½
	Mr Bourn ye Apothecary for Do		3	9
30 July	Mrs White ye Matron Houskeeping		19	1
1 Aug	Mr Sclater for Drugs	4	3	6
2 Aug	Mr Clutton for Do	1	10	0
1 Aug	Mr Bickerton for Hops		4	10
6 Aug	Mrs White ye Matron Houskeeping	1	4	5¾
13 Aug	Mrs White ye Matron Houskeeping	1	6	1
19 Aug	Mr Ald. Martin for Honey		4	2
20 Aug	Mr Thos Nanfan for Malt		10	8
	Mrs White ye Matron	1	2	7
	Mr Bourn ye Apothecary for Medicines		12	1
27 Aug	Mrs White ye Matron Houskeeping	1	0	2½
	Martha Head for Coales		18	0
13 Sep	Matron Bill for Houskeeping Aug 28		17	11½
	Do Do Do Sep 3	1	8	10½
11 Sep	Mr Bolus for Pillows		3	9
13 Sep	Mr Bourn ye Apothecary		19	7½
17 Sep	Mrs White ye Matron Houskeeping	1	4	2

Date	Description	£	s	d
13 Sep	Mr Sextie for Oil	1	5	0
20 Sep	Mrs White ye Matron Houskeeping	1	5	6
21 Sep	Saml Corbyn for Dimety for Pillows		7	3
18 Sep	Head for 6 tuns of Coales	2	13	6
1 Oct	Mrs White ye Matron	1	2	2
	Mr Bourn ye Apothecary Medicines		19	4½
2 Oct	Thos Corbyn for Medicines	1	16	0
15 Oct	Mrs White ye Matron Houskeeping	1	2	11
	Do Do for Octr 8	1	7	4½
22 Oct	Do Do for Oct		16	0½
22 Oct	Mr Bourn for Medicines		17	7½
	Cornwall for Car.		2	0
29 Oct	John King Secretary half a Years Salary due at Michaelmas last	5	5	0
1 Nov	More the Ironmonger for Sundrys	3	11	4
	Mrs White ye Matron for Houskeeping	1	4	9½
7 Nov	Saunders for Coales & Carr^d		6	8
6 Nov	Matron bill for Houskeeping	1	10	9½
8 Nov	for a Crate of Bottles	1	7	0
13 Nov	the Matron Houskeeping	1	4	6½
	the Apothecary for Medicines		19	4
	Mr Sargeant for Honey		5	0
19 Nov	Jos. Yarnold for Plumming		12	0
	Matron Houskeeping	1	10	9
	Robinson ye Mason	1	7	0
	Mr Farley for Lime		12	0
27 Nov	Mr Jn Soult	1	10	8
	Matron Houskeeping	1	6	9½
3 Dec	Matron Houskeeping	1	14	2
	T. Olivers for printing	6	19	10
	T. Cornwall for Carr^d		15	6
	Mr Bourn ye Apo. for Sundry		17	7½
16 Nov	Mr Bourn the Apothecary one Years Sallary due at Michaelmas last	15	0	0
1 Dec	for Coales	2	0	6
	W. Dickens ye Carpenter		10	11
10 Dec	J. Meredith for Sugar &c		11	8
	The Matron	1	10	9
	for Tow		6	0
	for Candles to Mr Bate		9	0
	Jno Hill for Chairs		6	8
17 Dec	Jno Holdship for Malt		10	8
	The Matron Bill for Houskeeping	1	12	0
	Mr Brooke half a Years Rent for the House due at Michs last	5	5	0
24 Dec	the Matron Houskeeping	1	12	9
27 Dec	Nurse Gosling half a Years Wages due at Christmas last	1	15	0
	pd her a gratuity for good behaviour		5	0
	Nurse Whetstone for half a Years Wages due at Christmas last	1	15	0
	pd her a gratuity for good behaviour		5	0
	Patience Perry for half a Years Wages due at Christmas last	1	10	0
	pd her a gratuity for good behaviour		5	0
	Mrs White ye Matron for half a Years Wages due the 5 of November last	3	0	0
	pd her a gratuity		10	0

1747

		£	s	d
1 Jan	Secretarys Expenses to Upton 2 days		5	0
	Horse hire Do		3	0
	Matron for Houskeeping	1	6	10
3 Jan	Apothecary a gratuity	1	1	0
7 Jan	Richd Squire for a Jack weight		2	0
	Matron for Houskeeping	1	5	4
9 Jan	Secretarys Expenses to Evesham & Pershore		6	8
14 Jan	Mr Russ. Laugher for Sundrys	2	2	0
	Mrs White ye Matron for Houskeeping	1	8	8
	Mr Bourn ye Apothecary for Medicines		15	11
15 Jan	Mr Smith for Charcoal		2	6
16 Jan	Secretarys Expenses for Wyck		2	8
15 Jan	Mr Smiths Exrs for Lamps		9	0
21 Jan	Matron for Houskeeping	1	2	7½
	Secretarys Expenses to Bewdley & Kid		6	7
29 Jan	Tho: Corbyn for Medicines	1	6	6
24 Jan	Expenses to Bromsgrove		4	10
	Shinton for Horse hire 7 days		10	6
28 Jan	Ald. Garway for Sheeting	5	18	6
	Matrons bill for Houskeeping	1	13	1½
	Mr Bourn ye Apo. for Medicines	1	17	3
29 Jan	Mr Tomlins for Spirits	2	12	0
5 Feb	Expenses to Stourbridge		7	10
6 Feb	Horse hire to Do		4	0
	Mrs White ye Matron Houskeeping	1	8	10¾
11 Feb	Mrs White ye Matron Houskeeping	1	8	9
12 Feb	Mr Andrews for quills			6
16 Feb	Wm Dickens for an Ambe		11	0
18 Feb	Mr Brook for Malt		10	0
	Matron for Houskeeping	1	15	5½
	J. Kings ye Secretary for Paper &c		6	4
21 Feb	Mr Smith ye Chandler for Candles & Ink pot			8½
25 Feb	Mr Dickenson for Sugar &c		12	8
	Matron Bill for Houskeeping	2	5	6½
	Mr Laugher for Wax		7	0
	Mr Bird for 2 Close Stools		15	6
5 Mar	Matron for Houskeeping	1	6	2
4 Mar	Mr Tomlin for Spirits	1	16	0
	Head for Coales Jan 26	2	18	6
	Birds Bill ye Carpenter Dec 23	18	1	0
11 Mar	Mary Seighton for Coales	1	5	6
	Matron Houskeeping	1	11	9½
13 Mar	Millington ye glazier		8	8
14 Mar	Jos: Higgins for Malt		10	0
18 Mar	Mrs White ye Matron Houskeeping	2	0	8
23 Mar	Russell Laugher tin Filings		12	5
25 Mar	Matron Houskeeping	2	11	10½
	Hall ye glazier		15	0
	Mr Edwards for Clyster Pipes		2	0
28 Mar	T. Edwards for grocery	1	1	11
	Mr. Mountfort for Bibles		15	0
4 Apr	Mr Bolus for Beds	21	0	0

		£	s	d
	Mr Ward for Do	10	15	6
	Mr Taylor for Do	10	15	6
	W. Dickens the Carpenter	5	16	6
	Davis the Mason	3	6	6
	Saml Corbyn for Drugs	4	8	6
	Do for John Corbyn for Malt		10	0
	Mr Lucas for Soap	1	5	0
	Mr Mayer for Rent	5	5	0
6 Apr	Ald Martin for Sundrys	1	0	0
	Mr Smith for Clos Stooll Pans		12	0
	Mr Perkins for Spirits	2	9	0
	Mr Soule Ironmonger for Sundrys	1	18	10
2 Apr	Wm Freme Ironmonger Sundrys	1	16	8
18 Apr	Gattrell for Carr of Goods		10	6
31 Apr	J. Holdship for Malt		10	0
20 Apr	Secretary half a Years Sallary at Lady Day	5	5	0
9 Apr	Apothecary Do	7	10	0
15 Apr	Sclater for Drugs	24	16	0
9 Apr	Tho: Bourn Apothecary for Sundrys	2	1	5
	Hope ye grocer	1	3	0
	Carried to the Treasurers Aud	612	17	8¾

Worcestershire Record Office, BA 5161/12.

Cures performed at Worcester Infirmary, 1754

An important aspect of encouraging subscriptions to a county infirmary was to advertise the wide range and number of cures achieved, and hospital annual reports, as at Worcester in 1754, invariably did so. A shorter list would also be published in the local newspaper, usually as part of an item on the infirmary's annual meeting.

Abscesses	15	Cough, and difficulty of Breathing	4
Albugo and Inflammation of the eyes	18	Deafness and Sopor from a Cold	1
Anasarca	1	Diarrhaea	4
Ascites	4	Dysentery	1
Asthma	4	Dysury	3
Atrophy	1	Epilepsy	2
Blood spitting	1	Eruptions scorbutic	4
Bones carious	2	Erysipelas	2
Burn in the arm	1	Fever eruptive	1
Catarrh	2	— hectic	2
Chin cough	2	— intermitting	5
Chlorosis and Inflammation of the Eye	1	— nervous, with extreme Lowness and Stupidity	1
Cholick flatulent, with a large Discharge of Blood by Vomiting and Stools	1	— with Pains in the Head and Stomach	1
Compression of the Windpipe from swell'd Glands	1	— petechial	1
		— pleuritic	1
Contusions and violent Sprains	20	Fluor Albus	1

William Russell, 1719–1801,
honorary surgeon at Worcester
Infirmary, of which he holds an
illustration. Unattributed.

Fractures	14	— in the Stomach and Bowels	18
Gout irregular	2	Piles	2
Gutta serena	2	Pthisis	1
Head-ach	2	Rheumatism	15
Heels sore, and oedematous Legs	2	Rickets	1
Hernia Scroti	1	Rupture in the Cornea	2
Hysteric Passion	3	— of the Eye, by a Fall	1
Jaundice	1	Rupture, inguineal	1
Incontinence of urine	2	Scalds	2
Indigestion	5	Sciatica	4
Itch	4	Shingles	1
— inveterate	1	Spasms, with difficult Circulation	1
Leprosy	6	Stone in the Bladder cut and cured	2
Lues	1	— and Gravel, and Costiveness	1
Mortification	3	Swelling, inflammatory	1
Obstructions	2	Tendons of the Hand thicken'd by a Blow	1
Ophthalmy scrofulous	3	Tremor, paralytic, of the Head, from	
Pain and weakness in the ankle and wrists	1	a suppress'd Eruption	1
— in the right Breast	2	Tumours	3
— in the Eyes, and Dimness	1	— scrophulous	3
— in the Head, and Syncope on Motion	1	Vertigo	1

Ulcers, fistulous	1	Worms	9
— putrid and scrofulous	25	Wounds	5
— in the throat	1		
Weakness in the Knee	1		
		Total Number of CURES	272

Worcestershire Record Office, BA 1558/19(111) Ref: 899:93.

THE HOSPITAL APOTHECARY'S DUTIES, 1779

When Birmingham Hospital opened in 1779, the trustees issued *The Statutes and Rules for the Government of The General Hospital, near Birmingham*, a 32-page pamphlet setting out subscribers' rights, patients' responsibilities and the duties of both honorary and paid staff. Such rules were generally copied from those followed at Winchester Hospital. Perhaps because of the duties or salary, hospital apothecaries did not usually remain very long in post and there were, for example, five men appointed at Birmingham in the hospital's first twenty years. The post was widely considered a first step in a medical career and helpful in establishing a practice.

APOTHECARY

I. That he shall not practice as an Apothecary out of the Hospital, nor dispense any medicines without the directions of the physicians or surgeons, except in cases of necessity, when they cannot be consulted.

II. That he shall fix a ticket on the bed of each patient, specifying the name of the patient, as also that of the physician or surgeon under whose care the patient may be, and the date of the Admission.

III. That he shall make a report of such patients as have been in the hospital two months, to the Committee, and deliver a list of such as have been received into the hospital during the foregoing week, and likewise an account of the number of beds that shall become vacant before the next day of taking in patients.

IV. That he shall not suffer the physician's books, or the pharmacopoeia to be inspected by any one, without leave from the physicians and surgeons.

V. That he prepare such chymical and galenical medicines as the physicians and surgeons shall direct, at the elaboratory; and that no borrowing or lending of Drugs, be permitted on any pretence whatsoever.

VI. That he give a list of the diet ordered for the patients to the matron each prescribing day.

VII. That he shall visit the wards every morning before the time of the physicians and surgeons, and be prepared to make a report of the state of any particular patients.

VIII. That he shall not be absent from the hospital without leaving a note with the matron where he may be found; that he and the matron never leave the hospital at the same time, and that neither of them be absent after eleven o'clock at night.

IX. That when any affairs of his own, require a long absence, he shall signify the same to the Committee, or weekly Board, and nominate another Apothecary to officiate in his stead, who shall be approved of by the physicians and surgeons.

X. That his salary shall be thirty pounds per ann. and ten pounds as a gratuity, provided he stays longer than twelve months, and his conduct has been approved of by the physicians and surgeons, as well as by the weekly and general Board; that he shall have his diet, washing and lodging at the hospital, together with the liberty of taking a pupil or apprentice, who shall not board in the hospital, unless approved of by the Governors, and a reasonable allowance be paid for his board.

XI. That he shall not buy any drugs or medicines without the order of the physicians or surgeons, unless when any particular drug be wanting, for which he shall bring in his account to the board in the course of every week.

Warwickshire County Record Office, CR 764/269.

PATIENTS ADMITTED TO BIRMINGHAM GENERAL HOSPITAL, JULY 1780

Of the ten midland counties, only Nottinghamshire was later than Warwickshire in establishing a county infirmary in the eighteenth century and its very geographical position must have contributed to the tardiness of Birmingham General Hospital's foundation. For Warwickshire's sick poor there was a choice of hospitals established in neighbouring counties in the 1740s (Northampton, Worcester, Shropshire), the 1750s (Gloucester) and 1760s (Stafford), as well as Oxford (1770) and Leicester (1771) within travelling distance. Treatment could be provided at any of these and a number of Warwickshire parishes subscribed to them.

At this time Warwickshire was unique among English counties in not having its infirmary in the county town but in the industrial capital, Birmingham. It is also unusual that the hospital did not come into existence because of clerical initiatives, as institutions did in many other counties, especially those in centres which were

Engraving of Birmingham Hospital, showing the new wing extensions, c. 1806.

also cathedral cities with substantial clerical communities. Plans for a hospital in Birmingham were announced in the local *Aris's Gazette* in November 1765, when John Ash MD, the town's most senior physician, called a public meeting; subscriptions were collected and construction by B. and W. Wyatt began on a seven-acre site. Local industrialists, such as Matthew Boulton and Samuel Galton, were early supporters. However, the trustees were obliged to stop building when they ran short of money and work could not continue until the scheme was funded by a music festival begun in 1778. The hospital opened with forty beds in October 1779. The town's population was then about 35,000.

The admission registers recorded a patient's home, medical condition, whether he or she was receiving in- or out-treatment and the name of the subscriber who had the right to recommend the patient. It is clear that the honorary physicians and surgeons undertook turns of duty and the admission registers noted by whom a patient was attended. The hospital's annual reports show its progress in terms of increasing numbers cured or relieved and money raised. Subscribers came from far beyond the county and some substantial bequests were made to the infirmary.

Patient	In	Out	Subscriber	Patient's home	Condition	Date out	Cured etc*
1 July 1780							
Thos Nash	228		W & W Walker	Darlaston	sore leg	22 July	C
Sarah Rogers	229		W. Dickenson	Bethlems End	sore legs	22 July	C
Sarah Freeth	230		Edw Thomason	B[irmingham]	sore leg	18 Sept	C
Wm Whitehead		305	Jos Glover	B	hare lip	8 Sept	OP
Phebe Forres		306	Wm Hunt	B	consumption	–	IP
. . . Horton (male)		307	Th Check Lea	B	–	2 Aug	C
Elizabeth Hands		308	Jas Sloane	B	fever	22 July	C
Thos Bagot		309	Rachel Barclay	B	nervous	26 Aug	C
Ann Mayo		310	Jos Glover	B	consumption	9 Sept	R
Eliz Tomlinson		311	Geo Turville	Tardebigg	scrophulous	8 Aug	R
Catherine Poole		312	J.S. Warren	B	consumption	26 Aug	R
Wm Taylor		313	Wm Humphreys	B	weakness	22 July	C
Mary Mills		314	T. Tomlinson	B	nervous	22 July	C
5 July							
Thos Crouch	231		G. Boone	–	bruised	22 July	C
Edw Deakin	232		M. Boulton Esq	Handsworth	contused leg	15 July	C
Thos Duncuff	233		Accident	B	burned foot	16 Sept	C
7 July							
Isaac Deeming	234		Accident	B	fractured thigh; amputated	16 Sept	C
8 July							
John Tomson	235		Mary Harris	B	inflamed eye	9 Sept	OP
Edw Bradeley	236		S. Galton & Son	Wednesbury	VD	25 July	D
Elizabeth Slater	237		J. & G. Bissett	Walsall	dis foot	22 July	C
Sarah Withers	238		Stephen Seager	B	sore leg	2 Sept	C
Martha Norgrove	239		Wm Russell Esq	Bromyard	pain in stomach	29 July	C
Samuel Penn		315	Charles Birch	B	pain in belly	–	R
Joanne Tucker		316	Charles Birch	B	pain in stomach	–	C
Joseph Edwards		317	Wm Bromley	B	cough	–	C

Patient	In	Out	Subscriber	Patient's home	Condition	Date out	Cured etc*
Elizabeth Clark		318	Ann Gold	B	sore throat	–	C
Thomas Newbold		319	T. Carless	B	VD	–	C
John Coley		320	Jos Webster	Sutton Coldfield	diarrhoea	–	C
Elizabeth Mansell		321	Robert Ward	B	pain in stomach	–	C
Mary Parker		322	S. Galton & Son	Aston	rheumatism	–	C
William Howes		323	John Allen	B	weak eyes	–	C
Mary Cottrell		324	John Lee	Handsworth	weakness	–	C
Elizabeth Thomas		325	S. Galton	B	pain in side	–	C
Diana Piper		326	Joseph Glover	B	cough	–	C
Sarah Jackson		327	Michael Lakin	B	sore eyes	–	C
13 July							
Wm Thomas	240		Wm Humphreys	B	contused neck	28 Oct	C
15 July							
Edw Bidford	241		Michael Lakin	B	sore leg	2 Sept	C
John Milward	242		William Smith	Beoley	dislocated elbow	2 Sept	OP
Mary Eades		328	Abel Humphreys	B	inflamed leg	12 Aug	IP
Richard Hughes		329	William Harvey	B	rheumatism	–	R
Elizabeth Fidoe		330	Henry Clay	B	asthma	–	R
James Male		331	Thos Bennett	Willenhall	rheumatism	–	C
John Timmins		332	William Hinton,DD	B	worms	23 Sept	C
Benj Richards		333	Thomas Wilson	B	consumption	–	R
William Hassall		334	William Hunt	Broughton	consumption	–	R
Edward Robbins		335	Joseph Oakley	B	nervous	–	R
Stephen Billingham		336	John Richards	B	nervous	–	R
James Dalton		337	Sampson Lloyd	B	nervous	–	R
Ann Flavel		338	John Taylor	B	consumption	–	R
Joanna Owen		339	Francis Goodall	B	scrophulous	–	C
Abigail Jones		340	Thomas Gill	B	fever	9 Sept	C
17 July							
Corpl Arthers	243		John Ash MD	–	VD	–	C
John (?) Mey		341	John Ryland	B	fractured arm	–	C
James Adie		342	Samuel Malkin	B	contused neck	6 Jan 81	C
22 July							
Thomas Star	244		Benjamin Blythe	B	swollen testicle	9 Sept	C
Thomas Medlam	245		Wm Handasyd	B	distended? testicle	26 Aug	C
Joyce Hughes	246		William Holden	B	sore leg	–	C
John Fenton		343	F. Parrott	Knowle	mouth cancer	–	C
James Barker		344	Mary Harris	B	–	–	R
Sarah Ratcliff		345	M. Lakin	B	–	–	C
Wm Scattergood		346	Richard Gibbs	Aston	dislocated finger	–	C
George Armitage		347	William Mobbs	B	–	4 Sept	IP
24 July							
Arthur Harris		348	Accident	B	contusions	–	C
John Ridgeway		349	Henry Perkins	B	–	–	C
28 July							
George Smith	247		Accident	B	fractured leg	9 Sept	C

Patient	In	Out	Subscriber	Patient's home	Condition	Date out	Cured etc*
29 July							
Mary Bird	248		John Wright	Oldswinford	ulcerated leg	12 Aug	C
Ellen Lightwood	249		John Wright	Oldswinford	VD	12 Aug	IP
Elizabeth Hall	250		Edw Horneby	W Bromwich	sore leg	23 Sept	C
Joseph Hopkins	251		Samuel Galton	Darlaston	sore leg	16 Sept	C
Sarah Wharton	252		Samuel Pemberton	S. Julians	pain in stomach	12 Aug	C
Elizabeth Briggs		350	Charles Lloyd	Oldbury	consumption	–	D
Charles Truss		351	John Francis	Elmbridge	–	–	C
Samuel Dean		352	Joseph Green	B	rheumatism	–	R
Thomas Harborne		353	William Fletcher	B	consumption	–	C
John Abnett		354	Nag's head Society	B	sore throat	–	C
Martha Lindon		355	Thomas Longman	B	–	–	C
Mary Corder		356	Daniel Ruston	B	consumption	–	R
Lydia Field		357	Edward Horne Esq	Halesowen	ulcerated breast	–	R

* C = cured; R = relieved; IP = became in-patient; OP = became out-patient; D = dead

Honorary medical staff attending patients admitted in July 1780:
William Withering MD throughout the whole month
Surgeons: Jeremiah Vaux 1–7 and 29–31 July   Thomas Tomlinson, jnr 8–13 July
George Kennedy 15–17 July   John Freer, jnr 17–29 July

Birmingham City Archives, HC/GH.

THE ACCOUNTS OF THE RADCLIFFE INFIRMARY, OXFORD, 1796

When John Radcliffe MD (1652–1714), a wealthy man and formerly physician to Queen Anne, died, he bequeathed funds to found the infirmary in Oxford, named after him, as well as the city's library, camera and observatory. The original endowment for the infirmary was £6,000 and it was built during the years 1759–67, with Stiff Leadbetter as its architect. It opened in 1770 and in 1778 admitted 551 in-patients and 284 out-patients. As the accounts for 1796 show, income was derived from investments (Old South Seas Stock and canal shares) and bequests (Dr Frewin's and Mr Blandy's), as well as from subscriptions and from Dr Radcliffe's trustees.

THE RECEIVER GENERAL, DEBTOR

	£	s	d
To Balance of the last Year's Account	407	2	3
By Dr. Radcliffe's Trustees	500	0	0
Subscriptions received for the present year, viz. 1796	1040	11	0
Arrears received	26	5	0
The Hon. Thomas Parker's Subscription	31	10	0
John Langston's Esq; Sarsdon, Ditto	31	10	0
Mr Blandy's Legacy,[7] in Part	500	0	0
Half a Year's Interest on £500 from the Oxford Canal Loan, a Benefaction given by Thomas Walker, Esq.	12	10	0
Collection at St. Mary's Church	91	12	0

	£	s	d
A Fine given by the Vice-Chancellor		5	0
A Benefit given by Mr. Jones	18	16	6
Half a Year's Dividend on £5775 O.S.S.A. to April 5	86	12	6
Ditto on £7275 Ditto, to October 5	109	2	6
One Year's Interest on £1550 from the Commissioners of the Paving Act	67	10	0
Ditto on £450 from the Oxford Canal Company	23	0	0
Ditto from the Court of Chancery, Dr. Frewin's[8] Benefaction	79	17	6
Cash from the Boxes		14	6
Sundries sold	9	16	6
A Soldier's Subsistence	2	12	0
One Year's Rent from Mr Brown		2	6
Receipts	3040	10	0
Expenses	2770	16	10
Balance due to the succeeding Receiver-General	£269	13	2

E CONTRA CREDITOR
By Disbursements, viz.

	£	s	d
For Bread and Flour	348	8	2
Butchers' Meat, 11,655 lb.	265	10	9
Malt, 244 Bushels	76	19	0
Hops, 100 lb.	7	8	2
Groceries	29	8	11
Candles, 258 lb. (remained in the House 35 lb.) remains in the House 16 lb.	10	4	3
Soap, 400 lb. (remained in the House 1cwt,1qr. 16 lb.) remains in the House 2qr. 10 lb.	15	7	11
Cheese, 27 cwt. (remained in the House 6 cwt. 3 qrs.) remains in the House 9 cwt.1 qr. 24 lb.	67	19	0
Butter, 442 lb.	21	13	4
Milk, 928 Gallons, 3 Quarts	30	17	0
Oatmeal, 14 Bushels	7	0	0
Canal Coals, 51 ton 2 cwt. 1 qr.	68	5	0
Faggots	7	4	0
	956	6	1

	£	s	d
By Salaries, Wages, and Gratuities	226	11	0
Medicines for the Apothecary and Surgeons	324	17	8
Extra Servants' Wages	11	7	6
Extra Nursing	23	5	0
Printing	12	13	0
Stationary		16	6
Casualties (*in which are included all Incidents not reducible in the above Heads*)	22	19	8
	622	10	10

	£	s	d
By Extra Expenses, viz.			
Several Tradesmen's Bills for Repairs	69	19	0
Mr. Wood for a Year's Water	10	0	0

	£	s	d
For twenty Pair of Patients' Sheets	12	1	4
Wine for the Patients	44	5	8
Looking after the Clock	1	2	6
Constables attending at St. Mary's Church		9	0
Assistants at brewing	2	8	0
Gardener	5	0	0
The Secretary's Bill of Expenses	1	4	5
	146	9	11
	1725	6	10
Dr. Frewin's Benefaction to the Physicians	79	17	6
	1805	4	4
Purchase of £300 Stock in the Old South Seas Annuities, April 6	203	12	6
Ditto of 1200 Ditto, June 23	762	0	0
Expenses £2770		16	10

Warwickshire County Record Office, CR 764/270.

A LETTER APPEALING FOR SUBSCRIPTIONS TO DERBY GENERAL HOSPITAL, 1810

Derby, the last midland county infirmary to open in 1810, had a distinguished board of twenty-four governors, initially chaired by William Mundy, a leading Derbyshire landowner. As funds were needed at its opening, in June a circular letter was devised that was sent to potential subscribers by the hospital secretary:

Sir,
The General Infirmary near Derby is now open for the reception of patients and much of the benefit to be derived from it must necessarily depend upon the degree of support it may receive from future donations and general subscriptions.
The Board of Governors have therefore thought it a duty which they owed to humanity to desire a direct appeal to be made to the benevolent feelings of those who, from their character and station in life, may be thought likely to contribute in any degree to the charitable objects of the institution – among the persons of this description whose names have suggested themselves to the Board, yours, Sir, naturally occurred and the Governors hope with confidence that the nature of this application will prove with you a sufficient apology for the liberty they have taken in directing me to make it.

Derbyshire Record Office, D1190.

LUNATIC ASYLUMS

In Moorfields, London, the notorious Bedlam had existed since the thirteenth century as a general institution for the sick, only later becoming an asylum for mental patients. It was unique in the eighteenth century, when provisions for lunatics were private arrangements, invariably involving physical restraint. Visiting Bedlam and paying to see the 200 inmates was a genteel entertainment, as shown in the final scene of Hogarth's *Rake's Progress* of 1735. When Richard Kay was a medical student in London in 1743 he described his excursion there and paying visitors provided a steady income for the asylum until 1770.

However, at Norwich in the early years of the century the generosity of a clergy widow, Mrs Mary Chapman, made possible the first 'public Bethel' in the provinces. It was endowed and opened in 1713 in compassion for 'distrest lunaticks', although not for 'such as are fools or idiots from their birth'. She died in 1724 aged seventy-seven and in her will left instructions for a governing body to be created so that the hospital might continue. Mary Chapman's estate was valued at £3,513 11s 4d, which was invested by the trustees for income and the Bethel also accepted gifts and bequests. In 1700 as England's second city Norwich had a population of nearly 30,000. Its general voluntary hospital was not to open until 1772. The majority of the Bethel's patients were female. Initially there were between twenty and thirty inmates but by 1783 it had fifty beds and there were two salaried physicians in attendance, one of whom, John Beever, MD, also ran a private asylum in the city. The Norfolk county asylum at Thorpe St Andrew was not built until 1811–14.

Apart from the Norwich Bethel, provincial public institutions for the insane were not to be founded until well into the eighteenth century (Newcastle upon Tyne in 1765, Manchester in 1766, York in 1777, Hereford in 1799), and all other asylums were privately run by either medical practitioners (Thomas Willis at Grantham, Thomas Arnold at Leicester) or by laymen as a business venture (Thomas Bakewell at Spring Vale, Staffordshire, the Harris family at Hook Norton, Oxfordshire). After an Act of 1714 pauper lunatics could be confined at parish expense, in workhouses, if they were 'furiously mad and dangerous'. The very wealthy could use the Mrs Rochester solution, providing private incarceration in the lunatic's own home, with constant attendance.

FOUNDING A LUNATIC ASYLUM AT HEREFORD, 1799

The General Hospital at Hereford was opened in 1776 and was one of the later county infirmaries to be established. In 1799 the hospital governors decided to set up a lunatic asylum near to the General Hospital, on the banks of the River Wye. Subscribers' names predictably indicate wide support from the county's leaders (the Bishop of Hereford, Viscount Bateman, the Earl of Oxford) and gentry. However, there were also a number of professional men who subscribed, including clergy, attorneys and medical practitioners, the most affluent of whom was undoubtedly John Matthews MD, who had married an heiress, gained a great estate at Belmont and become a Herefordshire gentleman. There were also a small number of benefactions from those living outside the county who either had local links or were generous towards such charities. Some large benefactions were left as legacies to the asylum. The father of Miss Cam, who bequeathed £200, had formerly been a physician at the General Hospital. The governors of Guy's Hospital in London contributed £21, presumably because much of Thomas Guy's fortune was drawn from his Herefordshire lands.

LUNATICK ASYLUM

As the Governors have adopted the Proposal of extending the Usefulness of this Charity by adding an ASYLUM for the Reception of LUNATICKS, the following BENEFACTIONS are offered for that Purpose – but they make no Part of the Infirmary Accounts.

N.B. *For the Satisfaction of Benefactors, we have pleasure in informing them, that the House is put in order and furnished, for the Reception and Cure of Patients.*

	£	s	
Published in the Printed Report, for 1787	471	19	0
BENEFACTIONS SINCE THAT TIME			
Edmund Eckley, Esq. Credenhill (*dec. paid*)	10	10	
Miss Eckley, ditto (*paid*)	5	5	
Lacon Lambe, Esq.(to make the above sum £500 *paid*)	12	6	
	500	0	
Rev. Mr Grand (*dec. paid*)	150	0	
Mrs Smith, of Hinton (*dec. paid*)	150	0	
A Gentleman of Hereford (*paid*)	100	0	
Abraham Seward, Esq. Sarum (*paid*)	100	0	
Rt. Hon. the Earl of Oxford (*dec. paid*)	21	0	
Rt. Hon. Lord Viscount Bateman (*paid*)	21	0	
Rt. Rev. Lord Bishop of Hereford (*paid*)	21	0	
Hon. Mrs Walsingham (*paid*)	25	0	
Hon. Edward Foley (*paid*)	10	0	
Sir Edward Boughton, Bart. *dec.* 2d Subscrip.	10	0	
Sir George Cornewall, Bart. (*paid*)	21	0	
Worshipful the Governors of Guy's Hospital (*paid*)	21	0	
Unknown, by Sir G. Cornewall, Bart. (*paid*)	21	0	
Richard Aubrey, Esq. Clehonger (*paid*)	21	0	
Rowles Scudamore, Esq. (2d subscrip. *paid*)	20	0	
Mr Wm. Perry, Hereford (dec. *paid*)	20	0	
Rev. Dr. Allen, Almely (*paid*)	10	10	
John Matthew, Esq. M.D. Hereford (*paid*)	10	10	
Thomas Cooke, Esq. ditto (*paid*)	10	10	
F.W.T. Brydges, Esq. Tibberton (*dec. paid*)	10	10	
Philip Westfaling, Esq. Rudhale (*dec. paid*)	10	10	
Michael Biddulph, Esq. Ledbury (*paid*)	10	10	
Thomas Coleman, Esq. Leominster (*paid*)	10	10	
John Peploe Birch, Esq. Garnstone (*paid*)	10	10	
Unknown (*paid*)	10	10	
Ditto, by the Rev. Mr Winston (*dec. paid*)	10	10	
Dr. Blount, Hereford (*paid*)	5	5	
William Matthews, Esq. Burton (*paid*)	5	5	
T.S. Powell, Esq. Pengethley (*dec. paid*)	5	5	
Thomas Brewster, Esq. Hereford (*dec.*)	5	5	
John Jones, Esq. ditto (*paid*)	5	5	
Thomas Downes, Esq. Letton (*paid*)	5	5	

	£	s
Thomas Garnons, Esq. Trelough (*paid*)	5	5
Rev. Mr Morgan, Ross (*paid*)	5	5
Mrs Clarke, Hill (*paid*)	5	5
James Hereford, Esq. Sufton (*paid*)	5	5
Somerset Davies, Esq. Wigmore (*paid*)	5	5
Rev. Mr Griffith, Ewithington (*paid*)	5	5
Dr. Symonds, Hereford (*paid*)	5	5
F.B. Thomas, Esq. ditto (*paid*)	5	5
Mr Philip Davis, jun. Leominster (*dec. paid*)	5	5
Mr William Wainwright, Hereford (*paid*)	5	5
Rev. Mr Taswell, ditto (*dec. paid*)	4	4
Rev. Mr Russell, ditto (*paid*)	3	3
John Nourse, Esq. Welton (*paid*)	3	3
Edmund Pateshall, Esq. Allensmore (*dec. paid*)	3	3
John Hanbury Williams, Esq. Colebrooke (*paid*)	3	3
Mr Downes, Attorney, Hereford (*paid*)	3	3
William Greenly, Esq. Titley (*paid*)	3	3
William Taylor, Esq. Tillington (*paid*)	2	2
William Money, Esq. Much-Marcle (*paid*)	2	2
Rev. Mr Prosser, Oxford (*paid*)	2	2
Mr Holder, Attorney, Ross (*paid*)	2	2
Mr Paytherus, Surgeon, ditto	2	2
Rev. Mr Powles, Ledbury (*paid*)	2	2
Mr Bird, Attorney, Hereford (*paid*)	2	2
Mr John Sharpe, ditto (*dec. paid*)	2	2
Mr Jones, Wyebridge-street, ditto (*paid*)	2	2
Mr Jones, jun. ditto (*paid*)	1	1
Mrs Russell, ditto (*paid*)	1	1
Penoyre Watkins, Esq. Brecon (*dec. paid*)	1	1
Mr James Maddy, Hereford (*paid*)	1	1
Mr Samuel Carless, ditto (*paid*)	1	1
Mr Price, Apothecary, ditto	1	1
Mr Price, Surgeon, ditto (*dec.*)	1	1
Mr Cooke, Grocer, ditto (*paid*)	1	1
Mr John Green, ditto (*paid*)	1	1
Mr Thomas Knill, ditto (*paid*)	1	1
Hugh Penry, Esq. ditto (*dec. paid*)	1	1
Mr Watkins, Tanbrook, ditto (*dec.*)	1	1
Rev. Mr Watkins, Weston (*dec. paid*)	1	1
W.F.H. Williams, Esq. Abergavenny (*paid*)	1	1
Thomas Turner, Esq. ditto (*paid*)	1	1
Mr Richard Williams, ditto (*paid*)	1	1
Mr Powell, Attorney, ditto (*paid*)	1	1
	1481	7

	£	s
A Gentleman unknown, by Lacon Lambe, Esq. towards furnishing the Asylum	£21	0
John Freeman, Esq. Letton, for ditto	50	0

Miss Cam's Legacy of £200, with £30: 8: 6 interest, has been lately received

ANNUAL SUBSCRIPTIONS TO THE LUNATICK ASYLUM

	£	s	d
Mrs Gregory, Woolhope	£2	2	0

Herefordshire Record Office, S60/8.

A VISIT TO NOTTINGHAM ASYLUM, 1814

The Grays were a prosperous middle-class solicitor's family, living in York in the second half of the eighteenth century. Mrs Faith Gray (1751–1826) kept a detailed social diary from 1764 until her death, and included accounts of the family's health, births, etc. Members of the family also travelled extensively in England and wrote to each other of what they had seen and whom they had met. Jonathan Gray (?b. 1779) wrote to his wife describing his visit to Nottingham asylum on his journey from York across the Midlands to London in 1814. He was accompanied by Daniel Tuke. The Nottingham asylum had only recently been built in the period 1812–14. Jonathan Gray had a considerable interest in the York asylum, of which he wrote a history, published in 1815. However, the family had long been involved with charities in York; William Gray, Faith's husband, became a director and gave £100 to the city's public dispensary established in 1788. Jonathan Gray was the secretary of the York Anti-Slavery Society when it was founded in 1823.

> We arrived at Nottingham at 5 to dinner . . . After dinner about ½p. 6 a note to Dr. Pennington[9] requesting permission to see the Asylum. The Dr. immediately called upon us, and took us thither. It is a new building, and stands delightfully on the slope of a hill, about ½ a mile from the centre of the town; without side the suburbs. It has only been finished about 2 years; & is on a most excellent plan.
>
> Tho' we took them by surprise we found everything clean & orderly. There are 54 patients. The building would hold 84. This Asylum is on a mixed plan of constitution, being partly built at the expense of the County as a place for Parish paupers, & partly by subscription for other Lunatics.
>
> Except in one or two instances of double bedded rooms, every patient has a distinct lodging room; & the provisions for air & ventilation are excellent; there are six spacious airing courts for the patients to walk in; & a large garden. . . .
>
> We introduced ourselves to Dr. P. as Governors of the York Asylum; which it appears was not the most flattering mode we cd. have adopted; tho' the Doctor's civility was equal to what it would have been under the most favourable circumstances of introduction. . . .
>
> This certainly is a place where any person might send their friends with satisfaction. The rooms for the opulent patients are handsomely furnished; & they are allowed their own servants if they wish it. Those for the poor are very airy, clean & comfortable. The bare mention of our mode of proceeding at York makes them stare with astonishment. The building &c. cost 20,000£. . . .
>
> Dr. P. rec[s]. 1 gns. per ann. for paupers besides 9s p. week which is paid to the institution: 2 gns. p. ann. from patients who pay less than 1gnaa. a week to the Inst[n] 4 gns. p. ann. from those who pay 1 gna. 6 gns. from those who are charged 1 gna. & a half; & 8 gns.p. ann. from those who pay 2 gns. or upwards p. week. Patients may be charged 3 gns. or more p. week according to their circumstances. There is an excellent Apothecary & Matron.

> A. Gray, *Papers and Diaries of a York Family, 1764–1839* (1927), pp. 134–5.

A VISIT TO BODMIN ASYLUM, 1841

Robert Barclay Fox (1816–55) belonged to a wealthy Quaker family that had settled in Falmouth, Cornwall, in the seventeenth century. With interests in shipping, mining, fishing and farming, they were considerable philanthropists. One of his ancestors was Edward Long Fox MD (1761–1835), who founded the asylum at Brislington near Bristol. Barclay Fox began his journal at school when he was fourteen and made daily entries until his marriage in 1844; thereafter entries were sporadic until 1854. The diary consists of ten volumes. With his friends, including John Stuart Mill and Thomas Carlyle, he travelled extensively in Britain, noting elections, scientific issues and religious events. Bodmin Asylum was built in 1818, with John Foulston of Plymouth as its architect; it was enlarged in 1842, 1847–8 and 1867. Barclay Fox died on 10 March 1855 at Gizeh, Cairo, where he had gone in a last attempt to recover his failing health.

23 August 1841 We went by Railway to Bodmin to breakfast. We took an hour & a half to go 8 miles, the train before us getting 3 times off the rail. Called on Hicks[10] who engaged us . . . to occupy the morning by a survey of the asylum. We spent about 5 hours in doing so, which contained more of interest to me than all the rest of our tour together. I was introduced to many of the patients and saw madness in many of its phases & many degrees. The more one sees of it the greater mystery does it appear. A madhouse is the most impressive sermon possible on the text 'I am fearfully & wonderfully made'. Hicks took us first to see a man styled Measter, who was boiling food for the pigs, apparently a hard working farmer. His mad point is a concern for the County rates. He considers himself the manager of the establishment & his intense concern at having to keep so many fellows in idleness is highly ludicrous. He abuses Hicks like a pick-pocket & tells him 'He will not put up with it, no longer. Take & send 'em off one to a time to Tor point & ship 'em aboard the *Royal Sovereign*. Send 'em to Americkey & swop 'em for balk, or put 'em to cultivate Dartymoor. They shall not stay here', &c. While listening to his extraordinary protest we saw poor Flamank wandering about the garden & throwing stones into a pond. Hicks called him & he came directly, recognized me & W. Hustler & greeted us warmly. He then informed us that Quaker & Quack doctor were words from the same root, but followed it up by asserting that the spirit of Quakerism & the Holy Spirit of God were one & the same. He then spoke of some nameless one who had deeply wronged him. I was lost in admiration at his deep pathos, & the occasional grandeur of his ideas; his wit was perfectly meteoric, so wild, so strange, so brilliant. We had wandered some way from the rest when we were called to speak to a religious enthusiast, a Bryanite, I believe, who was washing potatoes under the pump. He told us with an air of the strongest conviction of various extraordinary visitations to him, mostly in the form of clouds, some of which spoke to him. 'Do you know what clouds are?' asked Flamank. The latter was in a state of boisterous, uproarious merriment & turned all that the poor fanatic uttered into the wildest possible fun. In spite of it all, the other admitted that Flamank's sermon yesterday on the Pharisee & the Publican had affected him so that he was on the point of falling on his knees when the congregation went out. Flamank only laughed louder & said it showed his spiritual pride. . . . He went with us into the drawing room where his attentions to a young lady, whom he called his Queen, were the very quixotism of devotion. She was pretty & played her part well. Leaving them in the parlour, Hicks took me hastily over the asylum which seems well conducted, orderly, clean & ventilated. He introduced me to a singular character, called Sukey Provis, apparently a very plain Friend. She professes to be convinced, & made many enquiries of me respecting the state of the Society. Amongst the women was one poor, wild-eyed maniac, whose reason fled when her heart was broken: her lover had been false to her. I should think a madhouse contains more *character* within it than any other building. We all dined at the Asylum & met a large party there . . . We had a somewhat brilliant evening.

Barclay Fox's Journal, ed. R.L. Brett (1979), pp. 243–4.

CAUSES OF DEATH AT COLNEY HATCH ASYLUM, 1887

In 1827 a Select Committee of the House of Commons had revealed ill-treatment of the insane poor of Middlesex and the county's first pauper lunatic asylum opened at Hanwell four years later. The work of John Conolly MD and his regime of non-restraint there became a model for enlightened care of the insane in Victorian England. However, demand for places at Hanwell was so great that in 1851 a second county asylum had to be built at Colney Hatch; after 1889 it came under the control of London County Council and was known as Friern Hospital from 1973. Colney Hatch was to accommodate 1,250 patients and was, at a cost of nearly £300,000, the most expensive asylum ever built. The site covered 165 acres; the architect was S.W. Daukes.

Of the 190 patients who died at Colney Hatch in 1887 (see table opposite), only 6 (3 per cent) died from 'senility', while 83 (44 per cent) died from 'brain disease' and 28 (15 per cent) from 'thoracic disease', particularly tuberculosis. Post-mortem examinations were carried out on over 90 per cent of these deaths.

CAUSES OF DEATH.	Male.	Female.	Total.
CEREBRAL OR SPINAL DISEASES :—			
Apoplexy and Paralysis	3	26	29
Epilepsy and Convulsions	12	2	14
General Paresis	34	6	40
Maniacal and Melancholic Exhaustion or Decay	26	12	38
Inflammation and other Diseases of the Brain, Softening, Tumours, &c.	..	..	..
THORACIC DISEASE :—			
Inflammation of the Lungs, Pleuræ, and Bronchi	5	18	23
Pulmonary Consumption	10	14	24
Disease of the Heart, &c.	4	3	7
ABDOMINAL DISEASE :—			
Inflammation and Ulceration of the Stomach, Intestines, or Peritoneum	1	2	3
Dysentery and Diarrhœa	2	..	2
Pelvic Abscess	..	..	..
Exanthemata	..	..	..
Erysipelas	..	..	..
Cancer	..	1	1
Anæmia	..	..	..
General Debility and Old Age	3	3	6
Accidents (Poison)	..	1	1
Suicide (A female before admission)	1	1	2
	101	89	190

The thirty-seventh annual report of the committee of visitors of the county lunatic asylum at Colney Hatch for the year 1887, 1888.

PRISONS
DUTIES OF A PRISON SURGEON

The duties of a prison surgeon were performed part-time by a local practitioner who lived near the gaol and who would inspect prisoners and attend the sick as required in addition to his other patients. Gaol surgeons were appointed and paid by the county's magistrates at Quarter Sessions and, as the visits of the prison reformer, John Howard, revealed, levels of medical attention varied very considerably. The greatest risk, typhus or gaol fever, occasionally caused the surgeon's death, at as Worcester in 1783, where James Johnstone, junior, died after attending the prisoners during an epidemic. As the Weales' partnership agreement illustrates (p. 15), the gaol appointment was essentially a personal not a practice one. George Weale in fact succeeded another Warwick man, William Cole, in 1755, in providing 'physick' and over twenty years his fees averaged £5 a quarter, a sum which he was paid by contract from 1773.

The Gloucester prison surgeon's journal, 1796–7

1796

Tuesday 20 June I have visited the difft Classes of Prisoners and find they have no ailments Edwd Soul? is nearly recovered.

Friday 23 June On my visit the 21st – discharg'd Edwd Soul from the Hospital ward – I have been round the Prison the difft Appartments are clean, and the Prisoners in General healthy

Sunday 25 June On my visit yesterday, I desired Rid Wake might have a rice diet, he being unwell

Wednesday 28 June Yesterday and the day before I visited Rid Wake he is much better. Examined Wm Tandy he is better

Friday 30 June On my visit this morning gave Ann Pettyford medicine who was unwell last night

Monday 3 July I have seen Ann Pettyford daily she is better

Thursday 6 July Examined yesterday Tho Garn – he is clean there are no complaints

Sunday 9 July Nothing has happen'd since my last visit

Tuesday 11 July Examin'd yesterday Evening Robt Crook, and James Timbrel, they are clean

Wednesday 12 July Attended to examine Abm Organ, Morris Hill and Jno Dillon, they are clean. I have been over the House, find it in every respect clean.

1797

Wednesday 7 June Visited the Prison – and inspected all the lower part, also the Prisoners – find no complaints Dutton's wound keeps on the mending hand.

Friday 9 July Examined George Martin, and Rt Smith. Gave the Govr a certificate of their healths previous to their Transportation.

Sunday 11 July Neither yesterday, or today, I do not find any Prisoner with complaint, or anything amiss.

Tuesday 13 July I have been over <u>all</u> the Prison, which, for the most part is clean – and the Prisoners in in general healthy.

Thursday 15 July The Prisoners are all well – and everything according to its rules go on as it ought.

Saturday 17 July On my visit this morning found Jas Dutton unwell, and very low – he had found pain in the ulcer'd foot the evening before I examined the part, and found it, from the right side extended from the toes near halfway to the heel , in a state of inflammation, tending to gangrene, Directed for him to have every necessary in his case.

Sunday 18 July I saw Dutton several times yesterday – his foot I think is rather worse. Mrs Dutton being there would it not be more proper for her to stay to attend on him, – she knowing better how to do for him – having seen him in a similar situation? There are no other complaints.

Gloucestershire Record Office, Q/Gc/16/1.

The Gloucester city gaol surgeon's journal, 1827–8

1827

23 September Wright cured of the Itch & all the transports are fit for removal. No complaint in the Prison.

24 September Examined the transports & certified they were all fit for removal. No complaint.

1 November Visited the different departments of the prison. No complaint.

26 December Prisoners are in perfect Health.

1828

3 February Visited: Frith a boy who is subject to fits should not work on the Wheel at least not at those times when he may be expected to have them, they are periodical being influenced by the particular State of the Moon have given him Medicines the others are well.

22 March Two Felons are complaining – both Venereal disease & one has also the Itch. An old Man named White complains of Asthma – he should have but light work on the Wheel – Several of the convicted Prisoners complained of their Bread being short weight. I find on enquiry this is quite true & that Mr Turner has frequently return'd the loaves & got them changed.

3 April Visited

15 April Edwards has an inflamed Eye from cold, sent him an application for it. The others are tolerable.

16 April Charlotte Smith and Ann Clutterbuck are both Itch'd

21 April Visited the Prison

22 April Visited

29 April Visited the Prison

2 May Visited Browning is much debilitated by a Venereal disease he has been affected with & appears too much reduced to be able to work much at the Wheel – I advise his being allowed ½ a pint of Porter daily.

6 May Visited the Prisoners generally. Browning is better.

23 May Browning is quite well and may discontinue the Porter, and pursue the labour of the Tread Mill with the other Prisoners.

12 July Visited the Prison

22 August Visited the Prison
28 August Nicholas Salter has a venereal complaint which however is not a sufficient excuse for his not working on the Wheel.

There are two men's initials at the end of the days' comments; the practitioners appear to be Messrs Washbourn, apothecaries and druggists in East Street, Gloucester.

Gloucestershire Record Office, QBR/G3/G8/1.

The Horsley House of Correction surgeon's journal, 1843

14 April Joseph Purser age 22 P[auper] Constipation with fullness and pain in the belly to have calomel and Jalap John Curtis in bed – has a plentiful eruption in the Loins from the Tartar Emetic ointment which is likely to benefit him. The other Prisoners all well or convalescent.

The present quarter presents as usual many cases of slight and doubtful illness and a few of more serious and dangerous consideration – there have been several cases of Inflammatory remittent fever one of which John Humphreys was dangerous but ...... in recovery there have been several cases of Rheumatism confining the .... to bed and there has been one fatal case that of John Bown a man who came in with partial paralysis of the lower limbs – this prisoner had had dangerous seizures before coming into Prison which might be called fits and the attack in Prison with more comforts and attentions he could have had at his home proved incurable – during this Quarter there has been one case of Midwifery – Mary Ann ?Maun – one of the Prisoners
April 14 1843 Thos Stokes Surgeon

1 September
John Rowell age 28 P[auper] Deterioration of blood to the head Much better to day – Medicine & diet to be continued as before.
Joseph P?inter age 22 P[auper] Very much better
Edward Bidmead age 20 P[auper] Px Blue Pill & Opium at night – sore on the Penis to be washed three times a day with yellow wash
On Tuesday last I was requested by the Visiting Justices to meet them at the Jail, which I accordingly did, where they intimated to me that they were of the opinion they had exceeded limits of their authority when they ordered my <u>daily</u> attendance at the Prison on the 27th of July last, & they recommended me to discontinue my daily visits, which recomendation I have much pleasure in complying with. My attendance therefore at this Prison for the time to come will be regulated by the rules of 1842.
This day inspected the Prison found it clean, drainage very good, bedding clean & sufficient – examined the bread & found it good.

4 September Visited all the Prisoners-
Enoch Buck age 24 P[auper] Slight Diarroea To have Compound powder of Chalk & Opium
John Rowell age 28 P[auper] Deterioration of blood to the head Much better

Medicines as before
Joseph Pinn?er age 22 P[auper] Going on well
James Perry age 56 P[auper] Bad Leg
Jacob Bailey age 36 P[auper] Bad Legs

J.H. Wells, Surgeon

Gloucestershire Record Office, Q/Gh 2.

Littledean House of Correction surgeon's journals, 1843, 1845

19 August 1843 Sarah Tombs age 36 Nervous debility To take 1oz of purple & iron Mixture twice a day She is to continue with her tea & sugar with ½ a pint of Milk & 1 pint of good beer in the day.
Visited the prison this day & found the remainder of the prisoners well.
John Williams age 26 ⎫
John Broacher age 19 ⎬ recently admitted in good health
Wm Coates age 19   ⎭

Wm Heane, Surgeon

24 August 1843 Sarah Tombs age 36 Nervous Debility to continue mixture et Diet
John Jones age 36 Itch To be rubbed with Unguent Sulph twice a day and to take the Aperiant Piles tonight
Visited the Prison in the absence of Mr Heane in consequence of illness and find the remainder of the prisoners in good health John Hunt
20 March 1845 George Burgum age 30 Bad cough to continue
              Thos Jones age 55   do
              Wm Jervis age 20   do
Thos Watts age 63 recently admitted has a rheumatic pain in the left shoulder
Thos Field age 19 he has had an abscess of the finger he is not to perform any hard labour
Visited the prison this day & found the remainder of the prisoners well
23 March Visited the prison this day & found the prisoners all well
25 March Thos Watts age 63 Rheumatism of the right shoulder To take 10 grs of Dovers powder every night.
Visited the prison this day & found the remainder of the prisoners well

Wm Heane, Surgeon

Gloucestershire Record Office, Q/GLi 18/3.

NOTES

1. Charles Kimberley MD (1691–1754), a physician in Northampton.
2. James Stonhouse MD (1714–95), a physician in Northampton.
3. Dr Stratford has not been identified as a medical practitioner.
4. Edward Litchfield (before 1720–after 1783), a surgeon in Northampton.
5. John Murray (before 1725–after 1757), a surgeon in Northampton.
6. John Shipton (1680–1748), a London surgeon.
7. John Blandy, a gentleman from Kingston Bagpuize, Berkshire, had died in 1762.
8. Richard Frewin MD (1681?–1761) of Oxford left his books to the Radcliffe Library and his house for the Regius professor of medicine.
9. Charles Pennington, a Nottingham surgeon-apothecary, had earlier been apothecary to the county hospital.
10. Samuel Hicks was steward of the Cornwall Asylum at Bodmin.

VIII
CHARITIES, DISPENSARIES AND FRIENDLY SOCIETIES

❖   ❖   ❖

CHARITIES

England had an almost innumerable variety of charities, many dating from the medieval period, established to aid the poor with the necessities of life. Different centuries assessed necessity in different ways, so that whereas the Stuart philanthropist favoured almshouses, clothing charities and schools, a century later funds were bequeathed for apprenticing children, smallpox inoculation and attending lying-in women. In Victoria's England, homes to rescue 'fallen girls', industrial training and children's boot funds were favoured. Charities with a medical purpose were, however, fairly uncommon, with the exception of those for lying-in women, although occasionally a bequest would allow inhabitants of a particular parish to be admitted to a voluntary infirmary which a local benefactor had supported.

The city of Coventry had over fifty charities by 1900, with widows particularly preferred as recipients, although one charity existed to provide beds for in-patients at the Provident Dispensary. There were also two lying-in charities (founded in 1801 and 1810) and a district nursing institute, founded in 1883 to provide domiciliary attention in the area. The charities were the subject of a Royal Commission in 1909.

COVENTRY LYING-IN CHARITY, FOUNDED IN 1801

The object of this Charity is stated to be for the relief of poor industrious married women at their own houses. The income for the same period was: Subscriptions.
No woman is entitled to have a ticket except she reside in one of the parishes of Coventry, nor for the first child. In the original rules it is laid down that the child is to be baptized in the church of which the mother is a parishioner. This is not enforced now, though the Charity is still looked upon as belonging to the Church of England. The management is in the hands of a committee appointed at the annual meeting.
Subscribers of £1 1s. a year are entitled to two letters of recommendation. There is no wage limit, and no form of enquiry is used, nor is the home visited before the confinement.
The benefits include midwife's fee, 6s. 6d., grocery to the value of 1s. 9d., dinners for two weeks, costing 3s., flannel worth 1s. 9d., loan of clothes for mother and child, and medical assistance if needed. Every case is visited by the matron after the confinement has taken place, and visiting is also undertaken by members of the committee.
The income for the year ending March 31, 1907, was (after deducting £7 from S. Michael's Consolidated Charities):– Subscriptions £94, dividends (less £13 which appears under Endowed Charities) £36, proceeds of Fancy Dress Ball, £43; total, £173.
The expenditure was £192.
The number of cases dealt with during the same period was 184. As compared with 20 or 30 years ago the number of cases has somewhat declined.

COVENTRY DISTRICT NURSING INSTITUTION, FOUNDED IN 1883

The object of this Institution is to provide specially trained nurses to nurse the sick poor of Coventry and district in their own homes. The management is in the hands of a Council, elected at the annual meeting, and of a Managing Committee appointed by the Council. No relief is given by the nurses, but the Honorary Secretary has a small private fund, from which help is given in special cases.
    The staff in September, 1907, consisted of a superintendent and six nurses. During the year ending December, 1906, the number of fresh applications was 722, of which all but 18 came from the City of Coventry.
    A separate Nursing Association has recently been established for the parish of Foleshill, a portion of which is in the City of Coventry, and the Coventry District Nursing Institution has practically given up nursing in that part of the City.

In the same Home there is a staff of private nurses under the control of the Committee, and the expenses of rent, taxes, fuel and light are shared between the district nurses and the private nurses. A separate balance-sheet for each is issued.

The income of the District Nursing Institution for the year ending December 31, 1906, was: Subscriptions (including £21 from the Board of Guardians) £293, after deducting £85 from the Endowed Charities donations £57, after deducting £5 from Endowed Charities offertoried £22 and dividends; £6 total, £378.

The payments were £598. At the end of the year a sum of £129 was due to the bankers.

Report to the Royal Commission on the Poor Laws and Relief of Distress,
Parliamentary Papers, 1909, XXVIII.

DISPENSARIES
HENRY LILLEY SMITH AND THE PROVIDENT DISPENSARY MOVEMENT

By the early nineteenth century, medical demands on the parish, as Old Poor Law expenditure often exceeded income, meant that many sick poor were not treated, as commentators such as Sir F.M. Eden and the Revd David Davies noted. When Henry Lilley Smith (1788–1859) began practice as parish surgeon in Southam, a small market town in south Warwickshire, after a period in the army, he was particularly concerned at the high incidence of eye and ear diseases among the labouring poor and that many were unwilling to seek parish medical attention because of the stigma of pauperism. Smith began by establishing a charitable, self-supporting dispensary in 1818 at Southam. It was funded by donations from the wealthy and by small subscriptions from those of the labouring poor who could afford to do so. These subscribers, and those too poor to contribute, could thus be treated outside the poor law. The Southam dispensary was an immediate success and led to others being founded in several areas of the Midlands, such as Atherstone, Derby and Northampton. However, many medical practitioners objected to Smith's dispensaries treating poor subscribers who would otherwise have paid for their services. Smith in his later life undeniably made enemies when he supported some controversial causes, including universal education and allotment-owning, but also held some bizarre socio-religious beliefs. He died embittered and unappreciated, except by the poor.

SOUTHAM INFIRMARY,

FOR CURING DISEASES OF THE EYE AND EAR,

SUPPORTED BY VOLUNTARY CONTRIBUTIONS,

UNDER THE PATRONAGE OF

THE EARL OF WARWICK AND OF EARL SPENCER,

ESTABLISHED 1818.

At the Thirty-ninth Annual Meeting of the Governors of the Infirmary for Curing Diseases of the Eye and Ear, held July 2nd, 1857, The Rev. Temple Hillyard in the chair, it was resolved that the original Prospectus, Regulations, with Extracts from the Reports, should be re-issued, as there were many applications for information by new residents in the country.

PROSPECTUS

OF AN

ESTABLISHMENT OF THE NATURE OF AN INFIRMARY,

ON A SMALL SCALE AND AT A MODERATE EXPENSE,

AT SOUTHAM, IN THE COUNTY OF WARWICK,

FOR THE BENEFIT OF THE POOR AFFLICTED WITH

DISEASES OF THE EYE AND EAR,

BY

MR. H. L. SMITH,

OCULIST AND AURIST.

"The poor have *many* claims to the attention and benevolence of the rich; there are none more pressing or more generally admitted than those for assistance, when labouring under disease; and the variety of charitable institutions which distinguish this nation evince in how very few instances their claims are disregarded.

"The humane attention of the wealthy has been long and judiciously directed to the alleviation of the necessities of the indigent blind; but it remained long a subject of regret, that no Institution was established, even in the Metropolis, where gratuitous assistance might be administered to the poor for the prevention of blindness and the restoration of sight. It is only within these thirteen years, that, in London, an Infirmary has been established for the relief of the poor afflicted with diseases of the Eye and Ear; since which time, men, eminent for their skill and professional attainments, have devoted their time and attention to this highly interesting class of diseases, which, with few exceptions, had been previously consigned to the hands of presuming empirics, utterly unacquainted with the principles and practice of medical science. The late lamented Mr. Saunders, who established the *Eye and Ear Infirmary in London*, was the first to call the attention of the public to the magnitude of the evil, and to astonish them by the success of his exertions in restoring the use of organs, at once essential to manual occupation, and the sources of our most refined and intellectual enjoyments. This benevolent example has been followed with good effects to the community in many other parts of the kingdom, and Mr. Smith is induced, though with much diffidence, to believe, that a similar Infirmary may be established in the town where he resides, and in which he has practised the improved methods of his friend Mr. Saunders for the last seven years.

"Patients afflicted with disorders of the Eye are not prevented from travelling, and they will readily attend where they have a prospect of relief. The expenses of a small town are more likely to accord with their previous habits than those of a city, or the necessary rules of an Hospital. The disorders of the Eye and Ear, with which the poor are afflicted, seldom arise so much from their own imprudence as from accidental causes connected with their employment, over which they have no control; and as they rarely engage the attention of Medical Men visiting the parochial class, the patient is induced to use a few domestic remedies, which generally do harm, and the case becomes chronic.

"If Mr. Smith should meet with that support he anticipates, the principal energies of his professional life will be directed to the benefit of the poor who may be thus recommended to his care."

After the issue of the above prospectus, a large public meeting was held on the 18th of April, 1818; SIR GREY SKIPWITH, BART, IN THE CHAIR; and the following Regulations and Form of Recommendation were adopted:—

REGULATIONS.

This Institution is supported by Annual Subscriptions and by voluntary Contributions.

It is governed by the Patrons, Presidents, Vice-Presidents, Treasurers, Annual Subscribers and Benefactors of £5 5s. and upwards.

Annual Subscribers of £1 1s. and Benefactors of £5 5s. and upwards, have the right of admitting two Patients annually; and Annual Subscribers of 10s. 6d. one Patient.

Patients (except from a distance) are admitted on Mondays and Thursdays, between the hours of nine and twelve o'clock in the forenoon.

The services of the officers are *gratuitous*.

The Annual Subscriptions become due on the 25th May.

No.   FORM OF RECOMMENDATION:

To be signed by a Subscriber, with his Place of Abode, and dated.

I recommend
as a proper object of this charity.

No persons to be deemed objects of this charity but such as are necessitous.

Each Patient is expected to bring two shirts, two pair of stockings, and two night-caps.

Patients neglecting to conform with the Rules of the house and the directions given them, will be immediately dismissed.

Subscribers sending Patients must observe that the Funds of the Institution are not applicable to their Maintenance.—The terms of Board are, for the Men, 9d.; for the Women, 8d.; and for the Children, 6d. per day.

"The following extracts from the Fifth Report, made by Dr. Chandler, the then Rector of Southam, but now Dean of Chichester; and the Rev. W. C. Wilson, of Hardwick; explain the working of the Institution more fully than any of the subsequent ones.

"Five years are now completed since the first establishment of the SOUTHAM INFIRMARY for Diseases of the Eye and Ear, and this period being fully sufficient to ascertain the utility of the plan by the test of experience, it was the wish of the members present at the Annual Meeting held on the 7th of July, 1823, that a more detailed report of the design and of the actual state of the Institution should be laid before the Subscribers than can have been done in the brief accounts hitherto published.

"In compliance with their request that such a report should be drawn up by us, and with the assistance of such information on matters of a medical and professional nature as we have been able to obtain from Mr. H. L. Smith, the operating Surgeon, we beg leave to make the following statements:—

"We learn that it is not yet twenty years since the attention of the public has been directed to Institutions of this nature. Many are now established in various parts of the country, and from the multitude of patients to whom they have administered relief, it appears that the sufferers under a total or partial loss of sight must have been more numerous than could have been suspected, had not these Infirmaries brought them into notice.

"Most of the establishments alluded to, however, are unconnected with Hospitals, and consequently do not possess the full advantages that belong to those which are enabled to receive the patients into the house, and by that means keep them constantly under the superintendance and direction of the Surgeon. Such is the case with the Infirmary at Southam, where, by the liberality of the Subscribers, the patients are supplied with *lodging*, as well as medicine and medical attendance. It is however to be observed, that their board is defrayed by themselves, and the reason of this regulation is plain, since, if the whole of the expense of the establishment had been thrown upon the charity, it might have been too heavy since, if the whole of the expense of the establishment had been thrown upon the charity, it might have been too heavy a demand upon the benevolence of the public, while it might have afforded a temptation to some persons to continue burdensome longer than necessity required. Neither can this inconsiderable expense be a subject of just complaint with parishes which send their poor to the Infirmary, since, at all events, they are enabled, at a much reduced charge, to obtain a cure, and with a cure, the means of independent maintenance, for many who must otherwise have continued hopeless dependants upon the parochial funds. It may be mentioned that accidents affecting the Eye frequently befall labourers in cutting hedges, breaking stones in the road, hoeing turnips, &c.; and of this description of sufferers many have been removed from the parish books, or have been prevented from being placed there, by the happy relief obtained at this Infirmary.

"With respect to the local situation of this Institution, it may at first be thought that a parish containing so small a population as Southam is an unfit place, but it should be recollected that the Infirmary, as it proposes to take in the patients of a whole district, it designed to act in a sphere much larger than that even of the most populous towns, and that the spot where it should be established may be regulated by other considerations than the mere supply of cases from the immediate vicinity; and, in point of fact, cases are brought from many remote parts of the kingdom. It appears also, there are some advantages belonging to a small town in comparison with larger places, in the cheapness of provisions. Southam is also situated near the confines of the counties of Warwick and Northampton; and the Surgeon has been in the habit of paying periodical visits to the county towns of Warwick and Northampton, principally with a view of ascertaining on the spot who are proper objects to be sent to the Infirmary.* Of this practice, the advantages are not inconsiderable; it often saves the expense and trouble of sending cases that are hopeless, and thus prevents some feelings which have proved injurious to the interests of the Institution, since it has been found that persons who have come, or been sent, from a considerable distance, with fallacious hopes of receiving relief, have returned home with feelings of dis-appointment, and have so prevented the application of others, who would, in all probability, have been relieved. These visits of the Surgeon also afford to persons residing at a distance, and particularly to the overseers of distant parishes, an opportunity of making themselves acquainted with the management and internal arrangement of the Infirmary.

"With respect to the benefit received by the patients in the two departments of the Infirmary, we learn from the same information in which at the beginning of this statement we took leave to confide, and without which we could not have undertaken to make any report of its proceedings and success, that the cases of disorders in the Ear are less numerous than those in the Eye, and less easy to be cured; but in this department, even where complete cures were not obtained or expected, symptoms have been removed which are known frequently to precede serious and fatal disorders; and young persons labouring under deafness from peculiar causes, which would be more fitly described by Medical Men than we can venture to attempt, have been so far cured as to be capable of receiving instruction at school, and of taking and keeping services, to which they would otherwise have been quite unequal.

"The very nature of this Institution supposes that the persons so benefited are of the poorer classes—and so many are the individuals who are now placed in a situation to gain an independent livelihood, and who, but for the benefits of this Infirmary, would have been still suffering a deprivation afflictive to all, but to the poor doubly calamitous—and who would have lingered on a burden to themselves, to their friends, and to their parishes. But even in those cases where no relief has been given, if the failure be clearly owing to the nature of the disease, some consolation arises both to the friends of the patient and to himself; the former know that what skill can do has been tried—the latter, when he perceives that he is suffering under an irremediable evil, learns more easily to reconcile his mind to his lot, and to submit with more resignation to the dispensations of Providence.

* NOTE.—The Surgeon attends at the Warwick Arms, Warwick, at One o'clock every Saturday; at the George Hotel, Northampton, on the first Tuesday in every Month, at One o'clock; at Mrs. Claridge's, High Street, Banbury, on the first Thursday, at One o'clock; and at the Eagle Hotel, Rugby, on the first Friday, at Ten o'clock.

"The terms of Board are for the Men, 6s.; for the Women, 4s. 8d.; and for the Children, 3s. 6d. per week; and in this part of our statement we are particularly desirous to correct any mistaken suppositions which may have arisen that the several sums above specified are received by the Surgeon, whereas we would wish it to be understood that in this part of the management of the Infirmary he is no farther concerned than as directing the diet most proper for the several patients. The sums paid for their maintenance are wholly and solely applied to such purpose, under the management of the Matron; all balances, either of debt or credit, are confined to that account, and the books are subject to a monthly inspection of Ladies, whose punctuality and attention in the discharge of their office cannot be too highly praised.

"That the terms of the Board were not fixed upon improper calculations appears from the circumstance that, at the end of five years' housekeeping there is only a profit to the house of £5 9s. 6d., a sum which would indeed be somewhat increased if all the debts due were paid; but when the sums are to be collected from indigent patients, or from overseers of distant parishes, it has happened and it may probably be expected ever to happen, that there will be some deficiency. It would indeed be most desirable that the terms of the Board could be lower, as, although now proved by experience to be set at a rate scarcely more than enough to cover the expenses, still, it must be acknowledged that they tend to debar many proper objects from receiving the advantages of this Institution.

"In respectfully soliciting the Subscribers to fulfil their engagements, it may therefore be urged as a very powerful consideration, not only that they would enable the establishment to meet its ordinary expenditure, but they would create a certain surplus, which being handed over to the housekeeper's accounts, would ease the terms of the board to the poor patients, and give a greater facility of admission into the Infirmary to many whose exclusion must be a subject of serious concern.

"This review of the original design, and of the actual state of the Infirmary, exhibits, it is hoped, sufficient to satisfy all its friends and supporters that their bounty has not been bestowed in vain. We are of opinion, that it has proved itself useful beyond the expectation even of its first projectors, and therefore it would be a waste of words to solicit the Subscribers still to give it there own countenance, and to endeavour to make it known to others.

GEORGE CHANDLER, RECTOR OF SOUTHAM.

WILLIAM CORBET WILSON, VICAR OF PRIORS HARDWICK."

Here follows a list of the patients admitted, cured and relieved, with the expenses for each year from its commencement to the present time.

	Admitted	Cured.	Relieved.	Annual Expenses, Including Outfit. £ s. d.
Patients attended in Lodgings, before the erection of the Institution, to the 1st of June, 1818	31	136	116	353 14 8
Patients between the 1st of June, 1818 and 1819	274			
Ditto 1820	285	111	122	149 18 6¼
Ditto 1821	276	147	106	128 8 4½
Ditto 1822	395	254	109	120 5 6
Ditto 1823	352	225	101	130 9 4
Ditto 1824	276	115	135	126 3 8½
Ditto 1825	263	140	105	112 3 11½
Ditto 1826	294	170	76	113 2 1½
Ditto 1827	274	184	50	112 3 11

	Year							
Ditto	1827	...	...	31?	10?	60	112	3	11
Ditto	1828	...	...	331	190	68	119	18	4
Ditto	1829	...	...	309	176	64	113	12	4½
Ditto	1830	...	...	283	168	70	112	7	7½
Ditto	1831	...	...	295	184	90	130	12	6½
Ditto	1832	...	...	311	193	96	117	16	11½
Ditto	1833	...	...	305	187	110	125	18	7
Ditto	1834	...	...	324	210	105	137	10	3
Ditto	1835	...	...	318	234	50	117	9	2½
Ditto	1836	...	...	320	240	54	111	13	10
Ditto	1837	...	...	263	210	47	119	5	4½
Ditto	1838	...	...	281	196	67	118	3	0
Ditto	1839	...	...	342	209	104	116	9	7½
Ditto	1840	...	...	308	217	80	110	11	9
Ditto	1841	...	...	291	207	84	135	17	9
Ditto	1842	...	...	309	240	56	113	17	2½
Ditto	1843	...	...	354	321	22	120	1	6
Ditto	1844	...	...	368	317	18	107	12	3½
Ditto	1845	...	...	335	312	23	130	4	0½
Ditto	1846	...	...	325	309	14	113	1	4½
Ditto	1847	...	...	338	307	21	123	8	11½
Ditto	1848	...	...	327	300	18	120	10	0
Ditto	1849	...	...	335	306	29	122	10	2½
Ditto	1850	...	...	380	308	60	113	11	8
Ditto	1851	...	...	322	227	74	116	17	2½
Ditto	1852	...	...	329	243	86	118	1	8
Ditto	1853	...	...	341	250	90	114	7	3½
Ditto	1854	...	...	331	270	44	115	7	9½
Ditto	1855	...	...	318	250	47	133	18	6
Ditto	1856	...	...	291	256	20	130	11	8
Ditto	1857	...	...	315	261	33	111	0	0

The difference between the number Cured and Relieved, and the Total number admitted each Year, arises from—patients either not relieved—absenting themselves—three have died—and various other causes, always operating amongst the lower classes, many of whom apply from great distances.

The expenses of the Institution have averaged £126 per annum; or about 8s. 4d. for each patient; which includes Rent, Wages and Board for Matron and Servant, Washing for patients, Drugs, Spectacles, extra Nursing, Printing, Stationery, Insurance on Furniture, and all other expenses whatever.

The reports of the Surgeon and Secretary (which offices have been combined for the last two years in Mr. Smith), will shew the small expense at which these humble Institutions may be conducted. *It is incalculable the relief that would be afforded to suffering humanity by the establishment of similar small Institutions for the Diseases of the Feet, and the Diseases peculiar to hard-working child-bearing Women, who suffer much for the want of a special place of resort of this kind.*

Expenses	£	s.	d.
Matron's Wages ...	18	18	0
Matron's Board ...	13	1	0
Servant's Wages ...	2	2	0
Servant's Board ...	10	8	8
Rent of Infirmary ...	20	10	0
Sundries—Washing, Soap, Lights, &c. ...	16	13	2
Printing, Reports, Stationery, &c. ...	4	1	1
Matron's Bill for Postages, Money Orders, and House Stationery, ...	1	3	9
Insurance of Furniture ...	0	5	0
Carried forward	£87	2	8

	£	s.	d.
Brought forward	87	2	8
Collector's per centage ...	0	3	0
Coals ...	8	18	7
Repairing Surgeon's Instruments ...	0	11	0
Drugs and Leeches ...	9	17	0
Draper's Bill ...	3	6	9
Mason's Bill ...	0	10	0
Spectacles for Patients ...	0	11	0
	£111	0	0

In the hope of setting an example of the propriety and advantages of throwing open all the Charitable Institutions in the Kingdom to the Clergy—the following Resolution was adopted at the Annual Meeting in 1840:—

"Rev. Sir,—I am requested to send you a copy of the following resolution, unanimously agreed to at the annual general meeting, held this day, of the Governors of the Infirmary for Curing Diseases of the Eye and Ear, in hope that it may in itself prove useful, if any of your parishioners should be afflicted with these complaints; *and also, act as an example to other charitable institutions,* by pointing out a safe and extensive channel, by which their various benefits may be brought to the homes of the poor in distant and obscure places." The resolution was as follows :—"In consequence of several applications made for admission to this Infirmary by Clergymen and others, for their poor parishioners, many of whom reside at too great a distance to become regular subscribers, it was resolved, that for the future, the Clergy be permitted to recommend poor persons, as *out-patients,* without limit and without payment." It was further agreed, that a copy of the last resolution be forwarded to the officiating Ministers of the parishes within fifteen miles of Warwick and Northampton, with a list of the subscribers, in order that if it should be necessary to make such applicants *in-patients,* it may be known to whom they should apply.

T. S. WRIGHT, *Hon. Sec.*

That no harm has resulted to this novel and liberal extension of the Charity may be inferred, for although from lapse of time the greater part of its first subscribers have been removed by death, yet the number continues about the same. It should be observed, that from the beginning no Sermon has been preached and no Ball nor Bazaar held in its behalf; £50 was devised by the late James Arnold, Esq., in 1833, and £100 by Miss Landor, in 1853.

PATRONS.

THE EARL OF WARWICK. THE EARL SPENCER.

PRESIDENT.

HENRY WISE, ESQ. WOODCOTE.

LIST OF SUBSCRIBERS.

	£	s.	d.
Annesley, Rev. C. F. Eydon, Northamptonshire	1	1	0
Annesley, Miss	1	1	0
Atye, Miss Ellen, Ingon Grange, Stratford-on-Avon	1	1	0
Brooke, William de Capel, Esq. Market			

	£	s.	d.
Morewood, W. P. Esq. Alfreton Hall	1	1	0
Maynard, Rev. Robert, Wormleighton	0	10	6
Mills, Rev. H. Fillerton	1	1	0
Northampton, Marquis of	1	1	0
North, Colonel, Wroxton Abbey	1	1	0
Newdegate, Mrs. Arbury Hall	1	1	0
Otway, Rev. Cooke. Vicarage. Stoneleigh	0	10	6

Name	£	s.	d.
ford-on-Avon			
Broke, William de Capel, Esq. Market Harborough	1	1	0
Bracebridge, C. H. Esq. Atherstone Hall	1	1	0
Boddington, Miss, Kingsthorpe House	1	1	0
Botfield, Beriah, Esq. Norton Hall	1	1	0
Bromfield, Rev. H. Blockley, Worcestershire	1	1	0
Byron, Rt. Hon. Lady, Kirkby Mallory	1	1	0
Bouverie, E. Esq. Delapre Abbey	1	1	0
Bouverie, Miss Caroline	1	1	0
Biddulph, Rev. H. Birdingbury	0	10	6
Banbury Old Charitable Society	1	1	0
Blencowe, Miss, Portland Place, Leamington	1	0	0
Brixworth Union	1	1	0
Bracebridge, W. H. Esq. Sherbourne	1	1	0
Chamberlayne, H. T. Esq. Stoney Thorpe	1	1	0
Cotton, T. Esq. The Spring, Kenilworth	1	1	0
Colvile, F. Esq. Barton House	1	1	0
Cobbe, Rev. F. Spratton	1	1	0
Cartwright, Mrs. Edgcote	1	1	0
Coxe, Mrs. Hippisley, Southam	1	1	0
Cooke, Mrs. Beckley, Oxon	1	1	0
Downes, Rev. J. Northampton	1	1	0
Dicey, T. E. Esq. Claybrook Hall	1	1	0
Dickens, W. Esq. Cherrington	1	1	0
Duke, Hashleigh, Esq. Church Eaton, Stafford	1	1	0
Dashwood, Mrs. Dunstew, Oxon	1	1	0
Farmer, Mr. Bubbenhall	0	10	6
Fitzroy, Hon. Col. Grafton Regis	1	1	0
Golightly, Rev. Thos. Boddington	1	1	0
Goffe, Mr. Richard, Banbury	0	10	6
Goulburn, Rev. Dr. Rugby	1	1	0
Gazey, Mr. John, Banbury	1	1	0
Greaves, Mrs. Leamington	1	1	0
Holbeche, Rev. Chas. Farnborough	1	1	0
Hillyard, Rev. Canon, Southam	0	10	6
Heurtley, Rev. Dr. Fenny Compton	1	1	0
Harrison, Mrs. Warmington	0	10	6
Hibbert, W. Esq. Hilton Grange	1	1	0
Harrison, Rev. Bughrooke Rectory	1	1	0
Hale, Mrs. Kenilworth	1	1	0
Haddon, John, Esq. Leamington	1	1	0
James, Rev. H. Bilton	1	1	0
Knightley, Sir Chas. Bart. Fawsley Park	2	2	0
King, Bolton, Esq. M.P. Chadshunt	1	1	0
Knotesford, Rev. F. Stratford-on-Avon	1	1	0
Loveday, John, Esq. Williamscott	1	1	0
Lea, Rev. Thos. Tadmarton, Oxon	1	1	0
Leigh, Rt. Hon. Lord, Stoneleigh Abbey	1	1	0
Landor, H. Esq. Tachbrooke	1	1	0
Mordaunt, Lady, Walton Park	2	2	0
Marriott, Miss, Newton, near Rugby	1	1	0
Marriott, Rev. P. Cotesbache	1	1	0

Name	£	s.	d.
Newdegate, Mrs. Arbury Hall	1	1	0
Otway, Rev. Cooke, Vicarage, Stoneleigh	0	10	6
Palmer, Rev. Charles, Lighthorne	1	1	0
Percy, The Hon. C. B. Guy's Cliff	1	1	0
Pilkington, Rev. Canon, Stockton	1	1	0
Powell, Miss, Bitteswell	1	1	0
Robertson, A. Esq. M.D. Northampton	1	1	0
Rann, R. W. Esq. Leamington	1	1	0
Ryland, Miss, Barford Hill	1	1	0
Rugby Union	2	2	0
Risby Mr. Northampton	1	1	0
Scott, Rt. Hon. Lord John	2	2	0
Spencer, Earl, Althorpe	1	1	0
Sitwell, Rev. H.W. Leamington Hastings	1	1	0
Sutton, Miss Manners, Leamington	1	1	0
Smith, Rev. J. H. Leamington	1	1	0
Shuckburgh, Rev. C. B. Bourton House	1	1	0
Samuelson, Bernard, Esq. Banbury	1	1	0
Staunton, Wm. Esq. Longbridge	1	1	0
Shirley, Evelyn, Esq. Eatington	1	1	0
Sheppard, R. E. Esq. Church Stowe	0	10	6
Sawbridge, Mrs. East Haddon	1	1	0
Thornton, T. R. Esq. Brockhall	1	1	0
Thornton, Rev. W. Dodford	1	1	0
Taylor, Wm. Esq. Southam	1	1	0
Townsend, Rev. H. Honington	1	1	0
Townsend, J. Esq. Alveston	1	1	0
Tollemach, Lady Emily	0	10	6
Veysie, Rev. D. Daventry	1	1	0
Warwick, The Earl of	1	1	0
Willoughby de Broke, Lord, Compton Verney	1	1	0
Wise, H. Esq. Woodcote	1	1	0
Wise, Matthew, Esq. Leamington	1	1	0
West, J. R. Esq. Alscote Park	2	2	0
Watkins, C. C. Esq. Daventry	1	1	0
Watson, J. D. Northampton	1	1	0
Wyatt, Rev. C. F. Broughton	1	1	0
Wyatt, Miss E.	1	1	0
Welchman, R. F. Esq. Southam	1	1	0
Williams, Miss, Barford	1	1	0
Wyleys and Brown, Messrs. Coventry	1	1	0
Watkins, J. W. Esq. Badby House	1	1	0
Wise, Miss, Warwick	1	1	0
Walker, Mrs. Leamington	1	1	0

Donations since the last published List.

Name	£	s.	d.
The Duke of Grafton	5	0	0
Rev. R. G. Joston, Avon Dassett	1	0	0
Rev. J. Morton, Willoughby	1	0	0
Miss Newland, Stratford-on-Avon	10	0	0
Joseph Townsend, Esq.	1	0	0
Rev. Dr. Whorwood, Willoughby	5	0	0
A fine	2	0	0
The late C. H. Harrison, Warmington	1	1	0

BANKERS.

Messrs. Greaves, Greenway, and Smith, Warwick.
The Warwick and Leamington Banking Company.
The Northamptonshire Union Bank.

H. L. SMITH, Hon. Secretary.

F. SMITH, PRINTER, SOUTHAM.

THE COVENTRY PROVIDENT DISPENSARY, FOUNDED IN 1831

The object of this Dispensary is defined as being:– To ensure for its members, by the payment of one penny per week, for each member (adult or child), efficient medical advice, attendance, and medicine during illness. The benefits are limited to the families of working men and others of small means, where the head of the family does not earn more than a weekly average of £2 during a twelvemonth, or an annual income of £104.

Married women can be attended, when confined, by a doctor on payment of £1 1s., or by a midwife on payment of 10s., which may be paid by instalments, which must be completed at least one month prior to the expected confinement.

The children of members are entitled to all the benefits of the Dispensary at birth upon payment of a registration fee of 1s., which must be paid one month prior to birth. The ordinary subscription in such cases commences at the date of birth.

The management is in the hands of a committee of 24 members appointed at the annual meeting, together with the whole of the medical staff and the honorary secretary, who are *ex-officio* members.

In the Report for the year ending March 24, 1907, the number of members upon the books was stated to be 20,420.[1] The new members admitted numbered 1,863. At the time of our visit (September, 1907) it was computed that 7,000 or 8,000 members had seceded, owing to a dispute between the dispensary committee and the medical staff.

The receipts for the year were: Members' payments £3,520, midwifery fees £149, club payments £538, entrance fees £55, registration fees and certificates £29, surgical appliances £61, rents £12, and books £12 – total £4,376.

The payments were:– £2,738 to doctors and midwives, drugs £543, surgical appliances £71, and management £1,008 – total £4,360.

There is a reserve fund, which was credited during the year with £38 from rents, £45 from dividends, £19 bank interest, – total £141, and which amounted to £573 at the end of the year.

Report to the Royal Commission on the Poor Laws and Relief of Distress,
Parliamentary Papers, 1909, p.158.

The Report also covered Norwich and York as large towns, Kendal, Beverley, Lichfield, Ludlow and Bourne as smaller communities, the Rural Districts of Cullompton, Oundle, Cricklade, Fairford and Little Walsingham, as well as the Jarvis Charity at Staunton-on-Wye, Bredwardine and Letton.

FRIENDLY SOCIETIES

Friendly societies were essentially mutual insurance clubs providing cash benefits in cases of injury and sickness or to dependants on the death of a member. They existed in all parts of England, in towns and villages, and had certain critical features in common. Most had members from many different occupations, although usually of a definite social class, who could afford a particular level of subscriptions. In some very high-risk occupations, such as mining or lead-working, the friendly society would limit its members to that one trade. This was the closest a friendly society came to being a trades union, although modern and earlier commentators have often considered the two terms interchangeable.

However, friendly societies made no provision for unemployment or strike pay, although it is clear that friendly societies were feared, in the politically unsettled last decade of the eighteenth century, as a dangerous radical movement. In response to this suspicion, by an Act of 1793 (33 Geo III, *c.* 54) societies were required to register at their county Quarter Sessions, where they had to present their rules, often also stating the year in which they were first established.

Although friendly societies flourished after about 1750, there were a considerable but unknown number founded in the seventeenth century. They were single-gender organisations, often with a maximum limit to the total number of members, usually with a strict age range, and run on democratic lines, requiring all to share official duties. Most clubs excluded certain categories – bailiffs, debtors, paupers and criminals – and attendance at the monthly meetings was obligatory. Payment was refused to those who were responsible for their own illness – by fighting, playing football or from a venereal infection – and members were ejected if they made false claims. There were separate clubs, although fewer in number, for women.

The total membership of friendly societies is difficult to estimate, although some attempt was made to do so in the early nineteenth century, when contemporaries saw club membership as preventing poverty and avoiding dependence on the poor law. The societies had an important public role: they had an annual church procession and dinner, members were given a formal club funeral and they often carried emblems suggesting their names and origins. Some had decidedly political titles, such as the Loyal Britons or the True Blue Society. All the men's clubs met at a local public house, whose landlord was often the treasurer, and every member paid a fixed sum each month into the club box and was allowed beer worth a few pence on each occasion. Drunkenness, political comment and gossip about other members were strictly forbidden. Most clubs were solvent and paid small cash sums weekly so that claimants could avoid the stigma of receiving help from the parish.

Medical care was provided at the friendly society's expense by a local surgeon-apothecary, usually on a *per capita* basis, including his travel costs. Medical sickness certificates and letters survive for some areas. Most clubs required members to live within a short distance of the meeting-place. A surprising number of clubs were institutional subscribers to their county hospital – with nine contributing to the Radcliffe Infirmary, Oxford, in 1789, for example – giving their members rights of admission to the hospital.

ARTICLES AND RULES OF THE CANNOCK FRIENDLY SOCIETY

I. That the first meeting of this society being held on Tuesday, the first of August, one thousand seven hundred and eighty, the next, and every other club-meeting, shall be on the first Tuesday in every month, at the house of the said THOMAS BOULTON, between the hours of seven and nine o'clock in the evening, from Lady-Day to Michaelmas; and between the hours of six and eight from Michaelmas to Lady-Day. That each member shall pay *one shilling* to the box every club-night. That every member shall make his payments good in three club-nights; that such members as do not, shall be allowed one month's grace, for which they shall pay *six pence* to the box. That if any member offers bad money, knowing the same to be such, he shall be forever excluded. That *fifteen shillings* shall be paid out of the joint stock for liquor, on every club-night.

II. That on the club-night before the feast day, yearly, all members shall attend by six o'clock in the evening, at the club-room, in order to appoint the next four senior members, stewards, and other officers; and every absent member shall forfeit *six pence* to the box. That at every meeting, as above mentioned, the next four senior members shall be chosen to serve for the year ensuing; two as stewards, and two as constables. That if any member refuses to serve, he shall forfeit *two shillings and six pence*, and the next senior member shall be chosen in his room.

III. That all grievances or differences, which may happen in the club-room, shall be decided by the majority then present; but if the poll be equal, the high steward shall have the casting vote. That when the stock amounts to *two hundred pounds*, the overplus money shall, upon the feast day, yearly, be divided amongst the members, in due proportion, according to their entrance. That whenever the stock shall be reduced to *one hundred pounds*, the stewards shall give notice thereof to the society, and every member shall advance *one shilling* to the box, the club-night following, over and above his monthly payments: and every member refusing to advance the same, shall forfeit *five shillings*.

IV. That a box shall be provided at the society's expence, with three locks and three keys, in which the books of accounts, and papers belonging to the society, shall be deposited; one of which keys shall be kept by each steward, and the father of the club, for the time being. That the box shall never be opened by the stewards and father of the club, nor any papers taken out, unless there be three other members present. That if any keys are lost, the persons who lose the same, shall be at the expence of finding others; and upon refusal, shall be excluded. That the box shall be kept by the father of the club.

V. That the money shall be kept by the father of the club, who shall give sufficient security for the same. That for every *hundred pounds* lodged in his hands, he shall pay to the society *four pounds* per cent. per annum, and after that the same rate for every *fifty pounds*.

VI. That the stewards shall attend by seven o'clock in the summer half year, and by six o'clock in the winter half year, each club night; that in case they neither attend, not provide substitutes in their room, they shall pay *one shilling* each. That if the clerk does not attend at the same time, to take account of the money paid and received, or provide one in his room, he also shall forfeit *one shilling*; and if the constables do not attend at the same time, to assist the stewards, or provide two in their room, they shall, for every such neglect, forfeit *six pence* to the box. That the old stewards shall deliver up their keys to the new ones, the club-night after they are chosen; on which night they, the father of the club, and the clerk, shall make up their accounts, or pay the sum of *ten pounds* each over and above what is due from them, or be excluded.

VIII. That no person shall be admitted a member of this society; but who shall, at the time of his admittance, be above the age of eighteen, and under the age of thirty; and free from any unknown lameness, disability, or infirmity of body. That if after admission of any new member, it shall appear that he laboured under any bodily infirmity, concealed from the society, he shall be excluded. That every member shall be admitted at a public club-night, with the consent of the majority then present; and that he shall pay to the stewards *five shillings*, and receive articles free.

IX. That if any member be cast into prison for felony or murder, and be found guilty, he shall be excluded this society. That if any member of this society for fighting, excessive drinking, or whoring, after his admission, shall bring upon himself any distemper or misfortune, he shall be excluded.

X. That any member of this society, who has been duly registered, and paid his contributions for the space of one whole year, shall, by sickness, lameness, or any accident, or infirmity (not occasioned by wrestling, fighting, intemperance, or lewdness) be rendered incapable of working for his livelihood, he shall give notice of his disorder or condition to the stewards or clerk, and shall receive *seven shillings* a week from the box, from the time of such notice, until he shall be able to follow his business again. That if any member lives to be past labour, he shall receive *five shillings* per week. That the high steward shall regularly give to every sick, lame, or reduced member, an order upon the father of the club, for his said weekly allowance; and that the father of the club shall not pay any allowance to any member, without such an order. That if any sick member is in arrears to the box, such arrears shall be deducted out of his first week's pay: but if it should be found by experience, that the subscriptions to the box are insufficient to support the above . . . it shall be in the power of the majority of the members assembled on the first club-night after the feast, to reduce the same to such terms as they shall think fit and necessary.

XI. That if any member, who lives at a greater distance than six miles from the club-house, shall lay claim to the benefit of the box, notice of his disorder or condition shall be certified in writing, monthly, signed by the minister and churchwardens of the parish where he resides, and confirmed by some neighbouring surgeon.

XII. That upon the decease of any member, who hath been two years and upwards in this society, the sum of *five pounds* shall be paid out of the joint stock, to the deceased member's widow, nominee, or representative; and every member shall, on the next club-night, pay into the box *one shilling*. That if any member, who hath been admitted two years and upwards, shall bury his wife, he may receive *forty shillings*, and his nominee the other *three pounds* at his decease.

XVII. That four members be chosen each club-night, according to their entrance, to assist the stewards in visiting the sick: that the stewards, and such chosen visitors, or some of them, shall weekly visit every sick member, who lives within three miles of *Cannock*; and if the chosen assistants refuse to obey the orders of the stewards, they shall forfeit *six pence* each to the box.

XXII. That if any member of this society shall be known to work at his trade or calling, or any other business whatsoever, at the time he shall receive weekly benefit; or shall be seen disguised in liquor, or gaming in any public house, such pretended sick or lame member, upon due proof thereof, shall pay the sum of *fifty shillings* to the box, or be excluded. That if any member shall feign himself sick or lame, in order to receive the weekly allowance, he shall forfeit the like sum of *fifty shillings* to the box, or be for ever excluded.

XXIII. That on the club-night next before the feast, an able and experienced surgeon and apothecary shall be chosen by a majority of the members then present, to attend the sick and lame members of the society; that every member shall, yearly, on the feast day, pay to the said doctor, the sum of *two shillings*: that the doctor shall not be obliged to visit the sick or lame members, who live at a greater distance than six miles from the club house. That if the doctor detects any member feigning himself sick or lame, in order to impose upon the society, he shall immediately give notice thereof to the stewards or clerk.

XXIV. That if any member shall be guilty of suicide, his widow, nominee, or representative, shall not be entitled to any benefit from this society.

SPECIMEN LETTER AND CERTIFICATE OF LEA, DERBYSHIRE, FRIENDLY SOCIETY

To the MASTER & WARDENS of the Friendly Society, at Lea.

I do hereby give you notice, that on the   Day of   18   I was rendered incapable of Working by   therefore desire I may receive the benefit allowed by the Society during the time such inability continues. Witness my hand

     Day of   18   .

We whose names are subscribed hereto, do certify the Master and Wardens of the Friendly Society, at Lea, that on the   Day of   18 of   was rendered incapable of working by   and has continued to this   Day of   18   . Witness our hands.

A.B. Minister

C.D., E.F. Churchwardens

Derbyshire Record Office, D 1575/Box L.

SURGEON'S LETTER AND CERTIFICATE ABOUT A FRIENDLY SOCIETY MEMBER

Sir

I am requested by Samuel Redfern a member of the friendly society meeting at the Anchor Inn Doveridge to inform you that he has been ill, ever since the beginning of September, he has left his situation 2 weeks ago and is now so infirm, as to be unable to take an active part in any sort of business, and trusts you will have the goodness to apprize the members of the club, that he is now under the necessity of declaring himself on the club box.

     Yours

     J.M. Cater

to J. Riland, Minister of Yoxall

I do hereby certify that Samuel Redfern, member of the Doveridge friendly society, is, on account of Rheumatism and other infirmities incapable of following his occupation and is a proper object to receive the benefit of the club fund.

20 Nov 1824   J.M. Cater, surgeon, Abbot's Bromley

Derbyshire Record Office, D 1197A/PZ 31–26.

NOTE

1. In 1901 Coventry's population was nearly 62,000.

IX
PAUPER PATIENTS

❖   ❖   ❖

The cost of pauper parishioners who became ill was undeniably one of the greatest problems for the overseers of the poor. The parish was responsible for the necessities of life for those with settlement rights there and welfare expenditure covered food, rent, clothes, small cash sums and burial costs, as well as medical charges. The overseers could pay a local surgeon-apothecary either by an annual contract sum or on a *per capita* basis. Larger rural and urban parishes increasingly used the contract method of paying practitioners, thus omitting details of medical attention from their ledgers. However, until 1834 the majority of overseers continued to pay parish surgeons for individual cases treated. Overseers' accounts regularly record payments to midwives and nurses, as well as for sick parishioners' food, bedding, medicines and occasionally for sending them to a hospital or to a consultant. After the coming of the New Poor Law in 1834 accounts change drastically as the guardians administer relief.

OVERSEERS OF THE POOR ACCOUNTS, BUTLERS MARSTON, 1720, 1750, 1801

The Old Poor Law accounts for Butlers Marston, a remote rural Warwickshire parish, cover the years 1713–1820 in three ledgers. Until the later eighteenth century there were rarely more than ten regular paupers in the parish each year. However, after enclosure in 1771, with periods of high prices, harvest failure and population growth, the number of recipients doubled, as did overall expenditure. These extracts from the overseers' accounts for the years 1720, 1750 and 1801 show how the burden of medical relief increased. In the year 1720 there were only two regular paupers and the parish spent a total of £6 14s 5d, of which nearly a quarter was the surgeon's bill; there was a deficit of 17s 11d in the year. In 1750, when Mary Sabin claimed relief, there were only four regular paupers in the parish and £32 2s 9d was the total spent, of which her childbirth costs were £1 10s 6d, as well as £6 14s for her maintenance. In 1801, a year of widespread famine, there were 22 regular paupers out of a population of 200, costing a total of £383 10s, the second highest sum ever spent for the parish. Of this, the surgeon's bill for the year was £21 3s 3d.

	£	s	d
Recd one Leavy att one shiling the yard Land which comes to	4	19	0
had in mmy habe upon the old account		19	6
pd James Smith for keeping his sisters	1	0	0
pd for cloth to make smocks for Smiths daughters		6	8
pd for making two smocks			10
pd for two pare of stockins		2	6
pd for two pare of shoes		5	0
pfd for Caps and A handkarchif		3	0
gave to a Man which pretended to have the smallpox		1	0
for caring him on horse back to Kington[1]			6
gave to A woman with A great Bellie			6
gave to Goodey Napton to goe with her to Kington			6
gave Ann Ward to pay Thomas Napton to mend her house		1	0
gave to a woman with A great Bellie		1	0
gave Goodey Napton to goe with her to Pillarton[2]			6
for flanil to Bury John Collins child in[3]		1	2
gave to a woman with a great Bellie			6
for caring her to Cumbrook[4] on horse back			6
for keeping John Smiths youngest daughter twenty seven weeks	1	0	3
pd for keeping John Smiths eldest Daughter to Thomas Philips	1	19	0
pd Mr Henors[5] of Kington for the cure of Jane Smiths Leggs	1	10	0
Recd in all	5	18	6
pd in all	6	14	5
pd for a warrant and Expense		2	0

Mary Sabin's childbirth, Overseers' accounts, 1750

	£	s	d
feching the midwife & paying for Mary Sabin		6	6
her att her Lying inn		5	0
for malt & hops for Mary Sabin		3	4

Jas Mason for wood & fething water for Mary Sabin		10
dame pon for nursing Mary Sabin	6	0
for a coffin for Mary Sabins Child[6]	2	6
for a sroud & other things	4	10
To Wm Night for digging the grave & ringing the bell	1	6

Sick paupers, Overseers' accounts, 1801

	$£$	s	d
8 Apr Ann Collins funerl[7]	1	3	4
25 May pd Hannah Worral for nursing Mathos		3	0
John Jones when lame		3	0
25 July widow Mathos when ill[8]	1	14	0
pd Capps gerl for nursing Pricket		2	0
7 Aug bety Kinch for nursing Bayls week		2	0
18 Aug John Jones a day when lame			6
30 Aug for muton for Bayls			6
20 Sep pd Mary Newet for nursing Hannah Worral 2 weeks		2	0
23 Sep 1 pt of wine for mathos		1	9
27 [Nov] exps of Marey Capp beren[9]	1	10	6

Warwickshire County Record Office, DR 458/24–26.

MEDICAL EXPENSES OF THE POOR, 1795

In 1795 the Revd David Davies (1742–1819) wrote *The Case of Labourers in Husbandry Stated and Considered* to bring to public attention the practical details of how the poorest members of society were subsisting in a period of economic difficulty, high prices and war. Less well known than its contemporary, F.M. Eden's *The State of the Poor*, it suggested various means of improving the life of the poor, including education, more work for women and girls and membership of friendly societies. Davies acknowledged, however, that the most desperate could not afford even these modest improvements. He collected family budgets from fourteen English counties, including medical costs. He was rector of Barkham, Berkshire and gave many examples from this parish. Among annual outgoings he included medical expenses of £1 from the annual income of £7, or 2s 8¼d a week.

> *Lying-in*: the child's linen 3 or 4s.; the midwife's fee 5s.; a bottle of gin or brandy always had upon this occasion, 2s.; attendance of a nurse for a few days, and her diet, at least 5s.; half a bushel of malt brewed, and hops, 3s.; to the minister for churching 1s.; – call the sum 1 $£$ and suppose this to happen but once in two years; this is *per annum*   10s 0d
> *Casualties*: 1. In *sickness* there is physick to be paid for, and the loss of time to be allowed for:
> 2. *Burials*: poor people having many children, sometimes lose one: for both these together it seems moderate to allow *per annum*   10s 0d

David Davies, *The Case of Labourers in Husbandry Stated and Considered* (1795), p. 16.

A SMALLPOX PAUPER REMOVED, 1816

Richard Godsall became ill with smallpox in Badgeworth, Gloucestershire, many miles from his own Worcestershire parish, Powick, in which he would have had settlement rights and would have been entitled to assistance from the overseers of the poor. When he reached the hamlet of Twigworth, the overseer there had Godsall and his wife moved in a cart some ten miles away to the workhouse at Tewkesbury, where he died. A coroner's inquest was subsequently held at the Tewkesbury workhouse. The case was obviously regarded of sufficient interest to be reported in a distant East Anglian newspaper.

On Saturday se'nnight an inquest was held at the House of Industry, Tewkesbury, on view of the body of Richard Godsall, a labourer, belonging to the parish of Powick, in the county of Worcester, who died there the previous evening, of that most dreadful malady, the confluent small pox. From the testimony of the widow of this poor, unfortunate and neglected man, it appeared that he was taken ill at Badgworth, where he had been in employ a considerable time, on the Wednesday se'nnight preceding; and that on the following Sunday application was made, on his behalf, to the parish officers, assembled in the churchyard, after divine service, from the behaviour of whom he was induced immediately to quit the place, and proceed on his way to his own home. From the advanced state of the disorder, however, he could only reach the neighbourhood of Churchdown that evening, where he and his wife lay in a desolate barn, without necessary sustenance, and without more clothes than his usual labouring dress. On the Monday he with great difficulty reached the hamlet of Twigworth, in the parish of St. Mary de Lode, Glocester, where he could proceed no further, and applied to the overseer for relief, who put him into the hay-loft, where he lied all night among the hay and straw, without sheet or blanket, or covering of any kind save his own clothes. The disorder had now made such a rapid progress in his constitution that in the morning he exhibited a sad spectacle of human misery, totally blind, and so weak and emaciated that he was unable to stand. The overseer, notwithstanding, got him lifted into a cart and ordered him to be conveyed through several intervening parishes to Tewkesbury and there left. To save him from the jolting of the cart, his wife supported him in her arms the whole way, and when they arrived at Tewkesbury, the wretched state of the poor sufferer exceeded all description. He was immediately conveyed to the House of Industry, where the best medical aid and every solacing effort were promptly resorted to, but it was too late to save him, and he languished in increasing affliction until Friday morning. The Jury, after a minute investigation, returned a verdict "That the deceased being violently ill of the smallpox at Twigworth was removed from thence to Tewkesbury on the 29th. ult. and died of the said disease on the 1st instant, and that his death was greatly accelerated and hastened by such removal".

The Cambridge Chronicle, 15 November 1816.

WARWICK WORKHOUSE INMATES, 1819–23

The workhouse for Warwick's two parishes by 1815 was situated on the outskirts of the town in the Saltisford. It had a large common room and a good schoolroom for the inmates, as well as two workshops. There were rarely more than sixty people in the workhouse, with a resident master and mistress in charge. The building continued to be used until the new Union workhouse was opened in 1838 and it was then sold two years later. The register of inmates began in 1819 and ended in 1829; it was revised every year.

Male inmates

Name	Age	Infirmity	Arrived	Employed	Left	Died
William Neal	74	deaf & blind	8 10 1810	baker		5 5 1821
William Kenning	84	childish	19 8 1811			
William Egginton	69		18 8 1813	gardener		
William Thurman	62	rheumatism	29 7 1816			
William Bond	72		20 1 1816	shoemaker		13 7 1823
John Ryder	56	one leg	1793	minds the shop		
Thomas Attwood	69	childish	27 9 1817			4 4 –
Joseph Harris	70		6 6 1817	constable	20 12 1819	
Joseph Cockbill	70		16 12 1811	tailor	27 9 1821	
Joseph Freeman	22		17 4 1819	gathers dung		
Michael Boucher	48	one leg	6 7 1816	shoemaker		
Joseph Purden	48		20 7 1816	factory		
Thomas Washbrook	23		1814	labourer		5 4 –
William Job	14		1808	Mr Mowton	25 7 1821	
William Harris	15		27 10 1818	Mr Ward	10 10 1822	
John Taylor	15		21 1 1804	spins		
Richard Oudes	10		25 10 1819	spins	16 10 1819	
Joseph Flint	7		9 1 1814	knits	1 1 1823	
John Fily	6		7 6 1816	knits		
William Key	6		2 6 1814	knits		
Robert Howkins	5		18 1 1815			
William Bachelor	3		12 12 1817			
John Upton	1¾		29 6 1819			
John Parke	12	idiot	30 10 1819		11 2 1820	
Manton Parke	7		30 10 1819		11 2 1820	
Thomas Parke	5		30 10 1819		11 2 1820	
Abraham Parke	8 months		30 10 1819		11 2 1820	
.........Pearce	38		14 10 1819		14 5 –	
Thomas Wall	72		1 1 1820	sweep		24 5 1823
William Biddle	42		4 4 1820			8 4 1823
William Key	5		12 7 1820		18 7 1820	
Thomas Key	7		12 7 1820		18 7 1820	
William Cooke	13		1 8 1820	spins	25 9 1820	
George Herbert	6		2 8 1820			
William Carpenter	infant		9 9 1820		14 10 1820	
Joseph Tuck	10		14 9 1820		5 5 1821	
Ralph Morris	29		4 10 1820	sweeps streets	1 1 1821	
William Morris	5		4 10 1820		1 1 1821	

Name	Age	Infirmity	Arrived	Employed	Left	Died
William Nicholson	10		1 2 1821	spins	12 11 1822	
Thomas Nicholson	8		1 2 1821	spins	12 11 1822	
George Nicholson	2					3 9 1821
John Sanders	51	ill	9 4 1821		15 8 1821	
Marmaduke Bolton	28		5 5 1821	mill	20 5 1821	
Thomas Clarridge	17		24 6 1821	gravel pit	21 7 1821	
George Mortimore	42		7 7 1821	whitewashes house	10 10 1821	
George Mortimore	14		7 7 1821	Mr Thorns	14 9 1822	
William Warum	20		10 1 1822	gravel pit	12 7 1822	
Joseph Cockbill?	73		18 1 1822	tailoring		
John Key	37		31 1 1822	Old Park		
William Key	6		31 1 1822	pins	12 7 1822	
Thomas Key	8		31 1 1822	pins	12 7 1822	
John Job	infant		20 4 1822			
John Oades	1½		11 5 1822		14 4 18??	
Joseph Butler	67	idiot	20 12 1821			
William Laapworth	37	ill	30 3 1822			
John Prophet	58	ill	18 6 1822			3 8 1822
John Bennett	58	infirm	3 7 1822		7 10 1822	
Matthew Owen	40	blind	5 8 1822		16 10 1822	
John Kenney	50	insane	9 1 1823		27 3 1823	
Charles Dean	17	insane	20 3 1823		25 5 1823	
John Savage	60		24 5 1823	gardening	3 9 1823	
John Brian	9		4 4 1823			
Charles Brian	1½		4 4 1823			
Charles Dean	19		9 7 1823		7 10 1823	
John Bennett	49	ill	22 10 1823			

Female inmates

Name	Age	Infirmity	Arrived	Employed	Left	Died
Mary Harris	51		24 4 1810	makes men's beds	20 12 1819	
Ann Burnett	55	cripple	30 9 1811	washing	5 9 1825	
Elizabeth Moore	50	rheumatism	14 7 1811	washing	15 2 1820	
Sarah Baker	21		24 4 1810	goes out nursing	14 5 18..	
Phoebe Witts	27		1 7 1819	nurses her children	4 5 18..	
Sarah George	40	lunatic	5 9 1819			
Elizabeth Job	25		6 6 1817	nurses her children	4 5 18..	
Catherine Sabin	20		18 11 1816	spins	25 6 1821	
Mary Hall	20	cripple	29 7 1819	knits	3 6 18..	
Ann Allen	60	idiot	1774			
Elizabeth Toney	60	idiot	1779			
Sarah Bromage	76	childish	1784			9 6 1821
Mrs Walton	60	lunatic	9 2 1819		28 10 1820	
Sarah Hitchcox	58	lunatic	1801	took to Bethnal Green		
Ann Lowke	53		21 11 1812	in cutting room		
Ann Upton	23	ill	17 4 1817			29 12 1819
Harriet Culverwell	20	put to bed	5 11 1819		8 1 1820	
Ann Crook	60	idiot	1779			
Sarah Hinton	64		3 10 1810	goes out nursing		1 8 1821
Sarah Moore	20	cripple	14 7 1811	schoolmistress	15 2 1820	

Name	Age	Infirmity	Arrived	Employed	Left	Died
Charlotte Morris	17		27 7 1811	spins	12 8 1821	
Harriet Hopkins	16		20 9 1812	goes out nursing	4 5 18..	
Elizabeth Hancox	15		1804	spins	11 5 1822	
Phoebe Hale	14		29 7 1819	in cutting room	8 5 1822	
Martha Bennett	13		30 4 1817	goes out nursing	31 7 1822	
Margaret Mure?	12		23 4 1810	knits	20 6 1822	
Elizabeth Hopkins	9		5 5 1819	knits	5 6 1823	
Ann Hopkins	14		29 4 1819	spins	5 6 1823	
Sarah Smith	13		20 9 1817	spins	7 12 1822	
Ann Egginton	32	cripple/fits	18 8 1813			
Eliza Job	2		6 6 1817			
Ann Bratt	2		14 3 1818			
Harriet Herbert	1		28 10 1819			19 1 1820
Sarah Job	infant		20 8 1819			16 12 1819
Maria Witts	infant		17 9 1819		4 5 1820	
Susannah Culverwell	inf't		6 11 1819		9 1 1820	
Jane Rawlins	20	family way	24 11 1819	sews	15 2 1820	
Elizabeth Parke	37		30 11 1819	nurses her child	15 2 1820	
Mary Parke	13		30 11 1819	nurses	15 2 1820	
Harriet Parke	9		30 11 1819	knits	15 2 1820	
Elizabeth Parke	2½		30 11 1819		15 2 1820	
Harriet Taylor	16		14 12 1819	spins	22 1 1820	
Mary Russell	26		1 1 1820	spins	21 5 1820	
Mary Hall	21	scalded	13 1 1820		3 4 1820	
Jane Rawlins	1month		9 1 1820		15 2 1820	
Ann Warner	15		3 1 1820	spins	20 6 1821	
Widow Low	85	infirm	2 7 1820			18 1 1823
Mary Key	37		12 7 1820	nursing	18 7 1821	
Elizabeth Key	–		12 7 1820		18 7 1821	
Charles Key	–		12 7 1820		18 7 1821	
Mary Key	infant		12 7 1820		18 7 1821	
Sarah Carpenter	–	family way	13 7 1820		19 10 1820	
Mary Batchelor		family way	13 7 1820		15 7 1820	
Martha Randle		family way	14 9 1820		31 12 1820	
Ann Hopkins	15		6 10 1820	cleans rooms	25 6 1822	
Sarah Morris	29		4 11 1820	nurses children	1 1 1821	
Maria Morris	9		4 11 1820		1 1 1821	
Susan Morris	1¾		4 1 1820		22 1 1821	
Elizabeth Hewett	20	family way	16 11 1820		22 1 1821	
Harriet Hawkes Randle	infant	–	31 12 1820			
Harriet Hewett	infant	–	22 1 1821			

Warwickshire County Record Office, DR 126/687, 688.

MEDICAL CARE UNDER THE NEW POOR LAW

After the New Poor Law came into being in 1834, the first annual report that the Commissioners issued was a detailed and far-ranging survey, containing information about every aspect of pauper life; it stressed that the New Poor Law was working well and that the poor were better off. The *Report* is more than 400 pages in length, including illustrations of model workhouses, with some areas recorded in great detail. Medical care was, with apprenticeship, the only aspect of outdoor relief allowed after 1834, when all other assistance was to be received in the Union workhouse. The terms for medical relief and duties were precisely set out.

Medical relief

The guardians shall, from such period as they shall think proper, contract with some competent person or persons duly licensed to practise as a medical man or medical men, to be the medical officer or officers of the said Union, and to attend duly and punctually upon all paupers falling sick within the limits of the union, either in the workhouse or otherwise, and to supply such sick paupers with all necessary medicines and appliances whatsoever; but such contract may, if the guardians think proper, contain a clause, by which the said medical officer shall engage to attend, at a fair and reasonable charge per head, to be named in such contract, on all persons not belonging to any parish or place comprised in the said Union, whom by law any such parish or place may be bound to relieve, under suspended orders of removal.

The medical officer shall in every case, when required by the guardians or relieving officer, or by the pauper on whom he is attending, give a certificate under his hand of the sickness of such pauper, or other cause of the attendance of such medical officer, the extent and nature of such sickness at the time of giving such certificate, and its probable duration, and such other particulars as may show how far the applicant is prevented from attending too his usual calling.

The medical officer shall make a weekly return to the board of guardians, according to the Form hereto annexed, and shall also attend the board of guardians when summoned by them.

The medical officer's duties

1. To attend at the workhouse as such stated times as may be directed by the board of guardians, and also when sent for by the master or matron of the workhouse, in cases of sudden illness, accident or other emergency; and at all such other items as the state of the sick or lunatic patients within the workhouse may render necessary.

2. To examine into the state of the patients in the sick and lunatic wards; and also into the state of those sick paupers who have not yet been removed there, and also to examine into the state of the paupers on their admission into the workhouse.

3. To ascertain and report to the board of guardians the cause and circumstances of every death which may take place in the workhouse.

4. To give all necessary directions as to the diet, classification and treatment of sick and lunatic paupers, and to provide the requisite medicines, and to make up in writing, in the form and according to the instructions in schedule, a register of

the sickness and mortality which may have obtained amongst the paupers in the workhouse, together with such remarks on their general health and state as he may deem fitting, to be laid before the guardians at each weekly meeting of the board. In which book also the medical officer shall insert the date of every attendance at the workhouse.

First Annual Report of the Poor Law Commissioners for England and Wales,
Parliamentary Papers, 1835, XXVII.

REPORT ON THE SANITARY CONDITION OF THE LABOURING POPULATION OF GREAT BRITAIN

Sir Edwin Chadwick (1800–90) was an Assistant Poor Law Commissioner in 1832 and a year later became Chief Commissioner and a member of the Royal Commission to investigate the condition of factory children. He was secretary to the New Poor Law Commissioners from 1834 until 1846, a member of the Sanitary Commission (1839 and 1844) and of the Board of Health (1848–54). He was knighted in 1889. In attempting to change attitudes towards pauperism, he insisted that it was cheaper to eradicate poverty than simply to use the palliative of poor relief. His *Report* of 1842, with vivid descriptions of how the poor lived in different regions, showed that poverty was closely linked to ill-health, which in turn was exacerbated by the terrible sanitary conditions of much of the British population. The report's publication led to the passing of the Public Health Act of 1848.

The industrial town: the evidence from Leeds

Dr Robert Baker, a GP and sub-inspector of factories in Leeds, had already drawn up a 'Sanatory Map' of the town in 1840 and in 1838 had undertaken a house-to-house survey for the Corporation. Asked to prepare a report by Chadwick based on his work, Baker replied that he had 'no leisure but in the night' and he finally had to be pressed to complete the survey in November 1841.

In one of the streets of Leeds where stagnant water used frequently to accumulate after rain, and where there was perpetually occurring cases of fever of a malignant character, a deputation of females waited upon me in my capacity of town counsellor to ask if any remedy could be applied to this nuisance, which they declared was not only offensive but deadly. I directed then to communicate with the owner of the property, and to say that if the grievance was not remedied I should take further steps to enforce it. Never hearing again from the deputation, I presumed that the remedy had been applied, and had forgotten the circumstances until the house surgeon of the fever hospital in 1840, in noticing from whence fever cases were most frequently brought to the institution, remarked that "formerly many cases of malignant fever were brought in from _____ street, but for two or three years there had been none or not more than one or two".

In the houses of the working classes, brothers and sisters, and lodgers of both sexes, are found occupying the same sleeping-room with the parents, and consequences occur which humanity shudders to contemplate. It is but three or four years since a father and daughter stood at the bar of the Leeds Sessions as criminals, the one in concealing, and the other being an accessory to concealing the birth of an illegitimate child, born on the body of the daughter by the father; and now, in November, 1841, one of the Registrars of Leeds has recorded the birth of an illegitimate child born on the body of a young girl, only 16 years of age, who lived with her mother, who cohabited with her lodger, the father of this child, of which the girl had been pregnant five months, when the mother died.

The rural areas: the evidence from Bedfordshire, Lincolnshire and Dorset

Mr William Blower, the surgeon of the Bedford Union, described the 'influence of moral causes on the health of the population':

> Throughout the whole of this district, there is a great want of "superior cottage accommodation". Most of the residences of the labourers are thickly inhabited, and many of them are damp, low, cold, smoky, and comfortless. These circumstances occasion the inmates to be sickly in the winter season, but I have not yet observed them to generate typhus, the prevailing form of disease being principally catarrhal; such as colds, coughs, inflammations of the eyes, dysentery, rheumatism, &c. However, when any contagious or epidemic malaria occurs, the cases are generally more numerous.

The medical officer of the Ampthill Union stated:

> Typhus fever has existed for the last three or four months in the parish of Flitwick, and although the number of deaths has not been considerable as compared with the progress of the disease, new cases have occurred as those under treatment became convalescent, and several are still suffering under this malady. The cottages in which it first appeared (and to which it has been almost exclusively confined), are of the most wretched description: a stagnant pond is in the immediate vicinity, and none of the tenements have drains; rubbish is thrown within a few yards of the dwellings, and there is no doubt but in damp foggy weather, and also during the heat of summer, the exhalations arising from those heaps of filth must generate disease, and the obnoxious effluvia tends to spread contagion where it already exists. It appears that most of the cottages eluded to were erected for election purposes [the creation of new 40s freeholds carrying a vote], and have since been allowed to decay; the roofs are repaired with turf dug in the neighbourhood, and the walls with prepared clay, without the addition of lime-washing. Contagious disease has not been remarkable within the Union in any other spot than the one alluded to.

Mr T.P.J. Grantham, medical officer of the Sleaford Union, described the outbreak of typhus in a farm labourer's family:

> The domestic economy in this house was deplorable; eight persons slept in one small ill-ventilated apartment, with scarcely any bed-clothing; the smell arising from want of cleanliness, and the dirty clothes of the children being allowed to

accumulate, was most considerable. Considering the situation of the house, its filthy state, and the vitiated air which must have been respired over and over again, by its eight individuals sleeping in one confined apartment, it is not surprising that this family should have been afflicted with fever, and that of a very malignant type; the mother and one child fell victims to it in a very short time.

Mr John Fox, medical officer of the Cerne Union, described illness in his practice area:

The following shocking case occurred in my practice. In a family consisting of six persons, two had a fever; the mud floor of their cottage was at least one foot below the lane; it consisted of one small room only, in the centre of which stood a foot-ladder reaching to the edge of a platform which extended over nearly one-half of the room, and upon which were placed two beds, with space between them for one person only to stand, whilst the outside of each touched the thatch. The head of one of these beds stood within six inches of the edge of the platform, and in this bed one of my unfortunate patients, a boy about 11 years old, was sleeping with his mother, and in a fit of delirium jumped over the head of his bed and fell to the ground below, a height of about seven feet. The injury to the head and spine was so serious that he lived a few hours only after the accident.

CAUSES OF DEATH IN ENGLAND AND WALES IN 1838

In 1838 Neil Arnott and James P. Kay produced their 'Report on the prevalence of certain physical causes of fever in the Metropolis, which might be removed by proper sanatory measures' in the *Fourth annual report of the Poor Law Commission*.

COUNTIES	Number of Deaths during the Year ended 31st December, 1838, from										Proportion of Deaths from the preceding Causes in every 1,000 of the Population, 1841	Proportion of Deaths from all Causes of Mortality in every 1,000 of the Population, 1841
	1 Epidemic, Endemic, and Contagious Diseases				2 Diseases of Respiratory Organs			3 Diseases of Brain, Nerves, and Senses	4 Diseases of Digestive Organs	Total Deaths from the four preceding Classes of Diseases		
	Fever: Typhus, Scarlatina	Small-pox	Measles	Hooping Cough	Consumption	Pneumonia	All other Classes					
ENGLAND												
Bedford	155	75	40	66	457	97	57	304	131	1,382	13	22
Berks	204	288	21	86	739	231	162	467	201	2,399	15	25
Bucks	256	85	61	27	575	131	61	348	152	1,696	11	19
Cambridge	231	136	57	90	686	156	70	318	189	1,933	12	21
Chester	592	279	178	87	1,742	366	345	1,442	421	5,452	14	21
Cornwall	443	135	168	491	1,270	342	124	631	228	3,832	11	18
Cumberland	165	188	11	83	562	75	142	278	169	1,673	9	21
Derby	394	77	79	71	905	200	205	777	268	2,976	11	18
Devon	615	460	287	312	1,649	564	298	1,237	471	5,893	11	18
Dorset	137	255	80	58	571	146	106	380	159	1,892	11	19
Durham	347	316	139	304	1,007	362	207	1,138	274	4,094	13	21
Essex	417	460	83	163	1,250	276	234	782	268	3,933	11	19
Gloucester	352	457	440	244	1,395	578	476	1,142	510	5,594	13	20
Hereford	84	83	17	36	333	56	57	238	62	966	8	18
Hertford	160	116	45	48	620	107	90	453	155	1,794	11	20
Huntingdon	61	18	1	17	216	45	42	140	72	612	10	18
Kent	955	510	169	214	1,701	564	526	1,650	651	6,940	13	21
Lancaster	2,866	1,628	898	910	8,124	2,660	1,916	7,457	3,231	29,690	18	25
Leicester	273	98	17	70	941	243	154	668	314	2,778	13	21
Lincoln	370	138	29	88	874	248	242	1,090	358	3,437	9	17
Middlesex	4,422	3,359	487	1,749	6,220	3,097	2,334	6,643	2,492	30,803	20	27
Monmouth	328	321	49	91	481	183	78	550	100	2,181	16	24
Norfolk	515	126	63	109	1,388	325	281	793	395	3,995	10	19
Northampton	348	148	36	36	762	192	124	503	212	2,361	12	21
Northumberland	366	149	46	113	715	287	240	709	388	3,013	12	21
Nottingham	222	73	18	80	911	225	201	901	287	2,918	12	20
Oxford	222	81	51	59	655	108	152	389	180	1,897	12	21
Rutland	11	2	—	13	64	14	8	56	28	196	9	17
Salop	213	154	112	138	995	242	168	550	284	2,856	12	21
Somerset	560	710	401	46	1,446	426	373	982	473	5,417	12	21
Southampton	454	164	78	148	1,222	338	331	881	372	3,988	17	19
Stafford	610	249	182	268	1,809	539	419	1,251	597	5,924	12	18
Suffolk	480	325	53	158	1,306	315	184	538	275	3,634	12	20
Surrey	1,348	814	177	565	2,196	978	700	2,325	763	9,866	11	25
Sussex	391	80	159	88	1,047	222	181	863	295	3,326	11	18
Warwick	454	415	153	164	1,495	678	361	978	638	5,336	13	20
Westmoreland	41	40	6	41	248	33	44	154	46	653	12	21
Wilts	246	259	263	140	869	268	212	606	241	3,104	12	20
Worcester	381	305	122	258	990	353	235	645	446	3,735	16	29
York, E.R.	194	92	167	149	725	194	176	1,009	251	2,957	13	21
„ N.R.	123	28	69	114	550	102	135	553	187	1,861	9	17
„ W.R.	1,298	993	799	507	4,253	1,202	848	4,374	1,494	15,768	14	21
WALES												
North	660	575	4	210	1,227	102	223	1,311	198	4,510	13	18
South	1,613	1,004	199	398	1,834	129	277	1,200	380	7,034	14	21
Total, 1838	24,577	16,268	6,514	9,107	59,025	17,999	13,799	49,704	19,306	216,299	14	22
Total, 1839	25,991	9,131	10,937	8,165	59,559	18,151	12,855	49,215	20,767	214,771	14	21

Michael Flinn, *The Sanitary Condition of the Labouring Population of Gt. Britain by Edwin Chadwick*, 1964, pp. 103, 193, 86–7, 190, 83, 76–7, 228–31.

COMPARATIVE CHANCES OF LIFE IN DIFFERENT CLASSES, 1838–41, from Michael Flinn, *The Sanitary Condition of the Labouring Population of Gt. Britain by Edwin Chadwick*, 1964, pp. 103, 193, 86–7, 190, 83, 76–7, 228–31.

Classes	Total No. of Deaths under 20 Years of Age	Proportion of Deaths which occurred at the under-mentioned periods of Age			Proportion of Deaths under 20 Years to Total Deaths	Total No. of Deaths which occurred between 20 and 60	Proportion of Deaths which occurred at the under-mentioned periods of Age				Proportion of Deaths from 20 to 60 to Total Deaths	Total No. of Deaths which occurred above 60	Proportion of Deaths which occurred at the under-mentioned periods of Age				Proportion of Deaths above 60 to Total Deaths
		Between 0—5	Between 5—10	Between 10—20			Between 20—30	Between 30—40	Between 40—50	Between 50—60			Between 60—70	Between 70—80	Between 80—90	90 and upwards	
Gentry and Professional Persons, Children of																	
Manchester	21	1 in 3	1 in 24	1 in 54	1 in 3	13	1 in 18	1 in 14	1 in 18	1 in 18	1 in 4	20	1 in 6	1 in 8	1 in 14	—	1 in 2¾
Leeds	20	1 in 5	1 in 26	1 in 40	1 in 4	28	1 in 11	1 in 10	1 in 16	1 in 10	1 in 3	31	1 in 7	1 in 7	1 in 13	1 in 79	1 in 2½
Liverpool	61	1 in 3	1 in 11	1 in 23	1 in 2½	34	1 in 46	1 in 15	1 in 23	1 in 9	1 in 4	42	1 in 7	1 in 7	1 in 34	—	1 in 3¼
Bath	32	1 in 11	1 in 12	1 in 31	1 in 4½	29	1 in 29	1 in 24	1 in 24	1 in 12	1 in 5	85	1 in 5	1 in 6	1 in 5	1 in 146	1 in 1¾
Bethnal Green	33	1 in 5	1 in 20	1 in 13	1 in 3	21	1 in 25	1 in 17	1 in 25	1 in 14	1 in 5	47	1 in 6	1 in 5	1 in 9	1 in 101	1 in 2
Strand Union	21	1 in 6	1 in 29	1 in 29	1 in 4	37	1 in 9	1 in 9	1 in 10	1 in 11	1 in 2¼	28	1 in 7	1 in 9	1 in 22	1 in 86	1 in 3
Kendal Union	15	1 in 7	1 in 26	1 in 9	1 in 3	18	1 in 13	1 in 13	1 in 7	1 in 17	1 in 3	19	1 in 17	1 in 7	1 in 6	1 in 52	1 in 2¾
County of Wilts (Unions of)	25	1 in 9	1 in 40	1 in 13	1 in 5	32	1 in 15	1 in 15	1 in 17	1 in 13	1 in 4	62	1 in 5	1 in 4	1 in 12	1 in 119	1 in 2¼
County of Rutland (Unions of)	4	1 in 4	—	—	1 in 7	7	1 in 14	1 in 14	1 in 14	1 in 28	1 in 4	17	1 in 9	1 in 4	1 in 6	1 in 28	1 in 1¾
Total	232	1 in 5	1 in 19	1 in 19	1 in 3½	219	1 in 17	1 in 14	1 in 16	1 in 12	1 in 4	351	1 in 6	1 in 6	1 in 10	1 in 115	1 in 2¼
Farmers, Tradesmen, and Persons similarly circumstanced, Children of																	
Manchester	444	1 in 2	1 in 18	1 in 27	1 in 2	220	1 in 14	1 in 11	1 in 13	1 in 18	1 in 3¼	61	1 in 21	1 in 38	1 in 145	1 in 242	1 in 12
Leeds	425	1 in 2	1 in 18	1 in 18	1 in 2	238	1 in 12	1 in 14	1 in 14	1 in 19	1 in 3½	161	1 in 13	1 in 12	1 in 34	1 in 824	1 in 5
Liverpool	1,033	1 in 2	1 in 19	1 in 33	1 in 1¾	481	1 in 22	1 in 13	1 in 14	1 in 13	1 in 3½	224	1 in 16	1 in 22	1 in 51	1 in 869	1 in 8
Bath	78	1 in 4	1 in 24	1 in 30	1 in 3	109	1 in 11	1 in 7	1 in 9	1 in 9	1 in 2¼	57	1 in 9	1 in 12	1 in 40	1 in 122	1 in 4¼
Bethnal Green	142	1 in 2	1 in 20	1 in 28	1 in 2	92	1 in 15	1 in 11	1 in 12	1 in 11	1 in 3	44	1 in 13	1 in 15	1 in 93	1 in 278	1 in 6¼
Strand Union	99	1 in 3	1 in 20	1 in 25	1 in 2	71	1 in 16	1 in 22	1 in 10	1 in 9	1 in 3	51	1 in 9	1 in 13	1 in 22	—	1 in 4¼
Kendal Union	47	1 in 4	1 in 35	1 in 14	1 in 3	43	1 in 8	1 in 14	1 in 17	1 in 17	1 in 3	48	1 in 6	1 in 10	1 in 13	—	1 in 3
County of Wilts (Unions of)	54	1 in 7	1 in 27	1 in 15	1 in 4	65	1 in 22	1 in 14	1 in 10	1 in 12	1 in 3½	99	1 in 7	1 in 6	1 in 10	1 in 31	1 in 2¼
County of Rutland (Unions of)	174	1 in 3	1 in 30	1 in 17	1 in 3	108	1 in 15	1 in 16	1 in 19	1 in 19	1 in 4	168	1 in 8	1 in 7	1 in 9	1 in 90	1 in 2⅓
Total	2,496	1 in 2¼	1 in 20	1 in 23	1 in 2	1,427	1 in 15	1 in 12	1 in 13	1 in 14	1 in 3½	913	1 in 12	1 in 14	1 in 29	1 in 122	1 in 5
Agricultural and other Labourers, Artisans, and Servants, Children of																	
Manchester	3,106	1 in 2	1 in 22	1 in 19	1 in 1½	1,149	1 in 16	1 in 14	1 in 18	1 in 17	1 in 4	374	1 in 20	1 in 43	1 in 149	1 in 772	1 in 12
Leeds	2,245	1 in 2	1 in 14	1 in 14	1 in 1½	773	1 in 14	1 in 16	1 in 20	1 in 22	1 in 4½	377	1 in 20	1 in 23	1 in 62	1 in 485	1 in 9
Liverpool	4,004	1 in 1½	1 in 15	1 in 33	1 in 1¼	1,205	1 in 17	1 in 18	1 in 17	1 in 24	1 in 4½	385	1 in 27	1 in 47	1 in 102	1 in 1865	1 in 15
Bath	508	1 in 2	1 in 19	1 in 18	1 in 1¾	258	1 in 12	1 in 14	1 in 13	1 in 17	1 in 3	130	1 in 16	1 in 19	1 in 45	1 in 149	1 in 6¾
Bethnal Green	908	1 in 2	1 in 15	1 in 30	1 in 1½	228	1 in 18	1 in 23	1 in 21	1 in 31	1 in 5½	122	1 in 21	1 in 28	1 in 97	1 in 419	1 in 10¼
Strand Union	367	1 in 2	1 in 14	1 in 23	1 in 2	212	1 in 13	1 in 12	1 in 13	1 in 13	1 in 3	95	1 in 12	1 in 23	1 in 84	1 in 225	1 in 7
Kendal Union	186	1 in 3	1 in 19	1 in 11	1 in 2	113	1 in 13	1 in 14	1 in 18	1 in 14	1 in 3¾	114	1 in 11	1 in 9	1 in 15	1 in 207	1 in 3¾
County of Wilts (Unions of)	954	1 in 3	1 in 21	1 in 14	1 in 2	492	1 in 13	1 in 18	1 in 18	1 in 19	1 in 4	615	1 in 11	1 in 9	1 in 11	1 in 108	1 in 3½
County of Rutland (Unions of)	293	1 in 3	1 in 18	1 in 18	1 in 2¼	157	1 in 12	1 in 18	1 in 18	1 in 27	1 in 4	227	1 in 10	1 in 8	1 in 10	1 in 75	1 in 3
Total	12,571	1 in 2	1 in 17	1 in 20	1 in 1½	4,587	1 in 15	1 in 17	1 in 18	1 in 20	1 in 4	2,439	1 in 18	1 in 23	1 in 43	1 in 338	1 in 8

NOTES

1. Kineton, two miles away, was the local market town.
2. Pillerton Priors was the adjacent parish to Butlers Marston.
3. Daniel Collins was buried on 24 May 1720 aged thirteen.
4. Combrook was a neighbouring hamlet.
5. John Venour, a Kineton surgeon, died aged fifty-two in 1729, leaving £30 in his will to provide three cloth gowns a year for the poor of Wellesbourne, where he was born. There is a brass plate to his memory in Kineton church describing him as 'generosus peritissimus chirurgus' (a generous, most skilful surgeon).
6. Sarah Sabin, daughter of George and Mary, was baptised and buried in May 1720.
7. Ann Collins, aged twenty-five, was buried on 8 April 1801.
8. Widow Ann Matthews continued to be supported by the parish until the end of the accounts in 1822.
9. Mary Capp was buried on 10 November 1801, her husband in the following year.

X
MEDICAL PORTRAITS AND MEMORIALS

From at least the seventeenth century artists painted portraits and genre scenes showing the medical practitioner at work, while from an even earlier period monuments to commemorate respected physicians, surgeons and apothecaries were placed in English parish churches and cathedrals. However, only the most prosperous practitioners, virtually all physicians, had their portraits painted before at least the middle years of the eighteenth century and genre scenes seem to have been exclusively Dutch in origin until even later.

The majority of English sitters in the seventeenth century were overwhelmingly aristocratic, clerical and legal, although occasionally a medical portrait was created. An early example was that of John Patch, an Exeter surgeon, painted by the itinerant artist William Gandy (*c.* 1655–1729), in which Patch's professional skills

John Patch, *fl.* 1700–43, honorary
surgeon of Exeter Hospital, by
William Gandy.

John Ash MD, 1723–98, by Sir Joshua Reynolds, 1788. Ash was one of the founders of Birmingham Hospital and an honorary physician there. He holds a ground plan of the hospital, which opened in 1779 and can be seen in the background.

Below: The Mynors Family, by James Millar, oil on canvas, 1797. Robert Mynors (1739–1806) was a successful Birmingham surgeon who built Weatheroak Hall, Alvechurch, Worcestershire (shown in the background picture), now a golf club.

are indicated as he sits holding a scalpel, with a part-dissected forearm near him and an anatomical drawing close by. Most early portraits, however, show the sitter with some symbol of his profession in the painting, so that William Johnston MD (1643–1725) of Warwick was depicted by an anonymous artist wearing his academic robes, with a skull nearby. A painting such as B. Orchard's of Richard Morton MD (1669–1730) is unusual in that no professional emblems are shown, and the sitter is indistinguishable from his gentry contemporaries.

By the mid-eighteenth century, though, as medicine became increasingly prosperous and influential, many more medical portraits were commissioned and, indeed, virtually all the medical 'great names' of the period were painted, some several times, frequently by the leading artists of the day. Thus Sir Samuel Garth and William Stukeley MD both sat to Sir Godfrey Kneller, Jonathan Richardson painted William Cheselden and Richard Mead, Joshua Reynolds painted three physicians, John Ash, Rice Charlton and Abel Moysey, while Erasmus Darwin MD sat to Joseph Wright of Derby, and the royal surgeon, William Sharp, was depicted with his family by Johann Zoffany in 1779–81. An unusual provincial family group was that created by James Millar of Birmingham showing Robert Mynors (1739–1806), a local surgeon and his family in their newly built Worcestershire country house in 1797.

It is clear that in the next century certain artists specialised in medical portraiture, so that, for example, Sir Thomas Lawrence painted Matthew Baillie, Sir Astley Cooper, Sir Henry Halford and John Moore MD, while George Dance painted John Abernethy, William Coombe and John Moore. Among Sir Francis Chantrey's dozen medical sitters were Matthew Baillie, Sir Benjamin Brodie, Henry Cline and Sir Astley Cooper. However, many provincial hospitals commemorated their consultants with portraits, whose artists are now often unknown. Thus Worcester Infirmary has an anonymous portrait of the surgeon William Russell, holding the plan of the new hospital in his hand, while Birmingham Hospital has Reynolds's grand portrait of John Ash, also holding the infirmary's ground plan. A very unusual medical portrait was that of the physician Sir Alexander Morison, painted by the impressive Victorian artist Richard Dadd while he was confined in Bethlem for many years. The fashion for medical portrait tributes in hospitals has continued until the present day.

Busts and statues were a far more individualistic form of portraiture, since they could not be copied as engravings for wider circulation. Famous practitioners, such as William Harvey or Richard Mead, were sculpted, as were the 'Surgeon Princes' whose busts decorate the main staircase of the Royal College of Surgeons in London and indeed busts were a standard form of commemorating hospital consultants in their own infirmary. However, more modest provincial practitioners might also have a portrait bust where they were buried, as Claver Morris did at Wells Cathedral. A practitioner's cultural interests might also be recorded on a tombstone, as on those for Henry Harington MD (music) and John Wall MD (painting), both buried in Bath Abbey. Statues were also created of leading medical figures, often by public subscription, as at Leamington Spa, where Peter Hollins's large statue of Henry Jephson MD (1798–1868), who is considered to have made the town famous and

Monument to Henry Harington MD, 1727–1816, Bath Abbey. Harington was one of the first three physicians at Bath General Hospital and a founder member of the Bath Harmonic Society; he served as mayor in 1793–4.

John Wall MD, 1708–76, honorary physician at Worcester Infirmary, said to be a self-portrait. He was a founder of the Worcester Porcelain Company in 1751.

prosperous, was erected in gardens named in his honour at his retirement in 1848. Another heroic medical figure, Edward Jenner, is represented by R.W. Sievier's statue (1825) in Gloucester Cathedral.

However, it is perhaps in the cathedrals and parish churches of England that the greatest number of medical commemorations and monuments can still be seen, ranging from the simple brass or stone plaque, as for Richard Kay, to quite elaborate creations. Thus at St Bartholomew's, Edgbaston there is a wall monument to William Withering MD (d. 1799) showing the usual medical symbol, the caduceus, but with the snake entwined round a sprig of foxglove, from which Withering had discovered how to extract digitalis. Indeed, the caduceus is often the most noticeable indication on a church monument that it commemorates a medical practitioner, as at Worcester Cathedral, where two members of the Johnston family are buried. The monumental inscription was invariably very flattering, as on the tomb of John Wall, noting 'Nature gave him Talents, a benevolent Heart directed ye Application of them to the Study and practice of a profession the most beneficial to Mankind'. Again, Flaxman's monument in Salisbury Cathedral to Walter Long (d. 1809), a surgeon, shows allegories of Science and Benevolence. By the nineteenth century, though, sentimental funerary images predominate, often

Monument to Richard Sowray, BPhys, 1664–1708, St Mary's, Castlegate, York.

Monument to John Burton MD, 1709–71, Holy Trinity, Micklegate, York.

Monument to John Dealtry MD, 1708–73, by Richard and John Fisher, York Minster, inscribed with a poem by William Mason.

The Village Doctor by
H. Wigstead(?),
attributed to
Rowlandson, 1774.

showing a frail female figure bending over a classical urn, as in the tomb of John Dealtry MD in York Minster.

As an indication of how interested a consumer society had become in medical personalities, in the late eighteenth century Josiah Wedgwood produced a variety of jasper medallions of some famous practitioners for mass sale. His list of recent or contemporary figures included Mead, Sloane, Joseph Priestley and John Fothergill, but also some famous names from an earlier age, such as Herman Boerhaave (1668–1738) and John Woodward MD (1665–1728). Of these, Richard Mead's likeness appeared most often.

Cartoons, especially from the later eighteenth century, show many critical and scornful representations of practitioners and of medical procedures, although a practitioner had to be of a certain eminence to be recognised when depicted in a cartoon. However, many medical activities including dissection and vaccination, were thought worthy subjects for cartoonists, while some medical conditions were always considered darkly comic, so that venereal diseases, gout, obesity and often childbirth were caricatured. Thus, although William Hogarth carried out commissions to paint physicians' portraits (Benjamin Hoadley in *c.* 1738 and Thomas Pellett in *c.* 1735–9), his most trenchant comments were made through his widely sold engravings. In his three famous series, *A Rake's Progress*, *Marriage à la Mode* and *A Harlot's Progress*, venereal diseases are clearly depicted: the Rake ended his life insane as an inmate of Bedlam; the young Viscount Squanderfield was treated by a French quack, Mons de la Pillule, and Moll Hackabout, the young harlot, died 'poxed' at the age of twenty-three. Hogarth seems not to have admired the medical professions greatly, showing as the final episode in *The Four Stages of Cruelty* a dissecting room with John Freke as the surgeon-demonstrator. He also indicated his dislike of the unqualified in *A Consultation of Physicians*, subtitled *The Company of Undertakers* of 1737, where he caricatured the leading quacks of the day, John ('Chevalier') Taylor, Sarah Mapp and Joshua ('Spot') Ward. Rowlandson and Gillray were to continue this mockery in the nineteenth century. Cartoons, especially in the press, remained a powerful and popular way of instantly conveying a message, even as recently as in the publicity surrounding the establishing of the National Health Service in 1948. Although cartoons essentially depicted only the best-known figures and issues, they are comparable with portraits, busts, statues and monuments as another means of identifying very different aspects in the public perception of medical practitioners, both idolised and vilified.

CREDITS

The author and the publisher gratefully acknowledge permission from the following to reproduce the text extracts in this book:

R.L. Brett (ed.), Mrs R.L. Brett, for 'A visit to Bodmin Asylum, 1841' on page 141 from *Barclay Fox's Journal*.

W. Brockbank and W.F. Kenworthy (eds), The Chetham Society, for 'The Diary of Richard Kay of Baldingstone, 1744, 1749' on pages 104–5 from *The Diary of Richard Kay of Baldingstone, near Bury, Lancs.*

A.F.J. Brown (ed.), Essex Record Office, for 'The diary of Jonas Asplin, surgeon-apothecary, 1826' on pages 113–14 from *Essex People, 1750–1900*.

E. Cecil Curwen (ed.), Oxford University Press, for 'The diary of Gideon Mantell, surgeon-apothecary, 1818–31' on pages 110–11 from *The Journal of Gideon Mantell, surgeon and geologist, 1818–52*.

Vanessa S. Doe (ed.), Derbyshire Record Society, for 'The medical notes of James Clegg of Chapel en le Frith, 1729' on pages 99–101 from *The Diary of James Clegg of Chapel en le Frith, 1708–1755*.

Malcolm Elwin, Laurence Pollinger Ltd, for 'Sophia Curzon's letters to her aunt, Mary Noel, 1781–2' on pages 49–51 from *The Noels and the Milbankes*.

Adrian Henstock (ed.), The Thoroton Society, for 'The diary of Abigail Gawthern, 1803' on page 57 from *The Diary of Abigail Gawthern of Nottingham, 1751–1810*.

C.D. Linnell (ed.), Bedfordshire Historical Record Society, 'The diary of the Revd Benjamin Rogers of Carlton, 1730–39' on page 46 from *The Diary of Benjamin Rogers, Rector of Carlton, 1720–71*.

F.J. Manning (ed.), Bedfordshire Historical Record Society, for 'The births of children to Edmond and Christian Williamson, 1709–20' on pages 35–7 from *Some Bedfordshire Diaries*.

J.D. Marshall (ed.), The Chetham Society, for 'The autobiography of William Stout, 1736, 1742' on pages 61–2 from *The Autobiography of William Stout of Lancaster, 1665–1752*.

Frederick A. Pottle (ed.), Edinburgh University Press, for 'James Boswell in London, 1763' on pages 81–2 from *Boswell's London Journal, 1762–1763*.

F.N.L. Poynter (ed.), Pearson Education Ltd, for 'The journal of James Yonge, surgeon of Plymouth' on page 96 from *The Journal of James Yonge [1747–1721], Plymouth Surgeon*.

Roger Rolls, Bird Publications, for 'Nurses' duties at the Mineral Water Hospital, Bath, *c*. 1835' on page 41 from *The Hospital of the Nation*.

Matthew Storey (ed.), Suffolk Record Society, for 'The diary of Isaac Archer of
    Mildenhall, 1670–82' on pages 32–3 from *Two East Anglian Diaries*.

Frank Tyrer (ed.), Record Society of Lancashire and Cheshire, for 'The Great
    Diurnal of Nicholas Blundell of Little Crosby, 1725–28' on pages 44–5 from
    The Great Diurnal of Nicholas Blundell of Little Crosby, Lancashire, 1702–1728.

Joan Wake and Deborah Champion Webster (eds), Northamptonshire Record
    Society, for 'Letters to the 3rd Earl of Cardigan about his sons, 1727' on page 37
    from *The Letters of Daniel Eaton to the third Earl of Cardigan, 1725–1732*.

A.P. Watt Ltd on behalf of J.C. Beresford, B.W. Beresford and Ruth Longman for
    James Woodforde, Oxford University Press, for 'The diary of the Revd James
    Woodforde, 1784–91' on pages 51–3, from *The Diary of a Country Parson,
    1758–1802*.

The following record offices and libraries have given permission for their material to
    be reproduced: Birmingham Archives; Bodleian Library, Oxford; Bradford City
    Library; Coventry City Archives; Derbyshire Record Office; Gloucestershire Record
    Office; Hampshire Record Office; Herefordshire Record Office; Lichfield Record
    Office; Northamptonshire Record Office; Shakespeare Birthplace Trust Records
    Office; Somerset Archive and Record Service; Staffordshire and Stoke-on-Trent
    Archive Service; Warwickshire County Record Office; The Wellcome Library;
    Worcestershire Record Office.

SELECT BIBLIOGRAPHY AND FURTHER READING

Unless stated otherwise, London is the place of publication.

Abel-Smith, Brian, *A History of the Nursing Profession*, 1960
——, *The Hospitals, 1800–1948*, 1964
Abraham, James Johnston, *Lettsom, his Life, Times, Friends and Descendants*, 1933
Andrews, Jonathan, *et al.* (eds), *The History of Bedlam*, 1997
Aveling, J.H., *English Midwives*, 1872
Barry, Jonathan, and Colin Jones (eds), *Medicine and Charity before the Welfare State*, 1991
Berry, Mary, *Extracts from the Journals and Correspondence of Miss Mary Berry from the year 1783 to 1852*, ed. Lady Theresa Lewis, 3 vols, 1865
Blake, James Bailey, *The Diary of a Resurrectionist, 1811–1812*, 1896
Blundell, Nicholas, *The Great Diurnal of Nicholas Blundell of Little Crosby, Lancashire, 1702–1728*, ed. Frank Tyrer, 3 vols, The Record Society of Lancashire and Cheshire, n.d.
Borsay, Anne, *Medicine and Charity in Georgian Bath*, Aldershot, 1999
Boswell, James, *Boswell's London Journal, 1762–1763*, ed. Frederick A. Pottle, 1991
Brown, A.F.J., *Essex People, 1750–1900*, Chelmsford, 1972
Burnby, Juanita G.L., *A Study of the English Apothecary from 1660 to 1760*, Medical *History* Supplement no. 3, 1983
Bynum, William, and Roy Porter (eds), *William Hunter and the Eighteenth-Century Medical World*, Cambridge, 1985
Campbell, R., *The London Tradesman*, 1747
Chamberlaine, William, *Tirocinium Medicum*, 1819
Clark, Michael, and Catherine Crawford (eds), *Legal Medicine in History*, Cambridge, 1994
Clegg, J. (ed.), *Autobiography of a Lancashire Lawyer*, Bolton, 1883
Clegg, James, *The Diary of James Clegg of Chapel en le Frith, 1708–1755*, ed. Vanessa S. Doe, Derbyshire Record Society, vols 2, 3, 5, 1978, 1979, 1981
Cope, Zachary, *A History of the Royal College of Surgeons of England*, 1959
Curwen, E. Cecil (ed.), *The Journal of Gideon [Algernon] Mantell, surgeon and geologist, 1818–52*, Oxford, 1940
Davies, Celia (ed.), *Rewriting Nursing History*, 1980
Davies, David, *The Case of Labourers in Husbandry Stated and Considered*, 1795
Digby, Anne, *Making a Medical Living*, Cambridge, 1994
——, *The Evolution of British General Practice, 1850–1948*, Oxford, 1999

Dingwall, Robert, *et al.* (eds), *An Introduction to the Social History of Nursing*, 1988

Donnison, Jean, *Midwives and Medical Men*, New York, 1977

Dormandy, Thomas, *The White Death: a history of tuberculosis*, 1999

Durey, Michael, *The Return of the Plague*, 1979

Eaton, Daniel, *The Letters of Daniel Eaton to the third Earl of Cardigan, 1725–1732*, ed. Joan Wake and Deborah Champion Webster, Northamptonshire Record Society, XXIV, 1971

Eden, F.M., *The State of the Poor*, 3 vols, 1797.

Elwin, Malcolm, *The Noels and the Milbankes*, 1967.

Evans, Margaret (ed.), *The Letters of Richard Radcliffe and John James of Queen's College, Oxford, 1755–1783*, Oxford Historical Society, IX, 1888.

Farington, Joseph, *The Diary of Joseph Farington*, ed. Kenneth Garlick and Angus Macintyre, Yale, 6 vols, 1978–79

Flinn, Michael, *The Sanitary Conditions of the Labouring Population of Gt. Britain by Edwin Chadwick*, Edinburgh, 1964

Fox, Robert Barclay, *Barclay Fox's Journal*, ed. R.L. Brett, 1979

Gawthern, Abigail, *The Diary of Abigail Gawthern of Nottingham, 1751–1810*, ed. Adrian Henstock, The Thoroton Society, XXXIII, 1980

Gray, A., *Papers and Diaries of a York Family, 1764–1839*, 1927

Hamilton, Elizabeth, *The Mordaunts*, 1965

Hanway, Jonas, *An Earnest Appeal for Mercy to the Children of the Poor*, 1766

Hickey, William, *Memoirs of William Hickey*, ed. Peter Quennell, 1984

Hobby, Elaine (ed.), *The Midwives Book*, Oxford, 1999

Hodgkinson, Dorothy, *The Origins of the National Health Service*, 1948

Hunter, Richard, and Ida Macalpine, *Psychiatry for the Poor*, 1974

——, *Three Hundred Years of Psychiatry, 1535–1860*, New York, 1982

Kay, Richard, *The Diary of Richard Kay, 1716–51, of Baldingstone, near Bury, Lancs*, ed. W. Brockbank and F. Kenworthy, The Chetham Society, XVI, 3rd series, 1968

Lane, Joan, *A Social History of Medicine: health, healing and disease in England, 1750–1950*, Routledge, forthcoming.

——, 'A provincial surgeon and his obstetric practice: Thomas W. Jones of Henley-in-Arden, 1764–1846', *Medical History*, 31, 1987

——, 'Bradford Wilmer of Coventry, 1737–1813', *Social History of Medicine Bulletin*, III, 3, 1990

——, *Worcester Infirmary in the Eighteenth Century*, Worcestershire Historical Society Occasional Paper no. 6, 1992

Loudon, Irvine, *Medical Care and the General Practitioner, 1750–1850*, Oxford, 1986

Manning, F.J. (ed.), *Some Bedfordshire Diaries*, Bedfordshire Historical Record Society, XL, 1959

Martin, Peter, *A Life of James Boswell*, 1999

McLaren, Angus, *Birth Control in Nineteenth-Century England*, 1978

——, *A History of Contraception*, 1990

McMenemey, W.H., *A History of the Worcester Royal Infirmary*, 1947

Merians, Linda E. (ed.), *The Secret Malady*, Lexington, 1996

Morison, Kathryn, *The Workhouse*, RCHM, 1999

Morris, R.J., *Cholera, 1832*, 1976

Parry-Jones, William Ll., *The Trade in Lunacy*, 1972

Porter, Dorothy, and Roy Porter, *Patient's Progress*, 1989

Porter, Roy (ed.), *Patients and Practitioners*, Cambridge, 1985

——, *Health for Sale: quackery in England, 1660–1850*, 1989

——, *The Greatest Benefit to Mankind*, 1997

Ramazzini, Bernard, *A Treatise on the Diseases of Tradesmen*, 1706

Richardson, Harriet (ed.), *English Hospitals, 1660–1948*, RCHM, 1998

Richardson, Ruth, *Death, Dissection and the Destitute*, 1987

Rogers, Benjamin, *The Diary of Benjamin Rogers, Rector of Carlton, 1720–1771*, ed. C.D. Linnell, Bedfordshire Historical Record Society, XXX, 1949

Rolls, Roger, *The Hospital of the Nation*, Bath, 1988

Simpson, John, *The Journal of Dr. John Simpson of Bradford, 1825*, Bradford, 1981 (no editor named)

Small, Hugh, *Florence Nightingale, avenging angel*, 1998

Smith, F.B., *The People's Health, 1830–1910*, 1979

Stephen, Margaret, *The Domestic Midwife or the best means of preventing danger in childbirth considered*, 1795

Storey, Matthew (ed.), *Two East Anglian Diaries*, Suffolk Record Society, XXXVI, 1994

Stout, William, *The Autobiography of William Stout of Lancaster, 1665–1752*, ed. J.D. Marshall, The Chetham Society, vol. 14, 3rd series, 1967

Stuart, Flora Maxwell, *Lady Nithsdale and the Jacobites*, Innerleithen, 1995

Thackrah, Charles Turner, *The Effects of the Principal Arts, Trades and Professions . . . on Health and Longevity*, 1831

Thomson, H. Campbell, *The Story of the Middlesex Hospital School*, 1935

Towler, Jean, and Joan Bramall, *Midwives in History*, 1986

Turner, Barbara Carpenter, *A History of the Royal Hampshire County Hospital*, Chichester, 1986

Turner, Thomas, *The Diary of Thomas Turner of East Hoathley, 1754–1756*, ed. David Vaisey, Oxford, 1984

Waddy, F.F., *A History of Northampton General Hospital, 1743–1948*, Northampton, 1974

Whitmore-Peck, T., and K. Douglas Wilkinson, *William Withering of Birmingham*, 1950

Willoughby, Percival, *Observations in Midwifery by Percival Willoughby*, ed. Henry Blenkinsop, Warwick, 1863

Wilson, Adrian, *The Making of Man-Midwifery*, 1995

Woodforde, James, *James Woodforde, the Diary of a Country Parson, 1758–1802*, ed. John Beresford, Oxford, 1978

Woodward, John, *To do the Sick no Harm*, 1974

Yonge, James, ed. F.N.L. Poynter, *The Journal of James Yonge [1647–1721], Plymouth Surgeon*, 1963

INDEX OF NAMES

Except for those of medical interest, names within the extracts are not indexed

INDEX OF PLACES

INDEX OF TOPICS

vaccination 75, 79, 185
Velno's Vegetable Syrup 82
venereal diseases 33, 75–6, 132, 133, 134,
    145, 146, 185, 186; sufferers' accounts
    81, 82
Village Doctor, The (Wigstead) 185

wages: hospital staff 118, 120, 122–8,
    135–6, 158; labourers' 62, 90–1; nurses
    31, 41, 62, 63, 165, 167
Warwick workhouse: register of inmates
    (1819–23) 169
watchmakers 85, 88, 89
weavers: carpet 85, 86–8; handloom 88–90
Wells Cathedral 181
Westminster Hospital, London 7, 117
wet-nursing/nurses 35–6, 62
Whitehall Evening Post 14, 29
whooping cough 111–12, 176
widows/widowhood 70, 150, 167

Winchester Cathedral 117
Winchester Hospital 117
women: health/physique of 88, 89–90
woolsorters: and occupational hazards
    84
Worcester Cathedral 183
Worcester Infirmary 117, *124*, 131, 181,
    182; setting-up expenses (1745–7) 120,
    122–8; record of cures (1754) 128–30
Worcester Journal 25, 64, 65–6
Worcester Porcelain Company 105, 182
workhouses 74, 113, 114; and New Poor
    Law 172–5; nursing in 31; and
    pauperism 62–3, 64, 137, 168; register
    of inmates 169–71
wounds *see* injuries

York Anti-Slavery Society 140
York Asylum 137, 140
York Minster 184, 185